Study Guide

for use with

Fundamentals of
Corporate Finance

Third Edition

Richard A. Brealey
Bank of England and London Business School

Stewart C. Myers
Massachusetts Institute of Technology

Alan J. Marcus
Boston College

Prepared by

Matthew Will
Johns Hopkins University

 **McGraw-Hill
Irwin**

Boston   Burr Ridge, IL   Dubuque, IA   Madison, WI   New York   San Francisco   St. Louis
Bangkok   Bogotá   Caracas   Lisbon   London   Madrid
Mexico City   Milan   New Delhi   Seoul   Singapore   Sydney   Taipei   Toronto

McGraw-Hill Higher Education

A Division of The McGraw·Hill Companies

Study Guide for use with
FUNDAMENTALS OF CORPORATE FINANCE
Richard A. Brealey, Stewart C. Myers, Alan J. Marcus

3 4 5 6 7 8 9 0 CUS/CUS 0 9 8 7 6 5 4 3 2 1

ISBN 0-07-233781-8

www.mhhe.com

TABLE OF CONTENTS

CHAPTER		PAGE

PREFACE

The book you are using, <u>Fundamentals of Corporate Finance</u>, is by far one of the best textbooks you will encounter as a student of finance. Brealey, Myers and Marcus represent three of the top minds in finance. While each has a depth and specialty that sets himself apart from his peers, a more important trait may be the breadth of the knowledge each has in the field of finance. As a student of finance you are less concerned with the minutia of specific topics, than you are with the broad aspects encountered as a practitioner in this rapidly changing and dynamic field.

The supplements offered with <u>Fundamentals of Corporate Finance</u> illustrate the authors' commitment to excellence in topic coverage, both in depth and breadth. This <u>Study Guide</u> compliments the goal of the main authors and attempts to enhance the learning experience of each student. As with the main text, you will notice that the <u>Study Guide</u> is a student centric tool. Each word is designed to improve on the learning experience. After all, the test of a good "textbook" is not merely the thoroughness with which it covers topics, but how well it conveys the meaning of those topics to you, the student.

The format of the <u>Study Guide</u> is purposely created for ease of use. It tracks the outline of each chapter closely and in many ways can be used as a quick reference source. Many students have found that a quick review of the <u>Study Guide</u> before an actual reading of the chapter may improve comprehension. The thinking behind such a suggestion is that the tired old saying "you can't see the forest for the trees" may actually "hold water." The <u>Study Guide</u> paints a broad picture of the topics being covered, as well as introduces many terms and examples. We view this approach as part of an overall learning experience. The textbook, supplemental materials and your professor all combine to provide a comprehensive presentation of the field of finance.

You will quickly notice that each chapter is formatted in the same manner. A brief description of the topics to be covered in the chapter is presented at the beginning. It is relatively light reading designed to acclimate you to the environment in which the topic resides. This is followed by a "checklist." The checklist helps you organize your thoughts and proceed through the chapter, knowing where emphasis should be placed. Most chapters also provide a list of business information sources. This information is provided in order to help the reader put a face on the material. The biggest concern expressed in academia is "how relevant is this to the real world?" The business information sources will allow you to immediately link the topic you are covering with actual events and situations. The meat of the chapter is the chapter outline. Here you will see the textbook content outlined and summarized for you. Illustrations and formulas are woven throughout the outline in order to make it more comprehensible. A good technique is to periodically return to the chapter outline as you read the book and let it be your guide. After reading the chapter in the textbook you should be able to glance at the outline and fill in relevant content and examples on your own. Hopefully, the outline will seem almost simplistic once a comprehensive review of the chapter is complete. The chapters are concluded with completion questions and problems. The questions focus on concepts, while the problems are primarily numeric. Answers for each are provided at the end of the chapter. These questions and problems supplement the ones in the textbook and provide the user with extra practice.

In the final analysis, users of this <u>Study Guide</u> should find it a wonderful addition to the family of supplements that make up <u>Fundamentals of Corporate Finance</u> by Brealey, Myers and Marcus. The family of supplements and textbook, when taken in their totality, provide an excellent learning experience.

Professional courtesy dictates a concluding note. This <u>Study Guide</u> is the third in hopefully, a long series of supplements for the textbook <u>Fundamentals of Corporate Finance</u> by Brealey, Myers and Marcus. It represents an update and revision of prior editions. Significant credit must be given to the original authors, David R. Durst and Thomas E. Stitzel. The first draft of any manuscript is by far the most rigorous and challenging. It is my sincere desire that this revision be viewed as a worthy successor to their work and that the reader benefits from the changes and additions. As with any written endeavor, the ones closest to you bear the burden of your absence. Ironically, the benefit felt by the mass of readers to the written word is created and compiled in the most solitary of settings.

Biography

Matthew Will is an Instructor of Finance at Johns Hopkins University. He holds a B.S. in Actuarial Sciences and a M.B.A. in Finance, from Indiana University. He previously served as Coordinator of Research at the "Center for Real Estate Studies," based at Indiana University. In addition to his academic experience, Mr. Will has worked in the private sector for both Fortune 500 firms and small regional companies. He currently teaches courses in Corporate Financial Theory, Investments Analysis & Portfolio Management, Advanced Corporate Finance, and Derivative Securities. Mr. Will received the 1997 "Excellence In Teaching Award" from the Johns Hopkins University Business Division, and is co-author of "Innovative Investor" (McGraw Hill publishers), a software/textbook package covering investment and portfolio management topics. Mr. Will's other publications include "Powerpoint Slides" to accompany "Principles of Corporate Finance" by Brealey and Myers. In addition, he is the author of "Questions to Accompany Morningstar StockTools - 1998."

THE FIRM AND THE FINANCIAL MANAGER

INTRODUCTION

Like most first chapters of textbooks, the authors provide an introduction to the major areas of study and provide a brief overview of the topics and chapters which follow. Having a good overview of the scope of this course is important. One must have this overview or "big picture" because very soon each chapter will focus us on very detailed subjects. With a good understanding that this overview chapter provides, you will be able to see how the detailed chapter fits into the "big picture" of financial management.

This first chapter provides an orientation to the study of financial management or financial decision making. Given a choice or several alternatives in a business decision, which should I choose? The criteria for choosing, or decision criterion used in this text, is the selection of the alternative which produces the highest value or maximizes value. What creates value in business assets or securities? That is a major topic in this course and several chapters focus on valuation theory, or what we and a lot of other people think affects value. We think that the future cash flow returns associated with a business asset or security affect the value as does the timing and variability or riskiness of those cash flows. So 1) cash flows, 2) timing or when the flow occurs, and 3) variability or riskiness of the cash flows receives considerable time and space in a finance class.

The financial manager or financial decision makers in any business have two major decisions: 1) what assets should we invest in, or the investment decision, and 2) how should we finance the assets, or the financing decision. Both decisions affect the value of the business, so several chapters are devoted to each. The capital budgeting chapters focus on tools for making value-creating investment decisions, while other chapters focus on "financing" issues that are thought to impact value creation.

The choice of business organization has an impact upon the future cash flows, risk of the business, and the ability to raise capital. This choice has an impact upon the future value creating ability of the business, and thus it is important to discuss these concepts early.

LEARNING CHECKLIST

The major learning objectives of the chapter are listed below. Look at the list *before* reading the text and study guide chapter and *after*, just before you close the book or study session. Come back here and "check off" if you can discuss or write about the item in the learning objective, if you can tell someone else, in some detail, about the topic mentioned, or if you have done reasonably well in the text or study guide sample test questions related to the topic. In other words, if you can "check off" below, you know the material and are ready to test on it. Then it is time to move on to another topic.

After preparing this chapter, you should be able to:

_____1. List the advantages and disadvantages of the following forms of business organization: sole proprietorship, partnership, and corporation.

_____2. List and briefly discuss the business functions and major decisions associated with the financial manager.

_____3. Explain why, even with many stakeholder interests in a business, shareholder wealth maximization is a reasonable basis for major business decisions.

_____4. Explain what is meant by "agency problems," and how shareholders and boards of directors can provide incentives for managers to work toward shareholder value maximization.

SOURCES OF BUSINESS INFORMATION

Your professor has selected an excellent textbook package for you to learn financial management concepts. Finance is a really exciting subject and the concepts and principles discussed in the text are practiced every day by businesses, investors, governments, and financial markets and institutions. To keep up with this every day excitement, we encourage you to follow the current events of business and finance. While the library is a great, and prepaid source of recent business happenings, a subscription to publications such as The Wall Street Journal (WSJ), Business Week, Fortune, and other business publications is the best way to stay focused on recent business and finance events. In addition, you will learn about conditions in the job market, a hot topic for all business students. If the WSJ form is passed around, consider it an opportunity to see the ideas of this class and your other business courses come alive every day. From major business announcements to personal money management, reading these business publications on a regular basis is one good sign that you are developing a professional attitude and are serious about your future.

In chapters to come, this section is devoted to highlighting a few important business and finance publications, many located in your library and the internet, with which you should be familiar. In the earlier chapters, the important areas of the WSJ are featured along with a number of finance and business web sites that have become popular. Later, important references and periodicals are discussed. Many of you will have assignments beyond this textbook, usually focused on work in the library or the internet. We hope the materials in this section may be of assistance with those assignments, and for some, help you prepare for a lifelong interest in finance.

CHAPTER OUTLINE, KEY CONCEPTS AND TERMS

I.   **ORGANIZING A BUSINESS**

A.   The choice of business organization affects the risk and the potential return in the form of after-tax cash flows and thus, the value of the business.

B.   Compare and contrast the following business organizational forms by:
1.   The exposure or risks of personal assets from a business venture-- limited or unlimited liability.
2.   The ease and cost of organization and maintenance of the business organization.
3.   The expected life of the business under each form or business organization.
4.   The relative tax exposure of the earnings of the business.
5.   The relative ease of raising capital in financial markets.

	Sole Proprietorship	Partnership	Corporation
Who owns the business?	The Manager	Partners	Stockholders
Are managers and owners separate?	No	No	Usually
What is the owner's liability?	Unlimited	Unlimited (exceptions)	Limited
Are owners & the business taxed separately?	No	No	Yes

C. **Sole Proprietorship**
1. The sole proprietor business blends the personal and business assets of the individual toward a business venture.
2. The sole proprietor incurs unlimited liability (exposure of personal assets to business obligations), limited life, business and personal income/assets are viewed by taxing authorities as one, and because of these risks, has considerable difficulty raising funds in financial markets.

D. **Partnerships**
1. A partnership is an agreement of sole proprietors to pool their assets and talents in a business.
2. Like the sole proprietorship, partners are exposed to unlimited liability, limited life of the business, business income is combined with personal income for tax purposes; unlike a sole proprietorship, more than one person is involved, and thus, more capital may be raised in financial markets.

E. **Corporations**
1. A corporation is a legal entity separate from its owners called shareholders. The legal entity concept causes the corporation to differ considerably from the sole proprietorship and partnership: corporations are taxable entities, have perpetual lives, and are able to combine the capital of many shareholders, have greater organizational and legal costs, but are more likely to raise capital in financial markets.
2. Shareholder owners have limited liability, or their personal assets are free from the obligations of the corporations, and shareholders are more inclined to invest in riskier asset ventures to create value.
3. Shareholders vote for the board of directors, who in turn, appoint senior management, creating a separation of ownership and management of the business.
4. In a small, closely held business, the owner, board member and manager/worker may be the same person or family, while larger, corporations, with professional boards and management may have a broad base of shareholders or be known as public companies.

II.   THE ROLE OF THE FINANCIAL MANAGER

A.   The primary functions of the financial manager or financial decision-maker is to raise cash in financial markets (the financing decision), to invest cash (capital budgeting decision), to generate cash from efficient operations, and to allocate cash flows generated for reinvestment or to pay cash dividends.

B.   Funds are raised in financial markets by selling financial assets or securities to investors (stocks and bonds) and investing cash in, in the case of manufacturing firms, in real assets, or physical assets used to produce goods and services.

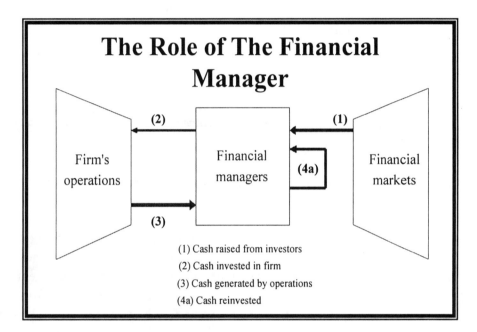

C.   The Capital Budgeting Decision
    1.   The decision as to the amount and which real assets to acquire is a capital budgeting decision.
    2.   Where cash if invested affects the amount of future cash flows generated, the timing of those cash flows, and the variability or riskiness of those future cash flows and thus, the value or worth of the capital budgeting decisions.

III. FINANCIAL INSTITUTIONS AND MARKETS

A. Financial Markets

1. Financial markets enable businesses to raise funds, enable investors to invest in financial assets, change or trade their portfolio of financial assets, and provide a continuous evaluation or valuation of the firm's securities.

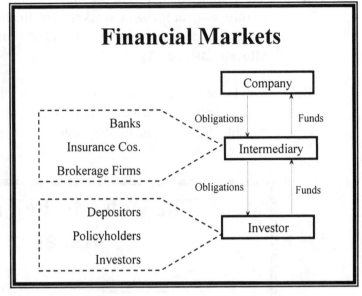

2. The initial sale of securities, where funds are acquired by the business, is called a primary issue or the securities are sold in the primary market.

3. Subsequent trading of the securities in the financial markets is said to trade on the secondary market, such as on stock exchanges or on the over-the-counter (OTC) market, where dealers trade inventories of securities held. Note: no new funds are raised by the firm in the secondary market; however, the firm's securities are evaluated or valued by the secondary market on a continuous basis.

B. Financial Institutions

1. A financial intermediary stands in between (is an intermediary) the saver/investor and borrower of funds, writing a **separate** contract for each.

2. Assets of financial institutions are financial assets such as loans and securities issued by borrowers; liabilities are contracts with investors or depositors.

3. Financial assets appear on two balance sheets as an asset (accounts receivable) and as a liability (accounts payable). Real assets, such as equipment, appear only on one balance sheet.
4. Besides functioning as an intermediary between lenders and borrowers, financial institutions:
   a. Serve as the center of the payments system of checks and electronic payments.
   b. Provide contract services permitting borrowers (loans) and savers (pension fund reserves) to transfer expenditures across time.
   c. Pool various risks in a portfolio, thus reducing the total variability or risk of the stock portfolio or auto insured customers.

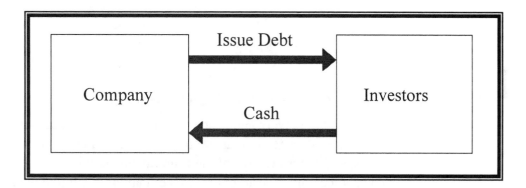

C. **The Financing Decision**
1. The maturity and type of funds raised in financial markets is the financing decision.
2. The selection and mix of long-term debt and equity securities in sold in capital markets determines the capital structure of the firm.

IV. WHO IS THE FINANCIAL MANAGER?

A. The financial manager refers to anyone responsible for a significant corporate investment or financing decision. The term is more oriented to the decisions rather than a specific title or job position. This book studies a number of financial manager decision areas, several of which, have a significant impact on shareholder value.

B.   The classic financial manager titles are the treasurer and the controller, with the former more associated with financing, cash management, and financial market relationships and the latter associated with more traditional accounting

functions of financial statements, budgeting, and auditing. The chief financial officer, in larger firms, oversees the treasurer and controller and is involved in formulating corporate strategy and financial policy.

C.   **Understanding Financial Markets and Institutions**

1.   Knowing the players and procedures of financial markets is an important factor for a financial manager, influencing the cost of funds, terms, and other features of the fund raising activities.

2.   The choice and investment returns of capital budgeting decisions affects the value of the securities issued by the business. Thus, investment and financing decisions are closely related.

V.   **GOALS OF THE CORPORATION**

A.   Shareholders want managers to make decisions based upon which alternative will maximize the value of the shareholders' investment.

1.   Making decisions that maximize focuses the financial manager on expected cash flows from investments, the timing of the cash flows, and the variability or riskiness of those cash flows.

2.   Other decision criterion, such as profit or market share maximization do not achieve value maximization. Making decisions based on profit maximization may focus on accounting income and not consider cash flow, is biased toward short run returns, perhaps ignoring the longer run implications of decisions, and ignores the relative riskiness of the alternatives.

B.   Ethics and Management Objectives -- shareholders and the public are concerned that managers operate within the law and maintain the reputation and ethical good standing of the business. Fair and ethical relationships build and maintain long run value.

    C.   **Do Managers Really Maximize Firm Value?**

        1.   Shareholders are concerned that managers work for maximizing shareholders' wealth and not managers' wealth and lifestyle. Agency problems exist when managers, as agents of shareholders, have a conflict of interest with shareholders.

        2.   There are many diverse interests with a "stake" in well being of a business: managers, workers, suppliers, customers, government, shareholders, etc. These stakeholders' interest may conflict at times; managers must work to resolve these diverse interests.

        3.   Compensation plans motivate managers to work for their own best personal interest and the best interest of the shareholders, thus resolving some agency problems.

        4.   The board of directors, elected by shareholders, oversees and at times, interferes, if managers do not act in the best interest of shareholders.

        5.   Managers whose company does not perform for the best interest of shareholders are candidates for a takeover by a new investor group.

        6.   Every public company and its managers are scrutinized and monitored by stock analysts. This specialist monitoring tends to focus managers on value creation.

VI.   **TOPICS COVERED IN THIS BOOK** -- Following the definition of the financial manager, this book first studies investment decision making, then financing decisions, then a variety of special issues. Please review the table of contents of your text.

COMPLETION QUESTIONS

1. Knowing which assets to buy involves a (*financing/investment*) decision.

2. Investment decisions are also called (*capital/cash*) budgeting decisions.

3. Knowing how to pay for assets is a (*finance/investment*) decision.

4. A business that is organized without partners or stockholders is called a _____.

5. A business that is owned by stockholders is called a _____.

6. Shareholders (*are/are not*) personally liable for obligations of the firm.

7. _____ assets are used to produce goods and services.

8. Financial assets are called (*tangible assets/securities*).

9. A firm may raise cash in the _____ markets.

10. The firm's mix of long-term financing determines its _____ structure.

11. Long-term financing is available in the _____ markets.

12. A new issue of securities is sold in the (*primary/secondary*) market.

13. The trading of existing securities among investors occurs in the (*capital/secondary*) market.

14. Shareholders want the firm to maximize its (*profits/market*) price.

15. In most large companies where managers are not major owners, a conflict of interest may occur. This is known as an (*agency/broker*) problem.

16. Anyone with a financial interest in the firm is known as a (*shareholder/stakeholder*).

17. The person in a company who is responsible for financing, cash management, and relationships with financial markets and institutions is called the (*controller/treasurer*).

18. The company officer who is responsible for budgeting, accounting and auditing is called the (*controller/treasurer*).

19.   The chief (*executive/financial*) officer oversees the treasurer and controller and sets overall financial strategy.

PROBLEMS

This section presents problems similar to those in the corresponding chapter of the textbook. Those problems serve to illustrate applications of concepts and formulas. In the case of the first chapter, there were no quantitative problems and the relatively few conceptual matters covered have been treated in the Completion section above.

ANSWERS TO COMPLETION QUESTIONS

1.   investment
2.   capital budgeting
3.   financing
4.   partnership
5.   corporation
6.   are not
7.   Real
8.   securities
9.   financial
10.   capital
11.   capital
12.   primary
13.   secondary
14.   market price
15.   agency
16.   stakeholder
17.   treasurer
18.   controller
19.   financial

CHAPTER 2

ACCOUNTING AND FINANCE

INTRODUCTION

In this second chapter the authors reinforce a number of basic accounting concepts that you established in your accounting courses. Accounting stresses generally accepted accounting principles (GAAP) as the basis for presenting financial statements. Historical cost, book value was one of the underlying basics of GAAP, but the financial manager and financial markets are focused on estimating market value. Accounting income differs from the financial manager's focus on cash flows, so the authors provide you with a finance perspective of accounting statements and the necessary adjustments needed for a value focus. Value is related to the future cash flows, the timing of the cash flows and the variability or riskiness of future cash flows. Note the futuristic orientation of finance versus the historical perspective of accounting statements.

The last part of the chapter keys on the federal income tax implications for proprietors (personal) and corporations. Taxes paid affects cash flows and cash flows impact value. Therefore, taxes affect value. Learn these few basics, such as marginal tax rate, average tax rate, after-tax concept, etc., for they will be used in future chapters.

LEARNING CHECKLIST

After preparing this chapter, you should be able to:

____1. Interpret the accounting information associated with basic financial statement such as the balance sheet, income statement, and the statement of cash flows.

____2. Distinguish between market and book value.

____3. Explain why accounting income may differ from cash flow in the period.

____4. Understand the basics of federal taxation of personal and corporate income.

SOURCES OF BUSINESS INFORMATION

The Wall Street Journal: The Wall Street Journal is a global business daily newspaper. We talk about finance in this class. The WSJ reports about people and organizations that *do* it and, make money doing it! The WSJ, besides the classic first page, has three sections: Section A is a newspaper with news and macro issues; Section B, entitled Marketplace, features companies and micro issues; and Section C, Money & Investing, focuses on financial market activity and issues.

In addition to the feature articles highlighted on the front page, there are many diverse and interesting columns in Section A. On the second page, the "Economy" section examines current economic events and issues. "Industry Focus" features business and industry analysis, while "International" provides news, discussion and analysis of our shrinking, more interdependent world. The "Leisure & Arts" section provides reviews and commentaries on a variety of areas including films, theater, books, television, sports, opera, and music. Finally, the "Review and Outlook" section provides the opinion of others on a variety of topics. Be sure and find the cartoon, "Pepper and Salt." "Politics and Policy" is assigned to the back page of Section A.

Business Internet Search Engines and Directories: All of the major search engines available from your browser, such as Netscape or Microsoft Explorer, have a business-related search area. Here you able to type in companies, products, industries, etc. and begin your assignments. From Yahoo, Infoseek, Excite, etc., located via the Netsearch button in Netscape, there are many other "search" sites that may help you. Directories are listings of specific sites, classified by topic. A few interesting ones are listed below and can be easily accessed via my website at http://www.mattwill.com

Bloomberg Financial Services	**Chicago Mercantile Exchange**
Zack's Financial Data	**Hoovers Online**
Chicago Board of Trade	**Edgar – SEC database**
NUMA Option Calculator	**Microsoft Investor**
CFO News Online	**CBOE**

CHAPTER OUTLINE, KEY CONCEPTS AND TERMS

I.   THE BALANCE SHEET

A.   The **balance sheet** presents the accounting value of assets and the source of money used to purchase those assets at a particular time.

The Main Balance Sheet Items

Current Assets
Cash & Securities
Receivables
Inventories

+

Fixed Assets
Tangible Assets
Intangible Assets

=

Current Liabilities
Payables
Short-term Debt

+

Long-term Liabilities

+

Shareholders' Equity

B.   Assets are usually listed in descending order of liquidity, or the ability to convert to cash.

   1.   Cash and marketable securities, accounts receivables, and inventories are current assets, each of which expect to cycle through cash over the next year.

   2.   Longer term fixed assets, both tangible assets like plant and equipment and intangible assets such as patents and trademarks, will not be converted to cash but are expected to generate cash over future accounting cycles.

C.   While the assets depict what is owned, liabilities and equity represent what is owed or who provided the funding for the assets.

   1.   Current liabilities, such as accounts payable, represent obligations requiring cash payment within the next year.

   2.   Current assets minus current liabilities is net working capital, or the extent to which current assets are financed with long-term sources of financing.

3. Long-term liabilities are debt obligations due beyond one year.
4. The difference between the accounting value of the assets and the liabilities is the shareholders' equity, representing the original capital contribution plus the earnings retained in the business. See Figure 2.1 for a good mental picture of the balance sheet.

D. Book Values and Market Values
1. Generally accepted accounting principles(GAAP) provide guidelines for preparing financial statements.
2. According to GAAP, assets and liabilities are usually "booked" at their historical or original cost value.
3. The *book value* of a business represents the accounting value or the balance sheet value. The book value of net worth or equity is the book value of assets less liabilities, or the historical contributions of owners including original cash contributions (sale of stock) and reinvested earnings (retained earnings.)
4. While book values are oriented to original cost, market value is oriented to value in use or economic value: the ability to generate future cash flows.
5. Shareholders and managers are concerned about the market value of their stock, so their focus is on a market value driven balance sheet.
6. The market value of assets minus the market value of liabilities is the market value of shareholders' equity. See the Jupiter Example 2.1 in the textbook.
7. Book values are based upon GAAP and market values of assets and liabilities, and thus net worth, are driven by economic value factors studied in later chapters. Seldom are they the same.

II. THE INCOME STATEMENT

A. The **income statement** is a financial statement listing the revenues, expenses, and net income of the firm in a period of time.

B. The income statement indicates where operating profit (EBIT) came from (revenues - operating costs - depreciation) and where operating income was

The Income Statement

Pepsico Income Statement (year end 1998)

Net Sales	22,348
COGS	9,330
Other Expenses	291
Selling, G&A expenses	8,912
Depreciation expense	1,234
EBIT	2,581
Net interest expense	321
Taxable Income	2,260
Income Taxes	270
Net Income	1,990

distributed (interest to creditors, taxes to governments, and profits to shareholders).

C. **Profits versus cash flow**

1. Shareholders and managers are concerned about maximizing shareholder value, which is oriented toward estimating and generating cash flows.

2. Cash flows and profits from an income statement usually differ because the income statement is interested in measuring profit in a specific time period and certain assumptions vary profit measurement from cash flow measurement.

3. Certain noncash expenses, such as depreciation and amortization, are allocated to a specific period to measure accounting profit. These noncash expenses cause profit to be less than what operating cash flow actually is and thus noncash expenses (noncash revenues) must be added back to (subtracted from) profit to estimate cash flow in a period. In addition capital expenditures, which are capitalized and depreciated or expensed over future periods incur cash outlays when purchased.

4. Another reason why profits and cash flow differ is explained by comparing cash accounting versus accrual accounting. Accrual accounting emphasizes profit measurement in a period: the revenue earned in the period; the expenses incurred in the period. Cash flow is oriented to cash collected versus disbursed in a period. Adjusting entries, accruals, receivables, prepaids, and payable cause accounting profits measured in a period to differ from cash flow in the same period.

5. Inventories produced or purchased may incur an outlay of cash, but not be expensed (cost of goods sold) until sold.

III. THE STATEMENT OF CASH FLOWS

A.   The **statement of cash flow** is a financial statement that shows the firm's cash receipts and cash payments over a period of time.

B.   **The statement of cash flow is divided into three sections.**

     1.   The cash flow from operations for a period is the sum of net income plus(minus) noncash expenses (noncash revenue) plus (minus) the net sources (uses) of cash from changes in various working capital accounts. Decreases (increases) in current asset (current liability) accounts are sources of cash. Increases (decreases) in current asset (current liability) accounts are applications or uses of cash during a period.

     2.   The investment cash flows represent added net (purchase less sale) long-term (capitalized) asset investment in the period.

     3.   The financing cash flows are listed last and include the net change in

---

The Statement of Cash Flows

Pepsico Statement of Cash Flows (excerpt - year end 1998)

Net Income	1,990
Non-cash expenses	
Depreciation	1,234
Other	382
Changes in working capital	
A/R=(303) A/P=253 Inv=(284) other=(47)	(381)
Cash Flow from Operations	3,212
Cash Flow for New Investments	(5,019)
Cash Raised by New Financing	190
Net Change in Cash Position	**(1,617)**

---

     debt outstanding, cash dividends paid, and the sale or repurchase of common stock.

     4.   Since every income statement ledger item and the changes in balance sheet ledger items in the period except the change in the cash/marketable securities account has been listed in the statement of cash flows, the balancing sum of net cash flows must equal the net change in the cash/marketable securities account in the period.

IV. ACCOUNTING FOR DIFFERENCES

A. While accounting is concerned with a presentation of earnings and book values according to GAAP, financial analysts, managers, and shareholders, current and prospective, are concerned with balance sheet and income statement adjustments which estimate market values and cash flows, respectively.

B. Areas such as valuable intangible assets, not normally listed on the balance sheet, conditional liabilities, such as pension commitments and stock options, are real variables affecting future cash flows and are a part of the value assessment process. There is a decided trend in GAAP toward accounting for market values and measuring cash flows.

V. TAXES

A. Taxes paid to governments affect cash flow available for shareholders. Usually there is a tax implication for every financial decision. The basic tax concepts which follow will assist in making the "tax adjustments" needed for the financial decisions studied in future chapters.

FOOD FOR THOUGHT - *If you were both the debt and equity holders of the firm, which would generate more cash flow to you? (assume Net Income = Cash Flow)*

	Firm A	Firm B
EBIT	100	100
Interest	40	0
Pretax Income	60	100
Taxes (35%)	21	35
Net Income	**39**	**65**

	Firm A	Firm B
Net Income	39	65
+ Interest	40	0
Net Cash Flow	**79**	**65**

B.   **Corporate taxes:**

> *Example* - *Taxes and Cash Flows can be changed by the use of debt. Firm A pays part of its profits as debt interest. Firm B does not.*
>
> | | **Firm A** | **Firm B** |
> |---|---|---|
> | EBIT | 100 | 100 |
> | Interest | 40 | 0 |
> | Pretax Income | 60 | 100 |
> | Taxes (35%) | 21 | 35 |
> | **Net Income** | **39** | **65** |

1.   The corporation is taxed on its taxable revenue adjusted for tax deductible business expenses, such as cost of goods sold, salaries, interest paid, and so forth. The tax table in Table 2.4 lists the marginal tax rates for each additional amount of corporate taxable income.

2.   The **marginal tax rate** represents the added taxes per dollar owed for each additional dollar of taxable income. The marginal tax rate is the relevant tax rate for financial decision making analysis. The concept is future oriented, consistent with financial decision making.

3.   The **average tax rate** represents the total taxes owed divided by income before taxes. The average tax rate is historical, after the fact, measure and not a valid decision making tool..

4.   Interest expense for the corporation is tax deductible; cash dividends paid to shareholders are not. The after-tax cost of a dollar of interest expense paid, with a 35 percent marginal tax bracket, is $1.00 times (1 - marginal tax rate of .35) or $.65. The cost of a $1.00 of dividends is $1.00. This special tax deduction for interest will have important implications when the financing decision of debt or equity is discussed.

C.   **Personal tax**

1.   Dividend and interest income for individuals (not corporations) is taxed as ordinary income at the appropriate marginal tax rate. See Table 2.6.

COMPLETION QUESTIONS

1. The financial statement that shows the value of a firm's assets and liabilities at a particular time is called the _____ _____.

2. Payments which are due to the company but which have not yet been collected are called accounts (*payable/receivable*).

3. Assets which are unlikely to be used soon or converted into cash in the near future are described as (*current/fixed*) assets.

4. The difference between a company's current assets and its current liabilities is called its net _____ _____.

5. The difference between assets and liabilities represents the amount of shareholders' _____.

6. GAAP stands for _____ _____ _____ _____.

7. The _____ statement shows the revenues, expenses, and net income of a firm over a period of time.

8. EBIT stands for _____ _____ _____ _____ _____.

9. Net income is either added to _____ _____ or paid out as _____.

10. Profits are different from cash flows mainly because of (*appreciation/depreciation*).

11. The practice of matching costs of producing goods with the revenues from selling them is known as _____ accounting.

12. The statement of cash flows shows the firm's cash receipts and cash payments (*at a particular point in time/over a period of time*).

13. Patents, trademarks, and franchises are examples of (*intangible/tangible*) assets.

14. The treatment of depreciation, reserves, and unfunded pension liabilities are examples of (*illegal/legitimate*) differences in accounting practices.

15. Additional taxes owed per dollar of additional income are computed from the (*average/marginal*) tax rate.

16. Interest paid by a firm is (*deductible/non-taxable*).

PROBLEMS

1. Prepare a balance sheet for Bonnie's Bedding from the following information. What is the shareholders' equity?
    Bank loans (short-term) of $200
    Cash of $100
    Inventory of $800
    Buildings and fixtures $1500
    Accounts receivable of $1200
    Mortgage loan of $1300

2. Nancy's Nursery had sales last year of $750,000. Her cost of goods sold was $500,000 and general and administrative expenses were $75,000. The other charges were $25,000 for depreciation and $30,000 for interest. Prepare an income statement for NN if she had an average tax rate of 40 percent.

3. A partial balance sheet and income statement for the past two years for North Ocean Bangles is shown below.

BALANCE SHEET, AS OF END OF YEAR
(Figures in $thousands)

Assets	1998	1999	Liabilities and Owners' Equity	1998	1999
Cash	100	200	Payable	200	400
Inventory	400	500	Short-term loans	300	400
Receivables	300	600	Long-term debt	1000	1400
Net Plant	2000	2400			

1999 INCOME STATEMENT
(Figures in $thousands)

Sales	1000
Cost of goods sold	700
General and administrative expense	100
Depreciation	50
Interest	60

a.   What is shareholders' equity in 1998 and 1999?
b.   What is net working capital in 1998 and 1999?
c.   What is the cash flow from operations in 1999?
d.   What must have been the new investment in fixed assets in 1999?
e.   If NOB has 50,000 shares outstanding what is the earnings per share for 1999?

ANSWERS TO COMPLETION QUESTIONS

1. balance sheet
2. receivable
3. fixed
4. working capital
5. equity, book
6. Generally Accepted Accounting Principles
7. income
8. earnings before interest and taxes
9. retained earnings, dividends
10. depreciation
11. accrual
12. over a period of time
13. intangible
14. legitimate
15. marginal
16. deductible

SOLUTIONS TO PROBLEMS

1. Arrange the accounts by major category and use shareholders' equity as the "plug" or balancing account. Remember that shareholders' equity (also called net worth) = assets - liabilities. These steps produce the following balance sheet:

BALANCE SHEET FOR NANCY'S NURSERY
(Figures in $thousands)

Assets		Liabilities and shareholders' equity	
Cash	100	Bank loans (short-term)	200
Accounts receivable	200		

Inventory	800	Mortgage loans	1300
Buildings and fixtures	1500	Shareholders' equity	1100
Total assets	2600	Total liabilities and equity	2600

2.
INCOME STATEMENT FOR NANCY'S NURSERY
(Figures in $thousands)

Sales	750
less Cost of goods sold	500
equals Gross profit margin	250
less Selling and general expenses	75
less Depreciation	25
equals Earnings before interest and taxes	150
less Interest	30
equals Taxable income	120
less Taxes (40%)	48
equals Net income	72

3

a. Shareholders' equity equals total assets minus total liabilities. For 1998 this is ($100 + $400 + $300 + $2000) - ($200 + $300 + $1000) or $1300. For 1999 it is $3700 - $2200 or $1500.

b. Net working capital equals current assets minus current liabilities. For 1998 this is ($100 + $400 + $300) - ($200 + $300) or $300. For 1999 it is $1300 - $800 or $500.

c. Cash flow from operations equals net income plus increases in current assets plus increases in current liabilities. Note that if current assets declined, the amount would be subtracted from net income. If current liabilities declined the decrease would be subtracted from net income. In this case, cash flow generated from operations equals net income of $80 plus the increase in current assets of $1300-$800 or $500 minus the increases in current liabilities of $800-$500 or $300 equals $280 cash flow.

d. Gross investment in fixed assets equals the increase in net fixed assets plus depreciation in 1999 or ($2400 - $2000) + 50 or $450.

e. Earnings per share equals net income divided by the number of shares outstanding. For 1999, EPS = $72,000/50,000 = $1.44

CHAPTER 3

THE TIME VALUE OF MONEY

INTRODUCTION

In this first chapter of Part Two entitled "Value," the time dimension of value is presented. The scope of business decisions covers a considerable length of time. The values of cash flows related to those decisions occurring over this wide time period are affected by the time value of money. Most decisions focus on doing something today, investments, with returns flowing over future time periods. It is important to understand that cash flows in different time periods are not comparable and must be adjusted to a common time period, usually to the present, before comparison and analyses can be performed. This adjustment reflects the opportunity cost of alternative investment and the adjustment focus in most decisions is the current period, the present.

This chapter starts the analytical or arithmetical dimension of business finance that gives this course its reputation. This is the chapter where you make it or break it. If you limp away from this chapter without mastering the concepts and a financial calculator, the next chapter is even worse.

The chapter starts relatively simple with compound interest and slowly builds. Arithmetic expressions are displayed visually via graphs, and simplified. Unknowns or "what am I solving for" that have plagued half of you since fourth grade are here again. If you have always guessed (what table should I use?), here is a suggestion. Draw a picture. Since these are "time" problems, draw a horizontal line and sketch the problem on the line. The present is on the left, future on the right, with payments (annuity) marked on the time segments of the line. Most of the problems have three variables and ask you to solve for the fourth. Identify the unknown on the time line then associate the interest factor tables with the situation. Better yet, use a financial calculator.

The cash flows discussed in the first part of the chapter are assumed to hold their purchasing power across time periods. Inflation, or the steady decline in purchasing power, is introduced in the last section of the chapter. If the purchasing power of money is declining in the future, then one should "discount" this cheaper value via a higher "I" and a lower present value.

This is the first "valuation" chapter and the authors have carefully included problems and examples in the chapter with valuation concepts, ideas, examples, etc., that will be presented formally in the next few chapters. Review the concepts to come in the next couple of chapters and treat this chapter as a building block to accomplish understanding of the valuation process.

LEARNING CHECKLIST

The real test of this chapter is your ability to work *and understand* the end-of-chapter and study guide problems. After you have worked enough problems, come back here and check off your ability to:

____1. Calculate the future value of money invested at a given interest rate.

____2. Be able to compare interest rates quoted over time such as calculating the annual effective rate when a monthly interest rate is given.

____3. Be able to calculate present value and future values (FV) and know how to distinguish between a present value versus a future value problem.

____4. Understand the difference between real and nominal cash flows and between real and nominal interest rates.

SOURCES OF BUSINESS INFORMATION

The Wall Street Journal: When you receive your first issue from your The Wall Street Journal subscription or pull your first copy from the newsstand, make sure you look over the entire issue completely. Last chapter we discussed Section A of the WSJ. Section B, along with the wide range of college courses, is where you have the opportunity to become an educated person. Hopefully by now you have the interest in learning new things on your own. That is what high school and college was all about. The rest is up to you. Section B, titled "Marketplace," has a variety of interesting subjects. Regular and feature columns entitled "Marketing and Media," "Enterprise," and "Law" provide an opportunity to "minor" in a variety of areas. You say that you have no time extra to read? Carry the WSJ with you for the next time the University puts you in a line. Consider waiting a gift of time and never be concerned about waiting again!

Finding Economic Data Online: Where can you easily and quickly find the current Consumer Price Index or current level of interest rates? Go see FRED! The FRED site is maintained by the Federal Reserve Bank of St. Louis (http://www.stls.frb.org/fred/). FRED stand for Federal Reserve Economic Data. The site provides anything from the latest to a series of interest rates, etc. You may download the data for statistical analyses or to load in a spreadsheet. The Invest FAQ web site (http://invest-faq.com/articles/analy-fut-prs-val.html) has information to aid in the understanding of present value and future value concepts. Visit Bankrate.com (http://www.bankrate.com/brm/default.asp), if you are looking for information on different interest rates for a variety of purposes. It also has some financial calculators. The FinanceCenter.com (http://www.financenter.com/) contains numerous calculators for evaluating many different financial decisions. The Financial Players Center (http://www.financialplayerscenter.com/Overview.html) calls itself the marketplace for financial knowledge. It has an introduction to the time value of money and several calculators.

CHAPTER OUTLINE, KEY CONCEPTS AND TERMS

I. FUTURE VALUES AND COMPOUND INTEREST

Future Values with Compounding

A. Cash flows occurring in different time periods are not comparable unless adjusted for time value.

B. The **future value** is the amount to which an investment will grow after earning interest. Future value = investment $\times (1+r)^t$

$$\text{Future Value of } \$100 = FV$$
$$FV = \$100 \times (1+r)^t$$

C. The expression, $(1+r)^t$, refers to **compound interest** or interest earned on interest at the rate, r, for t periods. An investment of $100 for five years at 6 percent interest compounded annually would be $100 $\times (1.06)^5$ = $133.82, with the $33.82 representing the accumulated interest.

D. If the $100 investment above earned 6 percent **simple interest**, or annual interest on the original investment, the sum of the original $100 plus accumulated simple interest would be $100 $\times$ .06 $\times$ five years = $30.00. Note that with compound interest an additional $3.82 is earned in the five year period. See Table 3.1 and Figure 3.1 for arithmetic and graphic analyses, respectively.

II. PRESENT VALUE

A. The value today of a future cash flow is called the **present value**. The present value computation solves for the original investment at a certain rate when one knows the future value. The present value is the reciprocal of the future value calculation. Present value $\times (1+r)^t =$ future value, while the present value $= 1/(1+r)^t \times$ future value. See Figure 3.3 for a graphical interpretation of this relationship.

$$\text{Present Value} = \text{PV}$$

$$\text{PV} = \frac{\text{Future Value after t periods}}{(1+r)^t}$$

B. The interest rate used to compute present values of future cash flows is called the **discount rate**. This will be an important variable when value determination is studied in the next chapter.

C. Present values are directly related to the future cash flows and inversely related to the discount rate, r, and time, t. The higher the future cash flows, the higher the PV; the higher the discount rate and longer the term, the lower the PV.

D. The expression, $1/(1+r)^t$, is called a **discount factor**, which is the PV of a $1 future payment. Discount factors for whole number discount rates and years, are calculated and available for use in Tables 3.3.

$$\text{Discount Factor} = \text{DF} = \text{PV of \$1}$$

$$DF = \frac{1}{(1+r)^t}$$

E. Cash flows occurring at different time periods are not comparable for financial decision making. The cash flows must be time adjusted, at an appropriate discount rate, usually to the "present" for comparison, summation, or other analysis.

F. **Finding the interest rate:**
   1. In the expression, $PV = FV(1+r)^t$, when the PV, FV, and t are known, $(1+r)$ may be solved arithmetically.
   2. The discount rate calculated is also called the annual interest rate, growth rate, and internal rate of return, depending on the situation.

$$PV = FV \times \frac{1}{(1+r)^t}$$

III. MULTIPLE CASH FLOWS

A. A future stream of cash flows associated with an investment may be compared or summed if adjusted to a common time period, usually the present.

B. The multiple cash flows may be the same amount and be equally spaced over the term (called an **annuity**), may be an annuity with cash flows assumed to be received forever (called a **perpetuity**), or the future cash flow stream may be unequal

C. The key point is that when discounted to the present, all future cash flows are standardized for comparison, for summing, and other analysis, such as net present value studied later.

$$PV = \frac{C_1}{(1+r)^1} + \frac{C_2}{(1+r)^2} + ...$$

IV. PERPETUITIES AND ANNUITIES

A. **How To Value Perpetuities**
1. The present value of a never ending equal stream of cash flows is called a perpetuity.
2. The PV of a perpetuity is equal to the periodic cash flow divided by the appropriate discount rate, or PV (perpetuity) = cash payments/r.

$$PV = \frac{C}{r}$$

B. **How To Value Annuities**:
1. An annuity is an equally spaced level stream of cash flows, such as $50 per year for ten years.
2. The present value of annuity is the difference between the PV of the cash flows in perpetuity less the PV of the cash flows beyond the relevant annuity period. Arithmetically, the PV of a t year annuity is:

$$PV = C\left[\frac{1}{r} - \frac{1}{r(1+r)^t}\right]$$

where C represents the annuity cash flows per period and r is the appropriate discount rate. The bracketed quantity in the formula above is called an **annuity factor**. Table 3.4 shows annuity factors with varied whole number r and t.

$$PVAF = \left[\frac{1}{r} - \frac{1}{r(1+r)^t}\right]$$

28

3. A financial calculator refers to annuity cash flows as payments.
4. A loan amortization problem uses the same expression above, solving for C, now the monthly or quarterly payments. The adjustment of annual to more frequent compounding or payments is to multiply the annual *t* by the number of payments per year and divide the *r* by the same number.

C. **Future and present value of an annuity**
   1. The future value sum of a series of consecutive, equal payments is called the **future value of an annuity** or:

$$FV = \left[C \times PVAF \right] \times (1 + r)^t$$

   2. The present value sum of a series of consecutive, equal payments is called the **present value of an annuity**, calculated by multiplying the future value of annuity, above, by $(1 + r)^t$

   3. With an **ordinary** annuity the cash flows (PMT or payments key in a financial calculator) are assumed to flow at the end of the period. An **annuity due** assumes the cash flows occur at the beginning of the period. (See the BGN or DUE key on your financial calculator).

V. INFLATION AND THE TIME VALUE OF MONEY

A. **Inflation** is an overall general rise in the price level for goods and services.

B. In the time value of money analysis above, interest rates were assumed to be "real" rates, and the cash flows over the time line were assumed to have the same purchasing power. With inflation the purchasing power of cash flows over a time line declines at the rate of inflation.

C. **Real versus Nominal Cash Flows**
   1. One measure of inflation is the Consumer Price Index (CPI). The annualized percentage increases in the CPI are a measure of the rate of inflation.
   2. Consumers and investors are concerned about the **real value of $1** or the purchasing power of the dollar or investment return in a period of time.

D. **Inflation and Interest Rates**
   1. Actual dollar prices or interest rates are called **nominal** dollars or interest rates. Bonds, loans, and most financial contracts are quoted in nominal interest rates.

2. Nominal rates, adjusted for inflation in a period, are **real interest rates**, or the rate at which the purchasing power of an investment increases.
3. The real rate of interest is calculated as follows:
4. The approximate real rate is the nominal rate minus the inflation rate.

$$1 + \text{real interest rate} = \frac{1 + \text{nominal interest rate}}{1 + \text{inflation rate}}$$

E. What Fluctuates: Real or Nominal Rates?
1. Investors and lenders include expected inflation rates in nominal rates to compensate for the loss of purchasing power.
2. Nominal rates include expected real rates of return plus expected inflation rates.

F. Valuing Real Cash Payments
1. Since nominal rates include real rates plus expected inflation, discounting nominal future cash flows by nominal rates will give the same answer as discounting real, expected inflation adjusted cash flows by the real interest rate.
2. Current dollar cash flows must be discounted by the nominal interest rate; real cash flows must be discounted by the real interest rate.

G. Providing For Retirement
1. Expected inflation is a significant variable in retirement planning, tuition savings plans, choice of vocation, or any long-term financial planning. Even a low rate of inflation can have a major negative effect on people who will receive relatively fixed nominal income or returns.

2. The actual purchasing power rate of return (real rate) on an investment is the nominal expected rate of return, $1+r$, divided by 1 + the expected inflation rate. With high inflation, the realized real rate may be negative.

H. Real or Nominal?
1. Most financial analyses in this text will assume nominal rates and will discount nominal cash flows. When one set of cash flows are presented in real term, such as the social security cash flows, then nominal cash flows and rates must be adjusted to compare, contrast, and mix the cash flows. As noted above, do not mix nominal and real or you will have-garbage!

VI. ANNUALLY COMPOUNDED INTEREST RATS VERSUS ANNUAL PERCENTAGE RATES

A. The **effective annual interest rate** is the period rate annualized using compound interest. If the one-month rate is 1 percent, the effective annual rate is 12 percent to the twelfth power for there are twelve months in a year. Thus, $(1.01)^{12} - 1 = .1268$ or 12.68 percent. The exponent used is the number of periods in one year.

B. The **annual percentage rate (APR)** is the period rate times the number of periods to complete a year or the interest rate that is annualized using simple interest. In the case above the one-month rate of 1 percent times the number of months in a year equals 12.68 percent. This is the APR.

C. To convert an annual percentage rate to an effective annual rate, divide the APR by the number of annual interest periods and annualize that period rate. In this example it is $1.0^{12} - 1 = .1268$ or 12.68 percent.

COMPLETION QUESTIONS

1. The amount to which an investment will grow after earning interest is a _____ _____.

2. When interest is earned only on the original investment it is called _____ interest.

3. When interest is earned on interest as well as on the original investment it is called _____.

4. The (*higher/lower*) the interest rate the higher will be the future value.

5. The interest rate that is annualized using compound interest is known as the _____ annual interest rate.

6. The interest rate that is annualized using simple interest is the _____ _____ rate.

7. The shorter the compounding period, the (*higher/lower*) will be the effective annual rate.

8. The value today of a future cash flow is called the _____ _____.

9. The _____ _____ is the interest rate used to compute present values of future cash flows.

10. The present value of a $1 future payment is called the _____ factor. It is always (*less/more*) than 1.0 for any positive interest rate.

11. The higher the discount rate, the (*higher/lower*) the present value of $1.

12. A stream of constant, or level, cash payments that never ends is called a _____.

13. The present value of an infinite stream of level payments (*is/is not*) infinite.

14. An annuity is a stream of cash flows that are _____ and spaced _____ .

15. The present value of a $1 annuity is called the _____ factor.

16. The perpetuity and the annuity formulas assume that the first payment occurs at the (*beginning/end*) of the initial period.

17. When a loan is repaid by a stream of level payments over its life, the loan is being _____ .

18. The amount of principal repayment from a typical home mortgage gradually (*decreases/increases*) over the life of the loan.

19. The expected rate of return that is given up by investing in a project is called the _____ cost of _____ .

20. Subtracting the present value of cash flows from the initial investment yields the _____ _____ _____ .

21. A risky cash flow in the future is worth (*less/more*) today than the same amount of a more certain cash flow.

PROBLEMS

1. Calculate the present value of $10 for the following combinations of discount rates and time periods:
   a. $r = 5$ percent, $t = 5$ years
   b. $r = 5$ percent, $t = 10$ years
   c. $r = 20$ percent, $t = 5$ years
   d. $r = 20$ percent, $t = 10$ years

2. Compute the future value of $10 cash flow for the same combinations of rates and periods as in problem 1.

3. Recently, the city of London was looking for a site on which to build a new airport. One location would have involved demolishing the 12th-century Church of St. Michael's. Suppose this edifice had been built for the equivalent of $240 and had increased 5 percent per year in value. What would be the worth today, 900 years later?

4. In 10 years, how much would a deposit of $100 grow to in a bank that pays compound interest at a 5 percent rate? How much of the ending balance would be interest earned on the interest paid?

5. Marlene and Jeff have a target of $100,000 in 20 years for their daughter Ariana's college education fund. How much do they need to deposit in a bank account today if they could earn 5 percent per annum?

6. Complete the following table by calculating present value, future value, periods, or interest rate for the missing cell on each line:

Present Value	Future Value	Periods	Interest Rate
$500		7 years	4%
$150	$201.59		3%
$320	$349.67	3 years	
	$2430	3 years	5%

7. What is the equivalent annual rate of interest of 8 percent compounded monthly as compared to semi-annual compounding?

8. Matthew's father agreed to give him an annual allowance of $1000 until he reaches his 18th birthday, 10 years from today. His older brother negotiated payments of $1200 until his 18th birthday which is 7 years from today. If both boys plan to save their money at a bank which pays 6 percent per annum, who has the best deal?

9. If you deposited $100 six years ago and your passbook savings account shows a balance of $200, what annual percentage rate has the bank been paying?

10. Using an interest rate of 8 percent, what would be the present value of cash flows of $500 in one year, $600 in two years, and $700 in three years?

11. Calculate the present value of the following annuities using a 7 percent discount rate:
    a. Five years of $100 per year with the first payment coming one year from today.
    b. Five years of $100 payments beginning two years from today.

12. What would be the monthly payment on a $10,000 auto loan to be repaid over the next 60 months if the monthly interest rate was one percent?

13. What would be the opportunity cost of capital for a property that is valued at $100,000 if it offers a return of $10,000 forever?

14. Matt has $100,000 and is expected to live for another 30 years. How much could he have to spend each year, before taxes, if he could earn 7 percent on his money and if he wanted to use it all up by the end of his lifetime?

15. Suppose Matt, as described in problem 13 above, wanted to leave a balance of $10,000 for his favorite charity when he dies. What would be his pre-tax income?

16. How much interest would you pay on a $100,000 home loan over 30 years if you made annual payments and the interest rate was 9 percent?

17. Suppose you want to buy a house and can afford monthly payments of principal and interest of about $1,000. If you finance the loan over 20 years at an APR of 12 percent, what is the maximum price you could pay?

18. What is the effective interest on a 1-year discount interest loan for $5,000 if the interest rate is 5 percent?

19. Olivia's Fashion Center offers a 2 percent discount on purchases for which cash is payed within 10 days after the purchase. The other choice is to pay the full price in one month. What is the effective interest rate of its customers who choose to defer their payments until one month?

20. Suppose a firm has bought a new $30,000 machine using a 4-year loan at a 10 percent interest rate. Complete the following table showing the loan repayment.

Time Period	Loan Balance	Year-end Interest Due On Balance	Year-end Payment	Amortization Of Loan
1	$30,000	$3,000	$9,464.12	$6,464.12
2			$9,464.12	
3			$9,464.12	
4			$9,464.12	

ANSWERS TO COMPLETION QUESTIONS

1. future value
2. simple
3. compound
4. higher
5. effective
6. annual percentage
7. higher
8. present value
9. discount rate
10. discount, less
11. lower
12. perpetuity
13. is not
14. equal, evenly
15. annuity
16. end
17. amortized
18. increases
19. opportunity, capital
20. net present value
21. less

SOLUTIONS TO PROBLEMS

1. Present values:
    a. $\$10/(1+.05)^5 = \$7.84$
    b. $\$10/(1+.05)^{10} = \$6.14$
    c. $\$10/(1+.05)^5 = \$4.02$
    d. $\$10/(1+.20)^{10} = \$1.62$

    Notice the time value of money--at an interest rate of 20 percent, a dollar received 10 years later is only worth 16.2 cents today.

2. Future values:
    a. $\$10 \times (1+.05)^5 = \$12.76$
    b. $\$10 \times (1+.05)^{10} = \$16.29$
    c. c. $\$10 \times (1+.20)^5 = \$24.88$
    d. $\$10 \times (1+.20)^{10} = \$61.92$

    Notice the power of compounding--at an interest rate of 20 percent, $1 grows to $6.192 in 10 years!

3. Today's value of St. Michael's would be $\$240 \times (1+.05)^{900} = \$2820$ trillion. That figure truly shows the power of compounding!!

4. In 10 years the balance would be $\$100 \times (1+.05)^{10} = \$162.90$. With simple interest, the earnings would be 5 percent of $100 or $5 each year for a total of $50. In that case the balance would be $150 so the interest earned on interest would be $162.90 - $150.00 or $12.90.

5. The deposit today equals the future value discounted back to the present or $\$100,000/(1+.05)^{20} = \$37,700$.

6. The future value = $\$55 \times (1+.04)^7 = \$657.97$.
    To find the number of periods, divide the future value by the present value.
    $201.59/$150 = 1.344. Then read from Appendix Table A.2 in the row where this value occurs. This is 10 years.
    The interest rate is found by the future value divided by the present value and raising this number to the reciprocal of the time period and then subtracting one to provide the decimal fraction. Thus $(\$349.67/\$320)^{1/3} - 1 = 0.03$ or 3 percent.
    The present value = $\$2430/(1+.05)^3 = \$720$.

7.   The eight percent rate on a monthly basis is .08/12 or 0.0067 percent per month. The annual percentage rate is therefore $(1 + .0067)^{12} - 1 = 0.0843$. With semi-annual compounding, the six month rate is .08/2 or 0.04 percent. The annual percentage rate then is $(1 + .04)^2 = 1.082$. Notice that the shorter the compounding period, the higher the annual percentage rate.

8.   The brothers' deal with their father is computed as the present value of an annuity. It is much easier to use a financial calculator or the present value of an annuity factors found in APPENDIX TABLE A.3 of the textbook. The latter is a simple multiplication. In Matthew's case this equals $1000 × 7.36 or $7360. Paul's arrangement has a present value of $1200 × 5.582 or $6698.

9.   When the interest rate is unknown it is probably easiest to use the tables from the textbook. The present value of $100 would be equal to the present value of $200 when that number has been discounted at the appropriate rate. In other words, $100 = $200 × discount factor. The discount factor equals $100/$200 or 0.5. Looking at the 6-year row of APPENDIX TABLE A.2, we find the interest is slightly higher than 12 percent.

10. Present values are:
          $500 × .926 = $463
          $600 × .857 = $514
          $700 × .794 = $556
          Total   =$1533

11. The present value of the annuities would be:
     a. $100 × 4.1 = $410.00
     b.   This is a two step calculation. First the present value of a six-year annuity would be computed and then the present value of a one-year annuity would be calculated and subtracted from the six-year amount.
          $100 × 4.767 - $100 × .935 = $383.20

12. The present value of $10,000 would be equal to the present value of the 60 monthly payments, M, figured at a monthly compounded rate of one percent. We need to divide the $10,000 by the present value of an annuity factor found in APPENDIX TABLE A.3. Note that the TABLE has the far left-hand column labeled "Number of years". This corresponds with an annual compounding period which is the situation found in most problems. In this particular case we have monthly compounding. We then have to mentally replace the "years" with "months" and use the 60 month factor at one percent. However, since the table only has entries up to 30 periods, the table factors must be separated into two, 30-month annuities and then combined on a present value basis. For months one to 30 the factor is 25.81. For months 31 through 60 the factor is the present value of 25.81 which is 25.81 × 0.742 = 19.15.

The present value factor for the entire 60 months is thus 25.81 + 19.15 = 44.96. The monthly payments are: $10,000/44.96 = $222.42.

13.   This is a perpetuity. The interest rate on a perpetuity is equal to the annual return divided by the present value of the perpetuity. Here it would be $10,000/$100,000 or 10 percent.

14.   The $100,000 is a present value and is equal to the present value of the annual withdrawals figured by including a 7 percent annual earning rate on the balance. Since the annual withdrawals are equal, this is an annuity problem. The $100,000 divided by the factor that is the present value of an annuity for the 30 periods. This is $100,000/12.41 or $8058. The balance remaining after the 30th withdrawal would be zero. Note that the amount of interest earned during the entire period would be 30 × $8058 - $100,000 or $141,740!

15.   The $10,000 to be left over at the end of 30 years has a present value of $10,000 × .131 or $1310. This amount should be subtracted from $100,000 so that the amount that can be allocated to provide the annuity for Matt's annual spending is $98,690. This cuts his yearly amount to $98,690/12.41 or $7953. In other words, by saving $8058 - $7953 or $105 per year for 30 years at 7 percent, Matt can accumulate $10,000.

16.   The first step is to compute the annual payments in a manner similar to that done in problem 13. Here the interest rate is 9 percent so the payments are $100,000/10.27 = $9737. This gives total payments of 30 × $9737 or $292,110. Remember that the annual payments included interest and principal. Since the loan was for $100,000 the interest must be $292,110 - $100,000 or $192,110. Think of this for a moment. The buyer in this situation pays almost double the principal as interest over the life of the loan.

17.   This requires calculating the present value of an annuity of $1000 monthly payments which will be the amount of the loan. The loan will be 90.818 × $1,000 or $90,818. With the down payment of $20,000 you could afford a house priced at no more than $90,818 + $20,000 or $110,818.

18.   The interest is paid at the beginning. It is 5 percent of $5000 or $250. The amount actually received in this loan is $5000 - $250 = $4750. The effective rate is $250/$5000 = .0526 or 5.26 percent.

19.   The "cash" customers will pay 98 percent of their purchase. However, if they delay payment for one month, they would forego the 2 percent discount in return for an additional 20 days. Since there are 365/20 or 18.25 periods in a year, they delay would cost 2/98 × 18.25 = 37.24 percent.

20. Note that the annual loan payment can be figured by dividing the loan amount by the present value factor of an annuity as determined from Table A.3. In other words, $30,000/3.1699 = $9,6412.12. For the second year, the loan balance equals the loan balance of the first year minus the amortization of loan, $30,000 - $6,463.72 = $23,536.28. The year-end interest amount equals the loan balance of the first year times the interest rate, $23,536.28 ×0.10 = $2,353.63. The principal repayment equals year-end payment minus the interest paid or $9,463.72 - $2,353.63 = $7,110.09. In the same way, the table for the third and fourth years as follows:

Time Period	Loan Balance	Year-end Interest Due On Balance	Year-end Payment	Amortization Of Loan
1	$30,000.00	$3,000.00	$9,464.12	$6,464.12
2	$23,535.88	$2,355.59	$9,464.12	$7,108.53
3	$16,427.35	$1,642.74	$9,464.12	$7,821.38
4	$ 8,605.97	$ 858.15	$9,464.12	$8,605.97
	0	0	---	---

CHAPTER 4

VALUING BONDS

INTRODUCTION

This chapter continues the cash flow and timing concepts in formal valuation of bonds. The valuation of bonds involves calculation of the present value of an expected annuity cash flow payments (interest) followed by the principle (future value) at maturity. Bond yields, both promised (yield to maturity) and realized (holding period return) are discussed, as is the inverse relationship between bond prices and interest rates. The discounted cash-flow model, studied in the last chapter, is extended to cover fixed rate bonds. Note that the same concepts are applied in valuing financial assets: cash flows, timing of the cash flows, and the riskiness or variability of cash flows in the form of the discount rate. The authors introduce a number of factors that affect the market rate of return, from expectations of future interest rates, default risk, and expected inflation. The bond market quotations, both Treasury and corporate, from The Wall Street Journal are presented, providing plenty of examples for learning.

SOURCES OF BUSINESS INFORMATION

The Wall Street Journal. In previous chapters this section has focused on the varied sections of The Wall Street Journal. Section C of the WSJ is the financial section of the paper. Titled "Money and Investing," this third section offers every student a lesson in the workings of financial markets every day. Match the WSJ tables with those in your text. See how the prices/yields have changed since then. In the "Credit Markets" section, also in Section C, a daily yield curve is presented along with recent yield curve plots to let you see how the term structure of interest rates have changed recently.

Moodys and Standard & Poors. These two entities publish information about bonds. Most people reference these sources rather than obtain the original debenture information on fixed income securities. Fortunately, the information is timely and relevant. So prominent is the information published by these two agencies that bond markets react to almost every change announced in their respective ratings.

CHAPTER OUTLINE, KEY CONCEPTS AND TERM

I. BOND CHARACTERISTICS
    A.   Terminology
        1.   A **bond** is a debt security that obligates the borrower or issuer to make specified payments (periodic interest payments and return of principal) to the lender or investor.
        2.   The bond promises to pay periodic interest or coupon to the bondholder at the contract rate of interest, called the coupon rate, plus return the face value principal amount borrowed at maturity.
        3.   For a fixed coupon rate bond, the coupon rate stays the same throughout the life of the bond. The coupon rate is the market rate, or discount rate, at the time the bond is issued. Thereafter, the market rate may vary; the coupon rate, which determines the periodic interest payment, stays the same.

II. BOND PRICES AND YIELDS
    A.   **Bond Pricing**
        1.   The price of a bond is the sum of the present values of the interest payment annuity plus the present value of the single cash flow or face value, usually $1000, at maturity. Using a financial calculator, solve for the present value with the coupon annuity expressed as a payment; the face value at maturity expressed as a single future value (FV).
        2.   Bond prices are quoted in the financial press as a percentage of their face value. Government bonds are quoted in 32nds after the decimal; corporate bonds are quoted in eighths.
        3.   When the coupon rate equals the discount rate, the PV price equals the original face value. When market rates of interest are greater (less) than the coupon rate, the PV of the bond is less (greater) than the face value.
        4.   Bond coupons are usually paid semiannually. To calculate the price of the bond on a semiannual basis, halve the coupon annuity payment and double the maturity of the bond.

$$PV = \frac{cpn}{(1+r)^1} + \frac{cpn}{(1+r)^2} + \ldots + \frac{(cpn+par)}{(1+r)^t}$$

B. **The Yield to Maturity**

1. The **current yield**, calculated by dividing the annual coupon interest by the price of the bond, is a rough approximation of the expected return on the bond. The current yield assumes that one will hold the bond forever or that the bond is a perpetuity.

2. A better estimate of the expected return on the bond is the **yield to maturity** or YTM. The YTM is the interest rate for which the PV of the bond cash flows (coupons and face value) equals the bond price. The YTM is the approximate market rate of return and assumes that one will hold the bond until maturity.

3. The two separate cash flows of the bond, the coupon and the face value, require that one estimate the YTM as in any equation with more than one unknown (two r values). Most financial calculators calculate the YTM, solving for r or I.

4. Bond coupon rates, for fixed rate bonds, determine the amount of annual coupon and remain the same over the life of the bond. Market interest rates, discount rates, and current borrowing rates change every day. Bond prices vary to give the new bond buyer the market rate of return.

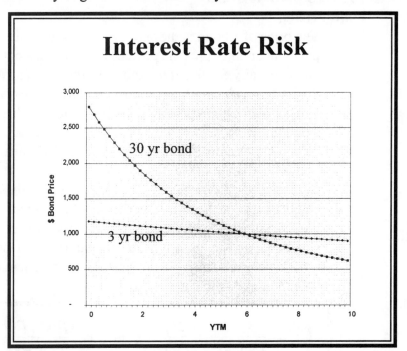

Interest Rate Risk

C. **Interest Rate Risk**

1. Bond prices (PV) vary inversely with changes in market interest rates.

2. The longer (shorter) the maturity of the bond, the greater (less) the change in the bond price for every change in bond discount rates.

3. If the bond is sold before maturity, the seller will receive the market price which, depending on the direction of market rates since the bond was

issued, will be higher or lower than face value. This is one dimension of interest rate risk or the variability of return from the expected YTM caused by selling the bond before maturity.

4. The actual **rate of return** earned on the bond investment or the holding period return on the bond may be higher or lower than the YTM.

D. **Reading the Financial Pages**
1. Government bond quotations list prices in terms of percent of face value with the value after the decimal representing the remainder in 32nds. Corporate bonds are quoted with the remainder in eights. Convert the fraction to decimal, add to the percentage price quote, and multiply by the face value, usually $1000, to determine the dollar price.
2. The prices of governments and other dealer traded bonds are quoted on a bid (price dealer will buy the bond) and ask (price the dealer will sell the bond) basis. See Figure 4.2.

E. **The Yield Curve**
1. The **yield curve** is a plot of an issuer's, such as the U.S. Government, bond yields (YTM) by time to maturity.
2. Expectations of future interest rates has a significant impact upon the shape of the yield curve, while time risks, such as interest rate risk, may also explain the shape of the yield curve.

F. **Default Risk**
1. The market yield to maturity on bonds, other than U.S. Treasury bonds, include a **credit risk premuim**, or added yield to cover the market's expected default loss on risk bonds.
2. The credit risk premium is the difference between the yield on a risky bond and a U.S. Treasury bond of similar maturity.
3. The higher the expected loss in yield from the risky bond, the higher the credit risk premium.
4. Bond rating firms, like Moody's and Standard and Poor's, rate the default risk of risky bonds.
5. High investment grades are in the range from AAA to BBB; speculative or **junk bonds** are rated below BBB.
6. The vertical yield difference between securities of varying default risk is the default risk premium.

COMPLETION QUESTIONS

1.   A _____ is simply a long-term debt.

2.   The amount of interest received each year by the bondholder is called the _____.

3.   The amount of principal that is repaid when the bond matures is also known as the (*book/face*) value, or (*par/real*) value, or (*market/maturity*) value.

4.   The coupon payment on a bond is an (*annuity/premium*).

5.   The coupon payment on a bond can be found as the sum of the (*future/present*) value of the coupon payments plus the present value of the final payment which is usually the (*face/market*) value.

6.   Most bonds in the U.S. pay interest (*annually/semiannually*).

7.   When the dollar amount of the coupon is divided by the market price of the bond the result is called the (*coupon/current*) yield.

8.   The (*current yield/yield to maturity*) is the discount rate that makes the present value of the bond payments equal to its market price.

9.   As interest rates rise the market prices of bonds (*fall/rise*).

10.   For a similar change in interest rates, the prices of longer-term bonds will change (*less/more*) than the prices of shorter-term bonds.

11.   The earnings on a bond over a year divided by the dollar amount invested is known as the (*rate of return/yield to maturity*).

12.   The fractions of bond prices are generally quoted in (*16ths/32nds*) of a dollar.

13.   The bid price quote is the price at which a bond dealer will (*buy/sell*).

14.   Entries in the financial pages showing government bond price quotes have a column headed "asked yield". This number is the same as the (*current yield/yield to maturity*).

15.   The relationship between time to maturity and yield to maturity is known as the _____ _____ _____ _____ _____. The graph of this relationship is called the _____ _____.

16.   Normally long-term rates are (*higher/lower*) than short-term rates. This means the yield curve is usually (*downward/upward*) sloping.

17. Two reasons why investors more often receive a higher return on long-term bonds compared to short-term bonds are because the former have (*less/more*) price fluctuations and because the proceeds from maturing bonds can be invested (*later/sooner*).

18. The additional yield that is promised on a corporate bond over a treasury bond having a similar coupon and maturity is called the _____ premium.

19. Bonds rated below investment grade are called _____ bonds.

20. The higher the bond rating or grade, the (*higher/lower*) the expected yield.

21. To measure returns in purchasing power terms, an adjustment to (*constant/nominal*) dollars is made to account for _____.

22. The rate at which the purchasing power of an investment increases is called the _____ interest rate.

23. Inflation will cause the purchasing power from an annuity to (*decrease/increase*) as time passes.

24. Two ways for a company to raise new money involve _____ and _____[1].

PROBLEMS

1. A 10-year old Bailey's bond pays $100 interest each year. Its last market price was $1064. What is its coupon rate, current yield, and yield to maturity?

2. What would be the coupon that Bailey would likely set on a new 10-year issue offered while the same market conditions as those specified in problem 1 above.

3. Bonnie is considering buying a bond having 15 years until maturity and a coupon of 9 percent. She wants a 10 percent yield to maturity. What is the maximum price she should pay for this bond?

4. Suppose there is a 9 percent coupon bond outstanding that matures in 5 years and offers a yield to maturity of 9 percent. What will be its price?

5. Jim purchased the bond described in the preceding problem for $950 a year ago. What is the rate of return that he would have received on this bond over the past year?

---

[1] Other correct terms are borrowing and equity.

6. If inflation this past year had been 4 percent, what would have been the real rate of return on the bond described in problem 5 above?

7. Small Industries' bonds sell for $885, will mature in 8 years, and offer a yield to maturity of 8 percent. What is the coupon rate?

8. Calculate the price of the bond that Bonnie was considering in problem 3 if interest rates rose dramatically causing the yield to maturity on that bond to suddenly increase by 1 percentage point to 11 percent?

9. Compare the situation faced by Debi who was looking at a 2-year bond that was identical to the one Bonnie was considering in all other respects. In other words, what would be the change in price for the short-term bond if interest rates rose by the same 1 percent from 10 to 11 percent?

10. Cathy started as an accountant 40 years ago at an annual salary of $4000. Her son-in-law expects to begin his accounting career earning $32,000. If the cost of living increased 7 times over the past 40 years, who entered the workforce with higher purchasing power?

11. If you expect to receive a 7 percent interest rate from a certificate of deposit, what real interest rate will you earn if inflation is 4 percent per year?

12. Suppose you plan to have savings totaling $1,000,000 when you retire in 30 years. What would be the purchasing power in terms of today's dollars of that amount if inflation averages 4 percent each year?

13. If you think you will live 25 years beyond retirement and the real interest rate during that period is 3 percent, what would be your annual annuity in today's dollars from the savings plan described in the preceding problem?

14. Neverend Life Insurance Co. has issued a perpetual bond with a coupon of 6 percent. What price would the bond sell for today if the required rate of return is 12 percent?

ANSWERS TO COMPLETION QUESTIONS

1. bond
2. coupon
3. face, par, maturity
4. annuity
5. present, face

6.   semiannually
7.   current
8.   yield to maturity
9.   fall
10. more
11. rate of return
12. 32nds
13. buy
14. yield to maturity
15. term structure of interest rates, yield curve
16. higher, upward
17. less, sooner
18. default
19. junk
20. lower
21. nominal, inflation
22. real
23. decrease
24. debt, stock

SOLUTIONS TO PROBLEMS

1.   The coupon amount or rate on a bond is fixed for its life at the time it is issued. In this problem the dollar amount is specified as being $100 per year.

The *coupon rate* is calculated by dividing the annual interest by the face value (also called par value): $100/$1000 = 0.10 or 10 percent.

The *current yield* is the coupon amount divided by the current bond price: $100/$1064 = 0.94 or 9.4 percent.

Yield to maturity (YTM) is a much more difficult calculation. YTM is the special interest rate that will make the present value of the bond's payments (the coupon and the principal) equal to the current price. Unfortunately there is no direct way to solve for YTM using an equation. A trial-and-error process is involved. However, financial calculators are programmed to this very quickly. Otherwise tables can be used but they require more time and computations. For example:

current price = present value
  = pv of coupon amount + pv of principal
  = coupon × annuity factor
  + principal × present value factor
  = $100 × factor + $1000 × factor

We know that since the current price is above par value that interest rate for this particular bond is currently below the coupon rate so the first guess is 8 percent.

$$\text{Present value} = \$100 \times 6.710 + \$1000 \times 0.463$$
$$= \$1134 \text{ which is not equal to the current price of}$$
$$\$1,064.50. \text{ Try 9 percent:}$$

$$\$1064 = \$100 \times 6.418 + \$1000 \times .422$$
$$= \$1063.80 \text{ which is very close to the price of } \$1064$$
so the YTM is 9 percent.

2.   Issuers of bonds must offer yields that are competitive. The convention is to set the coupon on new bonds at the yield to maturity offered by outstanding bonds of similar maturity, risk, and other factors. Since Bailey's has a bond outstanding with 10 years of life remaining and that yields 9 percent, it would chose a 9 percent coupon. This would allow it to sell at par value of $1000.

3.   Bonnie would pay an amount that would be below the par value so that the 9 percent coupon plus the gain from her purchase price to the par value (redemption value) would offer her required return of 10 percent (the yield to maturity). This price would be:

$$\text{pv of coupon amount} + \text{pv of principal} = \$90 \times 7.606 + \$1000 \times .239$$
$$= \$923.54$$

4.   The price will be equal to the present value of all future returns as illustrated in each of the preceding problems. Thus

$$\text{price} = \$90 \times 3.890 + \$1000 \times .650 = \$1000.1$$

Note this is within round-off error of $1000 which is par value. This reinforces the earlier statement that whenever the coupon and yield to maturity are the same, any bond will sell at par value.

5.
$$\text{Rate of return} = \frac{\text{interest} + \text{capital gain}}{\text{original price}}$$
$$= \frac{\$90 + (\$1000 - \$950)}{\$950}$$
$$= .1474 \text{ or } 14.74\%$$

6.
$$\text{Real return} = \frac{1 + \text{nominal return}}{1 + \text{inflation}} - 1$$
$$= \frac{1 + .1474}{1 + .04} - 1$$

7. Remember that
    $$\text{Price} = \text{coupon} \times \text{annuity factor} + \text{principal} \times \text{pv factor}$$
    $$\$885 = \text{coupon} \times 5.747 + \$1000 \times .540.$$
    $$\text{The coupon} = \frac{\$885 - \$540}{5.747} = \$60$$
    This means the coupon must be 6%.

8. The price at the higher yield to maturity of 11 percent will be:
    $$\$90 \times 7.191 + \$1000 \times .209 = \$856.19$$
    This compares with $923.54 in problem 3. It means that a 1 percent increase in YTM results in a decrease of $67.35 or 7.3%

9. Here we compare the value of the 2-year bond at a 10 percent yield with what happens if rates go to 11 percent. The original bond value would be:
    $$\$90 \times 1.736 + \$1000 \times .826 = \$982.24$$
    At 11 percent this bond would fall to:
    $$\$90 \times 1.713 + \$1000 \times .812 = \$966.17$$
    This is a drop of $16.07 or 1.6 percent which is considerably less than the decline of 7.3 percent figured for the longer-term bond. The conclusion is that longer-term bonds are much more volatile than short-term bonds for a given change in interest rates.

10. Cathy's son-in-law's equivalent purchasing power in comparison to hers would be $32,000/7 or $4571 which is substantially greater. It means that the starting salary of accountants, given these numbers, had outpaced the cost of living increases.

11. As in problem 6,
    $$\text{Real return} = \frac{1 + \text{nominal rate}}{1 + \text{inflation rate}} - 1$$
    $$= \frac{1 + .07}{1 + .04} - 1 = 1.029 \text{ or } 2.9\%$$

12. The cost of living would have risen by the 4 percent compounded annual rate for 30 years which would be $(1.04)^{30}$ or 3.243 times. This means the purchasing power would be $1,000,000/3.243 or $308,356.46.

13. The lump sum of $308,356.46 computed in the preceding problem would be equivalent to an annuity of $308,356.46/17.41 or $17,711.46 per year for 25 years if the real interest rate was 3 percent.

14. The bond pays a coupon of 6 percent or $60 per year. If the required return was 12 percent the bond would sell for $60/0.12 or $500.

VALUING STOCKS

INTRODUCTION

This chapter extends the valuation concepts explored in valuing bonds and applies them to equity securities. The same basic principles apply. Basic determination of cash flows and discount rates are at the core of valuing stocks. While bonds have default risk, stocks also have risk associated with the unknown nature of future cash flows.

These valuation techniques involve non-contractual and varied future cash flows, which are characteristic of all common stock. Covering an increasingly complex variety of cash-flow patterns from constant dollar (no-growth), constant growth (Gordon Model), and growth over a specific time period, the authors provide valuation techniques for a variety of common stock and business cash-flow patterns. The chapters which follow apply these concepts to specific value-creating, cash-flow generating projects.

As in prior chapters, the required/expected rate of return concept is reinforced. These rate-of-return discussions provide an important building block for the later study of capital budgeting and risk analysis.

SOURCES OF BUSINESS INFORMATION

The Wall Street Journal. The use of The Wall Street Journal as a source of valuation information is limited, relative to common stocks. Its primary use here is as a reporting tool. It does, however, report earnings announcements, dividend payments and other information used in the process of valuing stocks. The information provided, however, is more readily available and timely online.

Zacks. Earnings estimates have tended to dominate the scene in valuing stocks on the floor of the exchanges. Changes in earnings estimates alter the price of a stock instantly. Also deviations of actual results from consensus estimates cause immediate changes to stock prices. Zacks has emerged as a leading player in the tabulation of earnings estimates and distribution of this information.

Bloomberg and Lexis/Nexis. Real time news sources allow all market participants to react to the same information at the same time. It is very common for stock valuation experts to receive constant news feeds concerning a stock they are following

FINANCE ON THE TUBE. For many years there was only one television program available to keep stock investors up-to-date with current developments. Produced and presented by Louis Rukeyser, "Wall Street Week," every Friday evening was about the only way for the small investor to peek into Wall Street. Now there are several business news and investing programs on TV. Currently "Wall Street Week" is presented on public TV stations every Friday evening. Amid walnut paneling and marble columns, connoting wealth, Mr. Rukeyser offers an interesting commentary related to the week's political and investment results. Every week a panel of regulars, usually analysts and investment managers, discuss the previous week's investment results. A guest, usually another high profile Wall Street analyst or fund manager, is invited to give his/her assessment of the current market activities, and is asked for a prediction. For over twenty-five years, this program has attracted a large following of individual investors. One is able to pick up sound investment advice, strategies, and tips.

CNN has several business and investment related programs to offer. MoneyWeek and Business Day are two excellent business news and analyses programs. Business Unusual selects three or four businesses to highlight each thirty minute program. Focusing on "different" or "unusual" businesses, such as Steinway, the maker of pianos, each segment offers a history, recent developments, and assessment of the business.

CNBC offers several business news shows throughout the week. From Business early in the morning, to Squawk Box (financial trends), Money Wheel, Power Lunch (guess when it is presented), Street Signs (Wall Street of course), and finally Market Wrap provides an assessment of the current day's events from the investment world.

As a business student, learning about investments and businesses is an important part of your early training. The above programs and more not mentioned can provide the "street smarts" that a text will never mention. Check them out!

CHAPTER OUTLINE, KEY CONCEPTS AND TERM

I. STOCKS AND THE STOCK MARKET

A. Introduction
   1. Financial markets provide a source of financing for businesses and governments; a financial investment opportunity for individual and institutional investors.
   2. The initial, funds-raising sale of securities, usually with an investment banker, is in the **primary** market; subsequent trading between investors for liquidity, financial investing, and portfolio rebalancing is in the **secondary** market.

B. **Reading the Stock Market Listings**
   1. Figure 5.2 lists a number of stock quotations. Note price changes in eights, an "annualized" quarterly <u>dividend</u>, and the dividend yield as the annualized dividend divided by the closing price.
   2. Why do the dividend yields vary? Expected price appreciation and risk.

3. The price/earnings (P/E) ratio is the closing price divided by the earnings per share. Commonly used in valuation assessment, the ratio indicates the number of years of current earnings the market is willing to pay to own the stock.

II. BOOK VALUES, LIQUIDATION VALUES, AND MARKET VALUES

A. Terminology
   1. **Book value** of common stockholders represents the accounting value of assets less the accounting value of liabilities.
   2. Book value is biased toward historical or original costs.
   3. **Liquidation value** of common stockholders represents the quick sale of individual assets less liabilities owed.
   4. **Going concern value** represents the difference between a minimum liquidation value and actual or "true" value (market),the worth of an on-going business by investors considering, 1) future earning power of existing tangible and intangible assets and 2) the value of future investment opportunities of the firm.
   5. **Market value** represents the value assigned a firm by investors in a reasonable market driven by the expected level and variability of cash flows. When the market/book ratio exceeds one, the economic value of the assets exceeds the accounting value or the expected rate of returns to shareholders exceed their minimally acceptable rate of return.

III. VALUING COMMON STOCKS

A. Today's Price and Tomorrow's Price
   1. The expected and actual, realized rate of return to common stockholders comes from 1)cash dividends, DIV_1, and 2) capital gains or losses, P_1-P_0.
   2. Investors compare expected returns, based on expected dividends and price changes, with minimum required returns, comparable returns on similar securities (opportunity costs).
   3. If expected returns exceed comparable returns elsewhere, investors will want to purchase the stock, bidding the price up and the expected return down to the minimum acceptable return.
   4. At any market price, expected returns equal that required by investors.
   5. All securities of the same risk are priced to offer the same expected rate of return.

$$\text{Expected Return} = r = \frac{Div_1 + P_1 - P_0}{P_0}$$

B. The Dividend Discount Model
   1. The **dividend discount model**, or discounted cash flow model, states that share value equals the present value of all expected future dividends.
   2. With a specific investment time period or horizon, H, the intrinsic share value (value determined by the evidence) is:

$$P_0 = \frac{Div_1}{(1+r)^1} + \frac{Div_2}{(1+r)^2} + \ldots + \frac{Div_H + P_H}{(1+r)^H}$$

   3. The stock price at the horizon date, P_H, is the present value of cash dividends received beyond the horizon date.
   4. As the horizon date changes, the present value of the stock will remain the same as dividends are expected to grow at the rate of "r" (Example 5.2, Table 5.4, and Figure 5.3).
   5. At extreme horizon dates the present value of P_H becomes insignificant; thus the dividend discount model--share value equals the present value of future, expected dividends.

IV. SIMPLIFYING THE DIVIDEND DISCOUNT MODEL

A. **The Dividend Discount Model With No Growth**
   1. When all earnings are paid as cash dividends, no growth is possible (reinvestment = depreciation to maintain the current stock of capital).
   2. The stock value of a no-growth firm is the expected dividend capitalized (perpetuity) at the required rate of return or:

$$Perpetuity = P_0 = \frac{Div_1}{r} \text{ or } \frac{EPS_1}{r}$$

Assumes all earnings are paid to shareholders.

B. **The Constant-Growth Dividend Discount Model**
   1. The **Constant-Growth Discount Model** is an arithmetic expression calculating the present value of a perpetual stream of cash flows, DIV, growing at a constant rate of growth, g, and discounted at a required rate of return, r:

$$P_0 = \frac{Div_1}{r - g}$$

2. With a sustained positive growth rate in the economy and business activity, the Gordon Model and its assumptions are reasonable.
3. DIV_1 represents the dividend received at the end of period one.
4. The constant-growth formula is valid only when "g" is less than "r."
5. P_0 is directly related to DIV_1 and g; inversely related to r.

C. Estimating Expected Rates of Return
1. In constant-growth business situations, if g is capitalized in the market in higher stock prices, r may be a proxy for the market expected rate of return on similar risk situations.
2. The expected rate of return is a combination of the dividend yield, DIV_1/P_0, and capital appreciation rate, g.
3. The required rate of return, r, is a market- determined rate related to the risk-free rate adjusted upward for risk, given expectations of DIV_1 and g. The stock price, P_0, adjusts to equate the market-expected rate with the required rate of return.

D. What If Short-Term Growth Rates Don't Fit The Market?
1. The no-growth and constant-growth dividend discount models above assume two patterns of cash flows while reality presents the analyst with many variations. The dividend discount model is easily adapted.
2. Changing future dividend patterns from non-growth to constant-growth to variable-growth rates over a given horizon requires that the analyst estimate the stock price by forecasting the cash-flow patterns and discounting the cash flows at the market-required rate of return.
3. The terminal value, P_H, represents the present value of the cash flows beyond the horizon.

V. GROWTH STOCKS AND INCOME STOCKS

A. **Income vs. Growth Stocks**
1. **Income stock** returns are derived from the dividend yield, DIV/price, and are associated with businesses with a high **payout ratio**, the fraction of earnings paid out as dividends.
2. **Growth stock** returns are derived from a combination of no or relatively small dividend yields(low payout ratio) and a high **plowback ratio** (the proportion of current period earnings or free cash flow retained in firm), and earning high asset returns, in excess of that required by the market, on reinvested earnings.

3. The **sustainable** growth rate, g, discussed in the constant-growth rate discussion above, relates to the expected asset returns on reinvested capital adjusted for the proportion of earnings plowed back into the firm. Dividends (payout ratio) limit the level of reinvested capital and the growth potential of future earnings and dividends.

$$g = \text{return on equity x plowback ratio,}$$

where the return on equity is the expected return on equity capital plowed back into earning assets.

4. Similar stock prices ($41.67) will result from a 100 percent payout ratio and any less payout where the plowed back earnings earn just the required rate of return.

5. When rates of return on reinvested capital exceed the required rate of return, added value, often called "value added" or the **present value of growth opportunities** or **(PVGO)**, is capitalized in the market price of the stock.

B. **The Price-Earnings Ratio**

1. Higher price-earnings ratios are associated with higher expected growth opportunities and lower earnings-price ratios (earnings yield), reflecting that some portion of the required rate of return is expected to be derived from growth opportunities.

2. Expected future earnings are expected cash flows less any reinvestment associated with the economic depreciation of earning assets or earnings (cash flow) above that needed to maintain the earning power of the firm.

COMPLETION QUESTIONS

1. Owners of the corporation are (*debtholders/shareholders*) who expect a risk premium in the form of (*higher/lower*) returns compared to lenders.

2. Sales of new securities occur in the (*primary/secondary*) market.

3. Already-issued securities are bought and sold in the (*primary/secondary*) market.

4. Stock exchanges operate as an (*auction/dealer*) market.

5. The New York Stock Exchange member who buys and sells shares of companies assigned to him is known as a _____.

6. Investors may either place a price limit on their order or they enter a _____ order which directs their broker to execute at the best price that is immediately available.

7.   The term NASDAQ stands for _____ _____ _____ _____
        _____ _____.

8.   Periodic cash distributions from the firm to its shareholders are called (*dividends/interest*).

9.   Unlike bonds which normally pay a fixed amount of interest, common stockholders hope
        profits will grow enabling the firm to pay (*higher/lower*) dividends.

10.   The ratio of stock price to earnings per share for a company is called the _____
        _____ multiple.

11.   The term "odd lot" refers to (*the human race/trades for less than 100 shares*).

12.   According to the balance sheet (*book/market*) value is equal to assets minus liabilities. This
        is also called the net _____ of the firm.

13.   Because the value of a firm's assets as reported on their balance sheet is equal to their
        original cost minus the depreciation, their (*book/market*) value will often be very different.

14.   Net proceeds that would be realized by selling the firm's assets and paying off its creditors
        is called the _____ value of the firm.

15.   The actual value of a successful company is called its _____ _____ value.

16.   A firm may be worth more "alive than dead" due to its extra _____ _____,
        its _____ assets, and the value of its (*current/future*) investments.

17.   A financial statement that uses the actual or true value of all the firm's assets and liabilities
        is known as a _____ _____ balance sheet.

18.   The cash payoff to owners of common stocks comes from _____ and _____
        gains or losses.

19.   All securities of the same risk (*are/are not*) priced to offer the same expected rate of return.

20.   The _____ _____ model computes the share value as the present value of
        all future dividends.

21.   The present value of a stock (*equals/is greater than*) the present value of future dividends
        out to the investment horizon plus the present value of the forecasted stock price at the
        horizon. This relationship holds for (*any/only one*) horizon date.

22. When no growth of dividends is expected, the value of the stock will be equal to the dividend divided by the (*discount rate/yield to maturity*).

23. In the constant growth dividend model the share value is equal to next year's (*dividend/interest*) divided by the difference between the expected rate of return and the growth rate.

24. The (*payout/plowback*) ratio is the fraction of earnings that are paid out as dividends.

25. Growth stocks usually have relatively (*high/low*) payout ratios.

26. A company's growth rate is equal to the product of its return on (*assets/equity*) and its (*payout/plowback*) ratio.

27. If the present value of growth opportunities is positive, the required rate of return will be (*greater/less*) than the earnings-price ratio.

PROBLEMS

1. Peter's Pickle Chips (PPC) paid $2 in dividends this past year. Analysts expect this payment will grow at 6 percent annually for the indefinite future.
   a. What stock price is forecast with this model if a discount rate of 10 percent is appropriate (use the constant growth model)?
   b. What are the expected dividends for the next two years (i.e. DIV_1 and DIV_2)? What is the present value of these two dividends?
   c. What will be the estimated value of PPC two years from now? What is the present value of this price discounted to the present time (time zero)?
   d. Add the discounted price of PPC stock two years from now to the present value of the dividends in the first two years (i.e.. add the results of parts b and c). Compare the summation to the answer in part a, they should be equal (there may be small rounding error of a few pennies).

2. Suppose the Allman Brothers Grocery Stores Inc. currently has a $1.50 dividend per share. This dividend is expected to grow at 4 percent into the future and the appropriate discount rate for a stock with Allman's risk profile is 8.5 percent.
   a. What is the forecasted stock price for Allmans using the constant growth model?
   b. What happens to Allman's price if the discount rate rises to 10 percent?
   c. What happens to Allman's price if the expected growth in dividends rises to 5 percent? Use the original discount rate of 8.5 percent.

3. Fillmore West pays a $3 dividend right now and its stock sells for $43. The best estimate of Fillmore's required return is 13 percent. Given this information and using the constant growth stock price model, what is the constant growth rate for Fillmore?

4. Bankcity's perpetual preferred stock pays a $2 dividend and is priced to yield 13 percent. What is price of this issue according to the constant growth model?

5. Silver Creek Gold Company (SCG) has an average return on equity of 12 percent over the past five years. Analysts believe this rate is sustainable for the foreseeable future.

   a. If SCG's plowback ratio is 45 percent what is its expected growth rate?
   b. If SCG's dividend is expected to be $1.75 next year ($DIV_1$) and the required is 12 percent, what is the constant growth estimate for SCG stock price?
   c. What will happen to SCG's growth rate and stock price if they invest in projects that yield less than 12 percent?

6. Hacker's Cigarettes Company expects sales, earnings, and dividends to decline 5 percent into the foreseeable future due to rising taxes and falling demand. If their dividend is currently $3.50 and the required return is 15 percent, what would the constant growth model predict for Hacker's stock price?

7. Hardball Software stock sells for $46 with an estimated discount rate of 16 percent. Analysts estimate next year's dividend at $2.10 and Hardball plans to reinvest 75 percent of its earnings back into the business. What is Hardball's rate of return on its reinvested earnings (ROE)?

8. In the Wall Street Journal, you notice a cellular telephone stock that sells for $28.50 and earned $1.80 per share during the current year.
   a. What is the price/earnings (P/E) ratio for this firm?
   b. What return will you theoretically earn on this stock next year if you buy it at the above price and earnings do not change? (Recall that earnings belong to the shareholders). Does this seem like an adequate compensation for the risk of investing in stocks?
   c. In general, what do investors expect to happen to the earnings of firms that have high P/E ratios?

ANSWERS TO COMPLETION QUESTIONS

1. debt, stock , shareholders, higher
2. primary
3. secondary
4. auction
5. specialist
6. market
7. National Association (of) Securities Dealers Automated Quotation
8. dividends
9. higher
10. price earnings
11. trades for less than 100 shares
12. book, worth
13. market
14. liquidation
15. going concern
16. earning power, intangible, future
17. market value
18. dividends capital
19. are
20. dividend discount
21. equals, any
22. discount rate
23. dividend
24. payout
25. low
26. equity, plowback
27. greater

SOLUTIONS TO PROBLEMS

1. This problem illustrates forecast and valuation based on the constant-growth dividend discount model.

    a. $$P_0 = \frac{DIV_1}{r - g} = \frac{\$2.12}{(.10 - .06)} = \$53$$

    b. Dividends increase by 6 percent per year:

Present values of the second year's dividend:

$$DIV_2 = \frac{\$2.25}{(1+.10)^2} = \$1.86$$

c. $$P_2 = \frac{DIV_3}{r-g} = \frac{\$2.25(1.06)}{(.10-.06)} = \frac{\$2.38}{.04} = \$59.55$$

Present value of the above stock price (note: it is received at the end of year two, the same time the second dividend is received):

$$P_0 = \frac{\$59.55}{(1+.10)^2} = \$49.21$$

d. The summation of $49.21 + $1.93 + $1.86 = $53.00. You should see that the constant-growth dividend discount model used in answer a is simply a shorthand way of calculating the present value of all the future dividends in the special case of a constant growth in dividends.

2. It is evident after we do the math, but it should be intuitively obvious that rising discount rates reduce stock price and rising growth in dividends increases stock price. Keep your thinking cap on when you do these problems and it is easier to avoid silly mistakes (Like fat fingers that punch the wrong button on the calculator).

a. $$P_0 = \frac{DIV_1}{r-g} = \frac{\$1.50(1.04)}{(.085-.04)} = \$34.67$$

b. $$P_0 = \frac{DIV_1}{r-g} = \frac{\$1.50(1.04)}{(.10-.04)} = \$26$$

c. $$P_0 = \frac{DIV_1}{r-g} = \frac{\$1.50(1.06)}{(.085-.04)} = \$35.33$$

3. Since $P_0 = DIV_1/r-g$ we can substitute in the known variables and solve for the growth rate. Thus:

$$P_0 = \frac{DIV_1}{r - g} = \frac{DIV_0(1+g)}{r+g} = \$43 = \frac{\$3(1+g)}{(.13-g)} \text{ or } 5.6\%$$

4. Since the payout on this preferred stock issue does not grow (there are preferred stock issues that pay floating rate dividends) the g in our formula is zero. Thus:

$$P_0 = \frac{DIV_1}{r - g} \text{ and } P_0 = \frac{\$2}{.13} = \$15.38$$

5. A rough estimate of SCG's sustainable growth is that it will be able to earn the same return on its equity investments in the future that it has earned in the recent past. The earnings "plowed back" into the firm are called retained earnings (i.e. equity), the rest of the earnings are paid out as dividends and do not help the firm grow.

    a. For SCG:
        g = return on equity x plowback rate
        $= 12\% \times .45 = 5.4\%$

    b. $$P_0 = \frac{DIV_1}{r - g} \text{ and } P_0 = \frac{\$1.75}{.12 - .054} = \$26.52$$

    c. Investing in projects that return less than expected by shareholder (i.e.. required return) reduces the firm's growth rate and the stock price.

6. The constant growth model has trouble handling high rates of growth (it is not reasonable to expect a firm to grow at high rates for indefinite periods of time, competition always catches up), but the model has no trouble with negative growth rates, as Hacker's demonstrates:

$$P = \frac{DIV_1}{r - g} \text{ and } P_0 = \frac{\$3.50(1-.05)}{[.15-(-.05)]} = \$16.63$$

7. First solve for Hardball's growth rate:

$$P_0 = \frac{DIV_1}{r - g} \text{ so } g = r - \frac{DIV_1}{P_0} = 0.16 - \frac{\$3.10}{\$46} = \$.0926$$

Assuming it's reasonable to expect that Hardball's growth rate will be:

g = ROE × plowback ratio
.0926 = ROE × .75
ROE = .0926/.75 = 12.35%

8. a. P/E = $28.50/$1.80 = 15.83

    b. $1.80/$28.50 = 6.3 percent. This return looks low for a firm invested in a business as competitive as the cellular telephone market.

    c. Investors that pay high P/Es expect earnings will increase in the future. If the earnings do not increase then investors will have paid too much for the stock.

NPV AND OTHER INVESTMENT CRITERIA

INTRODUCTION

This chapter continues the valuation theme, but shifts to an internal, managerial focus oriented to the discussion and evaluation of several investment decision criteria. How should managers select long-term investments? In your economics class, profit maximization (PM) was used as the decision criterion. Profit maximization worked well under the simplistic assumptions of no risk and immediate returns from investment. PM is *not* an effective decision criterion in the real world of long-term and variable (risky) investment returns. A better decision criterion is needed. The net present value decision criterion fits the manager's needs to be concerned with long-term, multiple periods, variable or risky returns, and a focus on cash-flow returns. The net present value and internal rate of return decision criteria are consistent with shareholder wealth maximization, for they focus on expected cash flows, when the flow occurs, and the riskiness of the cash flow.

You must now make a transition from the former section and chapters related to valuation in a macroeconomic or general setting to this microeconomic setting related to making decisions within the business. Managers must assess the expected value added contributions of new investment projects. The net present value measures each project's expected contribution to shareholder wealth. This chapter is a continuation of the valuation theme from the last chapter.

LEARNING CHECKLIST

This chapter is a skills-specific chapter that focuses on training you to:

___1. Calculate the net present value of an investment and learn the NPV decision rule.

___2. Calculate the internal rate of return of a project and learn the IRR decision rule.

___3. Compare and contrast the NPV and IRR with the payback decision rule and book value rate of return decision rule, which do not always increase shareholder wealth.

SOURCES OF BUSINESS INFORMATION

Standard & Poor's Credit Week. A very important reference source of financial information about a company, state, city, etc., is the Standard & Poor's Credit Week. Standard and Poor evaluate the credit or default risk associated with the bonds, preferred stock, structured financing, commercial paper, issued by private corporations and governments. In the "Rating Action" section, new issues and revisions are presented. In the "Ratings Outlook," specific industries, geographic regions, types of debt are discussed and an outlook such as positive, stable, or negative is offered. The Credit Week includes a weekly "Credit Watch," which is numerous half-page summaries with financial data included for selected companies whose credit quality is being carefully reviewed. In the "Credit Trends" section, indexes of the last fifty-two weeks related to credit upgrades/downgrades are graphed and discussed. The S & P International Credit Week offers a quarterly analysis and perspective on international credit.

Practice Investing Online. There are several web sites that offer the chance to "play" investments by investing in a portfolio of stocks. **EDUSTOCK** gives you a hypothetical $100,000 to invest and it keeps track of your performance over time. Unlike other sites, this one lets you play along **free** and you can trade any stock you want. The site has a tutorial on the stock market. You can learn how the market works, how to select stocks, and manage a stock portfolio. It offers a "company profiles" section, providing important financial information needed to screen companies. This is a good investing starting point! See http://library.thinkquest.org/3088

CHAPTER OUTLINE, KEY CONCEPTS AND TERMS

I.   NET PRESENT VALUE

   A.   The Rationale
      1.   Net present value measures each project's contribution to shareholder wealth.
      2.   While there are several long-term investment decision criteria, the net present value method is favored because it tends to focus on building shareholder value and has the fewest limiting assumptions.

   B.   A Review of the Basics
      1.   **Capital budgeting decisions**, the process of choosing investment projects, are important because they usually involve large cash outlays with cash flow return over a long period of time. The *four* steps in the capital budgeting decision process are:
         a.   Forecast the future project cash flows, noting when the flow occurs.
         b.   Estimate the opportunity cost of capital. The **opportunity cost of capital** is the expected rate of return given up by investing in the project under review.
         c.   Calculate the present value of the future cash flows discounted at the opportunity cost of capital rate. The present value of the cash flows represents the maximum amount that investors would pay for the investment.
         d.   NPV Decision Rule: The present value sum of the future cash flows *minus* the investment outlay is the **net present value**. If the

net present value is positive (greater than zero), make the investment. If the net present value is negative, forgo the investment. If the present value is the maximum amount one would pay for the investment relative to the cost, the NPV represents the added value of the investment.

e. The expected net present value of a project is the added shareholders' wealth provided by the project.

$$NPV = C_0 + \frac{C_t}{(1+r)^t}$$

C. Valuing Long-Lived Projects
   1. Added net present values generated by investments are represented in higher stock prices.
   2. The net present value method is a proxy for financial market investor analysis of business investments.
   3. Projects that are expected to generate negative net present values will reduce shareholders' wealth by the expected negative NPV.

$$NPV = C_0 + \frac{C_1}{(1+r)^1} + \frac{C_2}{(1+r)^2} + \ldots + \frac{C_t}{(1+r)^t}$$

II. OTHER INVESTMENT CRITERIA

A. **Internal Rate Of Return**
   1. An alternative to the NPV method is the **internal rate of return**, which is the discount rate that, having discounted the expected cash flows, will produce a present value equal to the cost of the project. In this case, a discount rate that will generate an NPV of zero.

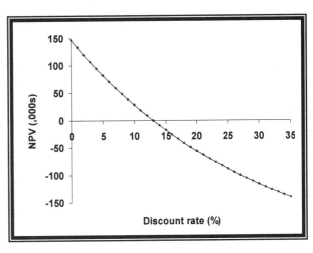

   2. The rate of return decision rule--invest in any project offering a rate of return higher than the opportunity cost of capital. See Figure 6.3 for an illustration.

A.   **A Closer Look at the Rate of Return Rule**

2.   The rate of return, or the **internal rate of return, or IRR**, or the discounted cash flow (DCF) rate of return, is the

$$\text{Rate of Return} = \frac{C_1 - \text{investment}}{\text{investment}}$$

discount rate at which NPV equals zero.

3.   If the rate of return is greater than the opportunity cost of capital, the NPV of the project is greater than zero.

4.   If the NPV of a project is less than zero (negative) the rate of return is less than the opportunity cost of capital.

5.   The rate of return rule and the NPV rule are equivalent.

D.   **Calculating the Rate of Return for Long-Lived Projects**

1.   The IRR of a single future cash flow (PV) or an annuity flow (PV of annuity) may be determined easily and arithmetically as the discount rate that equates the cost of the project with the present value of the future cash flows.

2.   The IRR of a multiple, uneven cash flow stream involves more than one unknown and is not easily solved arithmetically. One must iterate, often several times, selecting an expected IRR and discounting the cash flows until the NPV of the project is zero.

3.   The rate of return rule will give the same decision as the NPV rule as long as the NPV of a project declines smoothly as the discount rate increases. See Figure 6.2.

E.   **A Word of Caution**

1.   Do not confuse the IRR with the opportunity cost of capital. The IRR is the rate of return on the cash flows of the investment.

2.   The opportunity cost of capital is the minimum IRR acceptable to the firm. The opportunity rate of return is an estimate of the minimum acceptable rate of return demanded by investors in financial markets on similar risk investments.

F.   **Pitfalls of the Rate of Return Rule**

1.   While the IRR is easier to understand than the NPV, the NPV should be used as a final decision criterion for an investment.

2.   The IRR method has a number of theoretical pitfalls that encourages the use of the NPV method:

a.   Pitfall 1: mutually exclusive projects. Where **mutually exclusive projects** are facing the financial manager, one must be selected and the other deferred or passed by. In cases where competing projects serve the same purpose, select the project with the highest expected NPV. The IRR may give a conflicting choice relative to the NPV, which focuses more accurately on shareholder value. Analysis of the IRR on *incremental basis* will give decisions consistent with the NPV.

    b.   Pitfall 1a: mutually exclusive projects involving different outlays, same lives. Small projects may be erroneously selected over larger projects using the IRR. When NPV is higher as the discount rate increases, a project is acceptable only if its internal rate of return is less than the opportunity cost of capital.

    c.   Pitfall 2: lending or borrowing. The IRR does not distinguish between a lending (investing) or a borrowing (borrow and invest) situation, whereas the NPV clearly points out the negative aspects of the borrowing strategy.

    d.   Pitfall 3: multiple rates of return. Any change in sign (+,-) in period cash flows produces as many IRR's as there are changes in the cash flow directions of the investment. Many investments, such as oil or gas wells, entail added outlays after several periods of positive cash flows, producing the arithmetical possibility of multiple IRR's. Use the NPV, offsetting the discounted negative cash flows against the positive cash flows.

F. **Payback**

1.   A popular and relatively simple cash flow investment decision criteria is the **payback** defined as the time until cash flows recover the initial investment of the project.

2.   The payback rule states that the investment should proceed if the payback period exceeds a specified period.

3.   While cash flows are considered, the timing of the cash flows and the cash flows beyond the payback period are not considered. The payback method ignores the risk of the project cash flows and the opportunity rate of return of investors.

4.   The payback method is a popular, simple evaluation method for short-lived projects.

G. **Book Rate of Return**

1.   Another decision criterion, **book rate of return (accounting rate of return)** or the average accounting income per period divided by the book value of the investment.

$$\text{Book rate of return} = \frac{\text{book income}}{\text{book assets}}$$

2.   The book rate of return does not consider cash flows, the timing of the cash flows, nor the investors' opportunity rate of return.

III.   PROJECT INTERACTIONS

A.   **Special Situations**
1.   The capital budgeting decision analyses, to this point in the chapter, have considered mutually exclusive alternatives. In either Project A *or* Project B, the proper decision rule was to select the project with the higher NPV.
2.   There are other mutually exclusive decision analysis considerations that occur frequently that complicate our simple NPV rule. *Three* situations are discussed below.

B.   **Investment Timing**
1.   *When* to make an investment is a difficult decision in a dynamic world, where new cost-saving technology is always improving and NPV's are greater if delayed until later.
2.   The right time to purchase an ever-increasing NPV investment is indicated by the highest present value of future NPV's, found by discounting the estimated NPV's of projects made in future periods by the opportunity cost of capital.

C.   **Long-Lived versus Short-Lived Equipment**
1.   When comparing mutually exclusive projects that have unequal project lives, one must analyze the costs of the projects, the outlays and the annual costs of the projects.
2.   Calculate the **equivalent annual cost** of both machines. *Decision Rule:* Accept the project with the lowest equivalent annual cost.

$$\text{Equivalent annual cost} = \frac{\text{present value of costs}}{\text{annuity factor}}$$

3.   The equivalent annual cost is the annual (annuity or payment) project cost that equates the present value cost of the project (outlay and annual costs) at the opportunity rate of return. The equivalent annual cost is the level annual charge or cost necessary to recover the present value of investment outlays and operating costs.

C.   **Replacing an Old Machine**
   1.   Most equipment is replaced before the end of its useful economic life or its depreciable life (ACRS). Replacement decisions most often involve replacing old with new with different useful cash-flow lives.
   2.   Calculate the equivalent cost, annuity payment which equates the PV cost at the opportunity rate of return, of the new project's costs compared to the period cost of the old project.
   3.   If the equivalent period cost of the new project is less than the period cost of the old project, accept the new; if greater, delay the replacement and review later.

IV.   CAPITAL RATIONING

A.   **Capital Rationing Decision Criterion**
   1.   A business maximizes shareholders' wealth by accepting *every* project with a positive NPV.
   2.   The above statement assumes that only negative NPV's establish a limit on the capital budget of a business and that any financing needed can be raised in financial markets.
   3.   **Capital rationing** exists if there is a limit on the amount of funds available for investment. There are two forms of capital rationing: soft rationing and hard rationing.

B.   **Soft Rationing**
   1.   Soft rationing exists if businesses themselves, or their senior managers, place limits on the size of the capital budget.
   2.   Soft rationing limits can be relaxed if added NPV investments are available; financing is provided easily by financial markets.

C.   **Hard Rationing**
   1.   Hard rationing or limits on the capital budget are set by financial markets (investors).
   2.   With funding constraints, positive NPV projects are forgone.
   3.   With hard rationing, the firm must choose projects, to the limit of its financing ability, from among a list of projects with positive NPV's.
   4.   Within a hard rationing constraint, choose the projects with the highest **profitability index** to the limit of the financing budget. The profitability index is the ratio of the sum of present values of the project divided by the initial cost of the investment. It is a relative measure of the value (present value) of a project compared to its cost. The higher profitability index projects have higher PV's relative to the scarce capital invested.

D. **Pitfalls of the Profitability Index**
    1.   Using the profitability index decision rule in situations without capital rationing may give erroneous choices, similar to the IRR.
    2.   Using the profitability index without capital rationing wrongly favors small, short-lived projects over large, long-lived projects with higher NPV's.

COMPLETION QUESTIONS

1. The capital budgeting decision involves choices of (*investment projects/who to hire for staffing needs*).

2. The opportunity cost of capital is the expected rate of return (*earned/given up*) by investing in a project.

3. If the present value of a project's payoffs is (*greater/less*) that the investment outlay, the decision should be to go ahead with the project.

4. Managers increase shareholders' wealth by accepting all projects with a (*negative/positive*) net present value.

5. For most projects, the higher the discount rate, the (*higher/lower*) will be the net present value.

6. The common practice is to discount a project's cash flows at (*different/identical*) rates.

7. The internal rate of return (IRR) is the discount rate at which the project's NPV equals _____.

8. If the opportunity cost of capital less than a project's internal rate of return, the NPV will be (*negative/positive*).

9. For the IRR rule to work, the project's NPV must (*fall/rise*) as the discount rate increases.

10. When there are multiple changes in the sign of the cash flows over a project's life, the (*IRR/NPV*) rule does not work.

11. Two or more projects that cannot be pursued simultaneously are called _____ _____ projects.

12. The (*IRR/NPV*) rule can only be used successfully in selecting among mutually   exclusive projects if incremental cash flows are used.

13. The term capital (*budgeting/rationing*) refers to a limit on the amount of funds available for investment.

14. The ratio of the present value of a project's cash inflows to the investment amount is   called the _____ _____.

15. The time it takes for cash inflows from a project to recover the initial investment is   known as the _____ _____.

16. The payback calculation fails to account for (*cash flows/profits*) after the payback   period as well as the time value of money.

17. The book rate of return is equal to the average (*cash flow/net profit*) divided by the   average book value over a project's life.

PROBLEMS

Use the project information below to answer problems 1-9:

Year	Project C	Project D	Project E
0	$-10,000	$-14,000	$12,000
1	3,500	4,800	3,700
2	3,500	4,800	3,700
3	3,500	4,800	3,700
4	3,500	4,800	3,700

1.   Assuming an opportunity rate of return of 10 percent, calculate the net present value of the projects above. List the steps involved in calculating and interpreting the NPVs.

2.   Using the NPV rule, which project(s) above would you accept and why would you accept the project(s) if:

     a.   Projects C, D, and E were mutually exclusive?
     b.   Projects C, D, and E were not mutually exclusive?

3.   Calculate the internal rate of return for each project above. State the IRR decision rule. Which of the projects are acceptable using a 10 percent opportunity rate of return?

4.   If the opportunity rate of return were to increase, how high would it have to be to reject all three projects above?

5.	Calculate the profitability index for each project above.

6.	If only $15,000 were available for the projects above, which, if any, of the projects above would you accept? Why? (Hint: we are assuming a capital rationing situation).

7.	If the projects above were mutually exclusive, and without capital rationing, which would be selected for investment?

8.	Using the IRR and NPV calculations above, and with shareholder maximization as your decision criterion, which of the projects above would you select? Why?

9.	Calculate the payback period for each of the projects above. With shareholder maximization as your decision criterion, which of the projects above would you select? Why?

10.	Michelle could purchase a building for $400,000 and expects to sell it three years from now for $650,000. If alternative rates of return are expected to earn 14 percent in the period, should she buy this building? Use both the NPV and IRR methods and decision rules.

11.	If you were to pay $1000 for an art appreciation course that is expected to give you at least $200 per year in enjoyable benefits for life, what is your opportunity rate of return today if you refuse to take such a course?

12.	In the above question #11, if your opportunity rate of return were 10 percent, what is the NPV of the art appreciation class?

13.	A $100,000 machine with a useful life of three years is expected to produce cash profit before depreciation of $50,000 per year for three years. Assuming straight line depreciation, calculate the average rate of return on average book value.

14.	Two machines costing $100,000 and $112,000 are each expected to generate $35,000 in cash flows per year for five years. With an opportunity rate of return of 15 percent,

	a.	Which machine would you take if the machines were not mutually exclusive?
	b.	If only one of the machine investments will be made, which, if any, would you take?
	c.	What is the internal rate of return on each machine? What does the IRR decision rule indicate? With this information, which machine should you take if shareholder maximization were your basis for your decision?

15.	A $100,000 land investment made by Katie may be sold for $110,000 one year later. What is the rate of return on this one-year investment? If her opportunity rate of return is 15 percent, should she accept the project?

16.   A 10 percent coupon bond, $1000 face value, is purchased for $800 and will be held to maturity three years from today. Assuming interest paid annually one year from today, what is the internal rate of return on the investment?

17.   In the bond problem above, if your opportunity rate of return is 12 percent, would you buy the bond today? Why?

ANSWERS TO COMPLETION QUESTIONS

1.   investment projects
2.   given up
3.   greater
4.   positive
5.   lower
6.   identical
7.   zero
8.   positive
9.   fall
10. IRR
11. mutually exclusive
12. IRR
13. rationing
14. profitability index
15. payback period
16. cash flows
17. net profit

SOLUTIONS TO PROBLEMS

1.   Calculate NPVs at 10 percent opportunity rate of return. (4n, 10i, PV Annuity) = 3.170.

NPV Evaluation:

a.   List the expected cash flows and when they are expected--see project information.

b.   Find the present value of the future cash flows, discounting at the opportunity rate of return of 10 percent:

Project C: PV = $3,500 (3.170) = $11,095

Project D: PV = $4,800 (3.170) = $15,216

Project E: PV = $3,700 (3.170) = $11,729

c.   Calculate the NPV by subtracting the cost of the project from the PV of the discounted cash flows above.

Project C	Project D	Project E
PV $11,095	$15,216	$11,729
-outlay 10,000	14,000	12,000
NPV $ 1,095	$ 1,216	$ -271

The NPV of Project C and D are greater than zero and acceptable, while the NPV of Project E is less than zero.

2.   With reference to the NPVs of Project C, D, and E above.

a.   If only one project may be accepted (they are mutually exclusive), Project D with the highest NPV of $1,215 should be selected.

b.   If the projects above were not mutually exclusive or competing, accept all projects with positive NPVs. Projects   C and D will be accepted for the amount that we would have to pay. Project E has a negative NPV and should be rejected because the PV of $11,729 is less than the $12,000 that we must pay for the project.

3.   Let X = Unknown Interest Factor, PV Annuity, 4 years

Project C IRR: $10,000 = $3,500 X so X = $10,000/$3,500
X = 2.8571 IRR is approximately 15%. (Look on 4 year
PV Annuity line in Appendix, Table A.3)

Project D IRR: $14,000 = $4,800 X = $14,000/$4800
X = 2.9167 IRR is approximately 14%

Project E IRR: $12,000 = $3,700 X = $12,000/$3,700
X = 3.2432 IRR is approximately 9%

Financial calculator:

Project C	Project D	Project E
$10,000 PV	$14,000 PV	$12,000 PV
$ 3,500 PMT	$ 4,500 PMT	$ 3,700 PMT
4 n	4 n	4 n
Calc. I = 14.96%	Calc. I = 13.95%	Calc I = 8.95%

Under the IRR decision rule, accept all projects with IRRs greater than opportunity rate of return:

Project C = IRR of 15% which is > 10% opportunity rate; accept

Project D = IRR of 14% > 10% opportunity rate; accept

Project E = IRR of 8.95% < 10% opportunity rate; reject

4. Under the IRR decision rule, as long as the IRR equals the opportunity rate of return, shareholders will be earning their minimally acceptable rate of return, their opportunity rate. When the opportunity cost of capital exceeds the highest IRR of Project C or 15%, returns to shareholders will be below their minimally acceptable rate of return or be below what other, alternative investments would offer.

5. The profitability index for the projects are calculated below. The profitability index (PI) is calculated by dividing the PV sum of discounted cash flows by the cost (outlay) for the project. The PI decision rule is to accept projects with PIs greater than one; reject projects with PIs less than one. For competing projects under a strict capital rationing constraint, select the project with the highest PI.

Project C PI = $11,095/$10,000 = 1.11 > 1; Accept

Project D PI = $15,216/$14,000 = 1.09 > 1; Accept

Project E PI = $11,729/$12,000 = .98 < 1; Reject

6. Under this hard capital rationing situation, select the highest PI project from the acceptable projects. Project C has the highest present value per outlay.

7. Without capital rationing and assuming Projects C, D, and E are not mutually exclusive, select projects C and D with positive NPVs and IRRs greater than the 10 percent cost of capital.

8.   The NPV rule is consistent with shareholder wealth maximization. Projects C and D are acceptable with positive NPVs.

9.   The payback period is the length of time it takes the annual cash flows to cover or *pay back* the original investment.

Project C Payback Period = $10,000/$3,500 = 2.86 years

Project D Payback Period = $14,000/$4,800 = 2.92 years

Project E Payback Period = $12,000/$3,700 = 3.24 years

Under the payback period decision rule if one project is to be chosen, Project C, with the shortest payback period would be selected. All projects that pay back within policy limits will be acceptable under the payback decision rule. In this question, shareholder value is the decision criterion, so the highest positive NPV is favored. This means Project D first, then Project C will be accepted. The payback evaluation is not consistent with shareholder wealth maximization.

10.   NPV = -$400,000 + $650,000(14i,3n,PV$)
      NPV = -$400,000 + $650,000(.675)
      NPV = $38,750
      IRR: $650,000/$400,000 = 1.625   IRR is 17.6%
      Financial calculator: $400,000 PV
                                     $650,000 FV
                                     3 N
                Calculate I = 17.57%
         Decision Rules:
         NPV > 0; Accept
         IRR = 17.6% > 14%; Accept

11.   For a $1000 investment with a $200 annual return for life (perpetuity), the expected rate of return is:

         $200/$1000 = . 20 or 20%

12.   NPV = -$1000 + 200(10i,30n,PV Annuity)
      NPV = -$1000 + $200(9.427)
      NPV = $885.4 (30n)
      NPV = $993.4 (60n)

In problem 11, the expected return of 20 percent exceeds the opportunity rate of return of 10 percent and is consistent with a positive NPV, calculated in problem 12.

13. Average book rate of return = average annual income average annual book assets

Year	0	1	2	3
Gross Book Value	$100,000	$100,000	$100,000	$100,000
Cumulative Depreciation	0	$ 33,333	$ 66,666	$100,000
Net Book Value	$100,000	$ 66,667	$ 33,334	0

So the average annual book value is $50,000.

Year	1	2	3
Cash Profit before Depr.	$50,000	$50,000	$50,000
minus Depr.	$33,333	$33,333	$33,333
Net income	$16,667	$16,667	$16,667

Average book rate of return = $16,667/$50,000 or 33%

14. a. With the same cash flows and lower investment, the lower cost $100,000 investment seems better, but we must calculate the NPV of each project to see if the investments contribute to shareholder value or earn the shareholder opportunity rate of return.

NPV = -$100,000 + $35,000(15i,5n,PV Annuity)
NPV = -$100,000 + $35,000(3.352)
NPV = $17,320

NPV = -$112,000 + $35,000(15i,5n,PV Annuity)
NPV = -$112,000 + $35,000(3.352)
NPV = $5320
Accept both if not mutually exclusive.

b. If mutually exclusive, take the investment with the higher NPV, the $100,000 investment.

c. The IRR evaluation should give the same decision.

$100,000 = $35,000 (5n,PV Annuity, IRR?)
IRR: $100,000/$35,000 = 2.857 from Tables the IRR is 22 percent

Financial calculator: $100,000 PV
$35,000 PMT
5 n
Calculate I = 22.1%

$112,000 = $35,000 (5n,PV Annuity,IRR?)
IRR: $112,000/$35,000 = 3.200 from Tables the IRR is 17 percent

Financial Calculator: $112,000 PV
$35,000 PMT
5 n
Calculate I = 16.99%

The IRR for both investments is greater than the 15 percent opportunity rate of return and are acceptable. If mutually exclusive, take the $100,000 machine earning the highest NPV to maximize shareholder value.

15.   Rate of Return $= \dfrac{\text{Profit}}{\text{investment}} = \dfrac{C_1 - C_0}{C_0}$

$$= \dfrac{\$110,000 - \$100,000}{\$100,000} = .10 \text{ or } 10\%$$

With alternative investments of 15%, the investor would reject this investment opportunity.

16. | Year | Cash Flows | Interest Factors |
|------|------------|------------------|
| 0 | $- 800 | 1 |
| 1 | $ 100 | PV, single cash flow |
| 2 | $ 100 | PV, single cash flow |
| 3 | $1100 | PV, single cash flow |

Estimate the interest factors that, times the cash flows and summed, equals the outlay of $800 or NPV = 0. Or,

NPV=0 = $-800 + 100(3n,PV Ann.,IRR?) + 1000 (3n,PV Ann.,IRR?)

With two unknowns in the equation, one must estimate the IRR that generates a NPV = 0.

Financial calculator: $-800 PV
                                  $100 PMT
                                  $1000 FV
                                  3 n
                Calculate I = 19.4%

17.   The IRR of 19.4% exceeds the 12% minimum acceptable rate of return. Make the
       investment. Or,

       NPV = $-800 + $100 (12i,3n,PV Ann.) + 1000(12i,3n,PV $)
       NPV = $-800 + $100(2.402) + $1000(.712)
       NPV = $152.20 > 0, buy the bond at $800. The investor would have been willing to pay
       $800 + $152.20 or $952.20 for the bond, accepting a 12 percent IRR or expected yield to
       maturity on the bond.

USING DISCOUNTED CASH-FLOW ANALYSIS

INTRODUCTION

This chapter builds upon the last chapter and focuses on estimating the expected cash flows of an investment project. There are a number of general concepts and rather detailed procedures that you must master. One of the more important concepts is that of determining the "incremental" cash-flow impact of a new project. The standard question for you to ask is, "What changes, given the decision to make the investment?" The Blooper Industries example is a good discussion example that enables one to cover most of the concepts and rules developed in the chapter. Use the Blooper Industries example as a review to test your skills. When working the cash-flows examples, complete the analysis with an assessment of the NPV and IRR and their corresponding decision rules to accept or reject. This enables you to tie the last chapter and this one into a continuous process.

LEARNING CHECKLIST

In this skill-specific chapter you should be able to accomplish the following after reading the chapter and working the end-of-chapter problems:

____1. Differentiate cash flow from profits. Remember discount expected cash flows, not expected profits.

____2. Estimate the incremental cash flows of an investment project, including the incidental effects of an investment on other company cash flows.

____3. Be able to point out and deal with sunk costs and opportunity costs associated with an investment project.

____4. Remember to include estimated changes in net working capital for an investment (beginning and end) and to exclude the interest costs (financing costs) associated with financing a project. The opportunity cost of capital includes the cost of financing.

SOURCES OF BUSINESS INFORMATION

Federal Reserve Bulletin and Statistical Abstract. Two very important sources of business statistics, from interest rates, GNP, money supply, etc., are the Statistical Abstract, published by the U.S. Government, and the Federal Reserve Bulletin, published by the Federal Reserve System. The Statistical Abstract is organized around thirty-two major topics from population and employment (real economy) to banking and insurance (financial economy). The consumer and producer price indices for many years may be found here. The monthly Federal Reserve Bulletin has an appendix that tends to focus on financial statistics, including many tables associated with monetary policy and money supply data, interest rates, and international financial statistics.

CHAPTER OUTLINE, KEY CONCEPTS AND TERMS

I. DISCOUNT CASH FLOW, NOT PROFITS

A. Income statements measure historical performance according to generally accepted accounting principles, not in cash-flow terms.

B. Cash flows, when they occur, discounted at the opportunity rate of return is the proper method for net present value.

II. DISCOUNT *INCREMENTAL* CASH FLOWS

A. Include All Indirect Effects
  1. Project cash-flow analysis should consider the differential cash flows that occur given the acceptance of the project.
  2. Incremental cash flows represent the cash-flow changes that the new project creates, or the cash flow *with* the project *less* the cash flow *without* the project.

$$\text{Incremental Cash Flow} = \text{cash flow with project} - \text{cash flow without project}$$

  3. All differential cash-flow implications of the project must be considered, including the impact of the new project on *any* other aspect of the business cash flows.

B. **Forget Sunk Costs**
  1. Cash flows not related to the project are irrelevant in the project cash-flow analysis.
  2. Cash flows that occur regardless of whether the project investment is made are sunk costs and are not relevant to the current project.

C. **Include Opportunity Costs**
  1. Include opportunity cost cash flows, such as the value of land which you could otherwise sell, as a relevant cost of an investment project.
  2. The **opportunity cost**, or the best alternative value option of the land owned prior to the investment consideration, is a part of the investment outlay.

D. Recognizing The Investment In Working Capital
  1. The incremental **net working capital**, added current assets less added current liabilities, represents relevant cash-flow costs of initiating a project

and should be part of the NPV analysis. Working capital recovered at the end of the project is a relevant cash flow.

    2.   Ignoring working capital, or the fact that varying levels of incremental net working capital may occur throughout the life of the project, or ignoring the recovery of working capital are *three* common errors in project cash-flow analysis.

E.   **Beware of Allocated Overhead Costs**

    1.   Overhead costs, such as heat and lights, incurred whether the project investment is made or not, are irrelevant to the project cash-flow analysis.

    2.   Include only the additional or incremental cash-flow costs, only when they occur, in the project analysis.

III.   DISCOUNT NOMINAL CASH FLOWS BY THE NOMINAL COST OF CAPITAL

A.   If the discount rate or the opportunity rate of return used in project analysis is in nominal terms, versus inflation adjusted or in real terms, relevant project cash flows should be in nominal terms as well. One may use real, inflation adjusted discount rates and cash flows, but consistency in this matter is what is important.

$$1 + \text{real interest rate} = \frac{1 + \text{nominal interest rate}}{1 + \text{inflation rate}}$$

B.   Expected cash flows, if inflation is expected during the life of the project, must be adjusted upward to nominal values. The adjustment should reflect the added price changes in the prices of the products, labor costs, etc., rather than a general inflation rate, such as the Consumer Price Index.

IV.   SEPARATE INVESTMENT AND FINANCING DECISIONS

A.   When the cash flows of an investment are analyzed, *how* the investment is financed, or the financing cost of the project, is ignored.

B.   How the project is financed, and the financing costs, are variables affecting the opportunity rate of return, and are used to discount the cash flows. Financing the project and its impact is considered when calculating the opportunity rate of return, (studied later in the book).

C.   The value of the investment is considered by itself, independent of financing choice.

V. CALCULATING CASH FLOW

A. A project total cash flow is the sum of three components: capital investment, investment in working capital, and cash flow from operations.

B. Capital Investment - The money spent to begin any new project can be significant. Such large expenditures to start projects may produce tremendous value to the firm, however, the immediate impact may very well be a reduction in current cash flow. When determining the firm's total cash flow, the expenditures on new investments must be subtracted.

C. Investment In Working Capital - All new projects entail the conversion of cash assets into other types of assets. Items such as inventory, raw materials, and finished products drain cash from the firm. Coinciding with these asset conversions may be changes in accounts receivable and accounts payable balances.

D. Cash From Operations - The most recognizable source of cash is the firm's operations. Do not be deceived into thinking that this number can be pulled directly form the income statement. There are slight modifications, most notably depreciation, which must be made in order to arrive at a true cash flow. All of these adjustments are simple math, yet sometimes require investigative powers to locate all corporate transactions that impact the cash flow of a firm.

VI. EXAMPLE: BLOOPER INDUSTRIES

A. Work carefully through the Blooper Industries example, reinforcing concepts mentioned earlier.

Blooper Industries

	Year 0	1	2	3	4	5	6
Cap Invest	10,000						
WC	1,500	4,075	4,279	4,493	4,717	3,039	0
Change in WC	1,500	2,575	204	214	225	−1,678	−3,039
Revenues		15,000	15,750	16,538	17,364	18,233	
Expenses		10,000	10,500	11,025	11,576	12,155	
Depreciation		2,000	2,000	2,000	2,000	2,000	
Pretax Profit		3,000	3,250	3,513	3,788	4,078	
.Tax (35%)		1,050	1,137	1,230	1,326	1,427	
Profit		1,950	2,113	2,283	2,462	2,651	

(,000s)

B.   Calculating Blooper's Project Cash Flows
1.   All of the outlay, $10 million, is assumed to be made now or in the zero period, with no salvage value expected at the end of the project life.
2.   Note the changes in net working capital, or net added current assets needed, early in the project. Later, as the project winds down, net current assets are no longer needed and contribute to the positive cash flow.
3.   Revenues are estimated through the periods in which revenues are thought to be generated. Do not arbitrarily cut-off the periods of cash-flow generation.
4.   Lines four and five are assumed to be cash flow revenue and expenses, with depreciation to be the only noncash revenue/expense in the analysis.
5.   Project cash flows are the sum of *three* components: investment outlay of the project, investment in project net working capital, and project cash flow from operations.
6.   Cash flows from operations may be determined from the data *two* ways: calculate the sum of cash inflows and outflows, or add back depreciation (noncash expense) to net after-tax profit..

Blooper Industries

Cash Flow From Operations (,000s)

Revenues	15,000
- Expenses	10,000
– Depreciation	2,000
= Profit before tax	3,000
.-Tax @ 35 %	1,050
= Net profit	1,950
+ Depreciation	2,000
= CF from operations	3,950 **or $3,950,000**

C.   Calculating the NPV of Blooper's Project -- Cash flows are conservatively assumed to occur at the end of the year.

D.   **Further Notes and Wrinkles Arising from Blooper's Project**
1.   Nominal annual depreciation amounts, given inflation, yield lower real tax shield cash flow.
2.   Congress established depreciation schedules, called the **accelerated cost recovery system (ACRS)**, that provide an accelerated rate of depreciation,

depending on the class of asset, which offsets the reduced real value of the tax shield when inflation exists.

3. The half-year convention assumes that the asset was purchased at mid-point of the first year and retired by the mid-point of the year after the recovery period.

4. The ACRS provides a faster depreciation rate (double-declining balance) and tax shield recovery compared to the **straight-line depreciation** rate, which provides for equal depreciation amounts over the useful life of the project.

5. The ACRS depreciation tax shield affects cash flow and is relevant for capital budgeting analysis.

6. Salvage value cash flows involve the net cash received from the disposal *less* any taxes (sold for more than book value) on the sale or *plus* any tax shield (sold for less than book value) loss (book loss times the marginal tax rate).

Blooper Industries

Net Cash Flow (entire project) (,000s)

	Year 0	1	2	3	4	5	6
Cap Invest	-10,000						
Change in WC	-1,500	-2,575	-204	-214	-225	1,678	3,039
CF from Op		3,950	4,113	4,283	4,462	4,651	
Net Cash Flow	-11,500	1,375	3,909	4,069	4,237	6,329	3,039

NPV @ 12% = $3,564,000

COMPLETION QUESTIONS

1. Wise investment decision making relies, in part, on identifying (*cash flows/net profits*).

2. Capital expenditures (*are/are not*) deducted from revenues when calculating profits.

3. When sales are made on credit they are recognized in the calculation of (*cash flows/net profits*).

4. Cash flows for project evaluation (*are/are not*) determined by subtracting cash fl ows occurring without the project from those that would happen if the project were accepted.

5. Incremental cash flows (*do/do not*) include sunk costs.

6. Incremental cash flows (*do/do not*) include opportunity costs.

7. Changes in net working capital associated with the project (*should/should not*) be included in cash flow calculations.

8. If no additional overhead costs will be created, (*no/a proportion of*) overhead costs should be allocated to the project's cash flow.

9. To account for the effects of inflation, (*nominal/real*) cash flows should be discounted by the (*nominal/real*) interest rate.

10. Project financing costs (*should/should not*) be included in the cash flow calculations.

11. Revenues minus the total of expenses and (*depreciation/taxes*) equals cash flow from operations.

12. Cash flow from operations can be found by adding (*depreciation/ salvage value*) to net profits.

13. The reduction in taxes attributable to the depreciation allowance is called the depreciation _____ _____.

14. The depreciation tax shield (*decreases/increases*) cash flows.

15. The Accelerated Cost Recovery System (ACRS) enables a firm to realize (*depreciation sooner/more total depreciation deductions*).

16. In comparison with straight line depreciation, ACRS (*decreases/increases*) the value of the depreciation tax shield.

17. The salvage value of an asset that has been fully depreciated is treated as a (*gain/loss*) for tax purposes.

18. When only one project will be selected from two or more choices, the projects are said to be (*interdependent/mutually exclusive*).

19. When a project decision concerns when to make an investment, the choice should be the year that offers the (*highest/lowest*) NPV of benefits.

20. The _____ annual cost calculation is used to evaluate projects that do the same thing but which have unequal lives.

PROBLEMS

1. Mel's Music, Inc. expects to sell $500,000 of instruments and supplies this coming year. Depreciation on his furnishings and rental instruments will be $50,000. He will pay $300,000 for labor and the items he sells. The rent on his store is $60,000 and he figures taxes will be 40 percent of taxable income. Compute his expected net profit.

2. Use the three methods outlined in the textbook to compute the operating cash flow for Mel's.

3. MaryAnn's Medical Supplies had sales last month of $100,000 and operating expenses of $90,000. During that month she reduced her accounts receivable by $12,000 and increased her bank loan by $8,000. What was the net cash flow for her business?

4. Jason's Jump Rope Company (JJRC) decided to purchase a new delivery vehicle for $100,000. If this asset is depreciated according to Accelerated Cost Recovery System for a 3-year recovery period, what would be the book value of the truck at the end of the second year?

5. Suppose JJRC sold the vehicle described in problem 4 for $40,000 three years after it was purchased. Assuming the tax rate is 40 percent, what would be the net cash realized from the sale?

6. Jackie's Jelly Beans, Inc. (JJBI) is considering buying a new mixing machine for $50,000. It would replace an existing machine having a trade-in value of $10,000 which is also equal to its book value. Production cost savings with the new machine are estimated to be $20,000 per year. The life of the new mixer is 10 years and it would have a zero market value at that time. The cost of capital is 12 percent, the tax rate is 40 percent, and straight line depreciation is used. What are the project cash flows?

7.   For JJBI in the above problem:
      a.   Calculate the net present value (NPV).
      b.   Calculate the internal rate of return (IRR).

8.   Tell how the NPV and IRR would change if the accelerated cost recovery schedule (ACRS) were used instead of straight line depreciation for the data presented in problem 6. You don't need to actually make the calculations, just describe the effect of using ACRS.

9.   What would be the equivalent annual cost of the machine described in problem 6?

10.   Geree is considering buying a personal computer system for her home use for $5,000. She estimates the pc will have a 3-year useful life and that it will have no significant value at the end of 3 years.. She can also lease the system for the same period for $1,000 annually. Which is the lowest cost alternative if her opportunity cost is 14 percent?

11.   Suppose Geree's husband, Shell, thinks he can negotiate a better lease arrangement for the computer. What would be the maximum payment for each of the three years that would be necessary to make the two options have an equal cost?

ANSWERS TO COMPLETION QUESTIONS

1.   cash flows
2.   are not
3.   cash flows
4.   are
5.   do not
6.   do
7.   should
8.   no
9.   nominal, nominal
10.   should not
11.   depreciation
12.   depreciation
13.   tax shield
14.   increases
15.   depreciation
16.   increases
17.   gain
18.   mutually exclusive
19.   highest
20.   equivalent

SOLUTIONS TO PROBLEMS

1. From data given in the problem, the following statement can be prepared:

INCOME STATEMENT FOR MEL'S MUSIC, $	
Revenue	500,000
Variable Expenses	300,000
Fixed Expenses	60,000
Depreciation	50,000
DEBIT	90,000
Taxes (40%)	36,000
Net Income	54,000

2. Net income plus depreciation approach:
$$\$54,000 + \$50,000 = \$104,000$$

Cash inflow - cash outflow analysis: (this method simply subtracts all of the cash outflows from the cash inflows)
$$\$500,000 - (\$300,000 + \$60,000 + \$36,000) = \$104,000$$

Depreciation tax shield approach: (this case adds the after-tax cost of the net cash flows to the tax savings of the non-cash charges)
$$(\$500,000 - \$300,000 - \$60,000) \times 0.60 + \$50,000 \times 0.40 = \$104,000$$
Note that all three methods result in the same value.

3. MaryAnn's sales efforts generated $100,000 - $90,000 or $10,000. She also generated cash by reducing her accounts receivable by $12,000 and $8,000 by increasing her bank loan. These actions provided $20,000 so her total new cash was $10,000 + $20,000 or $30,000.

4. A complete depreciation schedule is shown because a part of it is needed for the next problem.

YEAR	ACRS, %	DEPRECIATION, $	YR-END BOOK VALUE, $
1	33.33	33,333	66,667
2	44.45	44,450	22,217
3	14.81	14,810	7,407
4	7.41	7,410	0[1]

The book value at the end of the second year is $22,217.

5. At the end of the third year JJRC shows a book value of $7,407. The firm realized $20,000 from the sale of the vehicle so there is a taxable profit of $20,000 - $7,407 or $12,593. Taxes would be 40 percent of this or $5,037. The net cash from the sale would be $20,000 - $5,037 or $14,963.

6.

Cost of new mixer	$50,000
less trade-in allowance	10,000
Net outlay	$40,000
Annual savings	$20,000
less depreciation ($50,000/5)	10,000
Taxable income	$10,000
Tax	4,000
Net profit	$ 6,000
add depreciation	10,000
Cash flow	$16,000

---

[1]The book value calculation is $3 due to round off error. The zero amount shown is correct.

The $40,000 outlay is followed by net cash flows in years 1-5 of $16,000. Note that the cash flow would be reduced by any additions to working capital. This is illustrated in problem 11 of the textbook.

7.   a.   The NPV $= \text{(PV factor)} \times \$16,000 - \$40,000$
            $= 3.605 \times \$16,000 - \$40,000 = \$17,680$

     b.   IRR: Remember that:
                 PV of inflows - PV of outflows = 0
                 PV factor $\times \$16,000 = \$40,000$
                 PV factor $= \$40,000/\$16,000 = 2.5$
            the IRR is almost 29 percent.

8.   Think what happens when accelerated depreciation is used in place of straight line depreciation--the higher charges occur earlier. This means greater deductions leading to lower taxable income and lower taxes and lower net profit in the earlier years. However, the cash flow is higher! This is because the only change to cash flows is a reduction in the outflow for taxes in the earlier years. Note that the total amount of depreciation is unchanged. ACRS thus makes it possible to shift cash flows from later years to earlier years. Since money has a time value, we would rather have it sooner. The result is to increase the project's NPV and the IRR as well. This is the explanation why the ACRS was instigated to stimulate capital investment by improving the returns to expanding businesses.

9.   The equivalent annual cost is the cost per period with the same present value as the cost of buying and operating the new mixer. In this case the 5-year annuity that is equivalent to the investment outlay is:
            $= \$50,000/\text{PV of annuity}$
            $= \$50,000/3.605 = \$13,860.$

10. The cost of buying: $= \$5,000 - \$1,000 \times \text{PV factor}$
                           $= \$5,000 - \$1,000 \times 2.914$
                           $= \$2,086$

     The cost of leasing: $= \$1,000 \times \text{PV factor}$
                            $= \$1,000 \times 2.914$
                            $= \$2,914$
     So it is cheaper to buy the computer.

11. The maximum lease payments would be the annual amounts whose present value is equal to the net present value of the purchase option. Thus:
            $\$2,086 = \text{lease payment} \times \text{PV factor}$
            lease payment $= \$2,086/2.914 = \$716$

PROJECT ANALYSIS

INTRODUCTION

Past chapters focused on the general concepts and specific techniques of the capital budgeting evaluation. This chapter extends those ideas to a more realistic setting within a business. In every business, large and small, the capital budget is assembled, negotiated, reassembled, and finally is presented to senior management and the board of directors. A small proprietor may assess the value of new equipment by herself over morning coffee. As the business grows, the people, dimensions, and breadth of competing opportunities grows exponentially! All this is planning, estimating, and setting a course in an uncertain future. A plan should not be a single point in a very uncertain future, but provide a basis for considering alternative results to varying future conditions. "What if" analysis, scenario analysis, break-even analysis (accounting and NPV), etc., are techniques searching for a "feel" for the future. A capital plan should consider several alternative economic situations; a review of new investments should consider the most critical variables that will "make or break" the success of the project. In addition to the useful planning techniques, the chapter offers a good planning perspective for you as a future manager: We do not know what the future holds, but we have a good feel for the results, and are ready, when specific things happen. Read and study the chapter within a planning format and overview, rather than looking at a series of specific planning techniques.

LEARNING CHECKLIST

After preparing this chapter you should be able to:

____1. Appreciate the practical problems of capital budgeting in large corporations.

____2. Be able to define and differentiate sensitivity analysis, scenario analysis, and break-even analysis.

____3. Recognize the importance of managerial flexibility in the capital budgeting process.

SOURCES OF BUSINESS INFORMATION

Value Line Investment Survey. If you are doing any research on specific industries or companies, the Value Line Investment Survey offers a compilation of financial and operating data, and an analysis of the future prospects, for over 1700 companies. The analysis of each individual corporation is thorough and comprehensive, but is contained in a one-page presentation. Industry analyses provided here are important for reviewing career opportunities. The Investment Survey, besides considerable financial and operating information about a company, offers information about the investment opportunities of the company's stock and the relative riskiness of the company. Use this reference next time you have a company- or industry-specific assignment. The Value Line Weekly Investment Survey provides weekly updates to the Investment Survey.

Data From SEC EDGAR Web Site. Internet data or text files can easily be downloaded with the help of any internet browser. One can download a whole page or selected material. For example, go to the Federal Reserve Board of St. Louis clicking on the underlined text. Then click on "FRED" the historical database of economic and financial data. Next, click on the link entitled "Data files" index of historical data series available. Then proceed to click on "Monthly Interest Rates" and then "6-month Certificate of Deposit Rate. "You will now see the requested time series. To download this information do the following:

Downloading Software from the Internet. If you don't have a compression/expansion utility already, that should probably be first on your list, because much of the other software will be in a compressed format to speed up the download time and you'll need to expand it in order to use it. Visit http://www.shareware.com/ to download such software.

If you are using a Mac, the file will automatically be downloaded to your desktop. If you are using Navigator for Windows, the "Save As" window will open allowing you to choose a destination for the file. Be sure to note where it is so that you can find it after the download is finished. If you are using Explorer, the "File Download" window with a warning about viruses will open first. Choose "Save it to disk" and then the same "Save As" window will open as in Navigator. To install the program, find the file and double click it. You will be prompted as to how to finish the installation.

CHAPTER OUTLINE, KEY CONCEPTS AND TERMS

I. HOW FIRMS ORGANIZE THE INVESTMENT PROCESS

    A.   The Process
        1.   There are two important steps in the investment process: the capital budget and project authorization.
        2.   They include the planning and proposals of investment, followed by evaluation and approval.

B.	Stage 1: The Capital Budget
1.	The **capital budget** is a list of planned investment projects.
2.	The list may be compiled from the bottom up (divisions and departments) or from the top down (strategic planning).
3.	Project plans from the bottom up bear the specific knowledge of people close to the customer and other business dimensions; senior management has the perspective of corporate strategy and the big picture of the firm's operations.

C.	Stage 2: Project Authorization
1.	*Four* different project areas are common in a business:
a.	Outlays required by law, such as safety equipment, or projects required under company policy are evaluated to find the lowest cost.
b.	Maintenance or cost reduction projects, such as replacement decisions.
c.	Projects related to expanding the capacity of existing business activity.
d.	Investment projects in new products or services.
2.	The required outlays, number one above, are mandated and the lowest cost for compliance is the decision rule. The other three types of projects should use the NPV method as a decision criterion.

D.	Problems and Some Solutions
1.	Making sure that assumptions are consistent among competing proposals is important. A top-down set of assumptions, such as an economic forecast, focuses assumptions in a narrow, consistent range.
2.	Keeping the manager reward system consistent with shareholder returns encourages a long-run focus in investment evaluation, and helps eliminate conflicts of interest.
3.	Competition for scarce funds may lead to an inflation of estimated project cash-flows or benefits, and an overstatement of the estimated project NPV.
4.	Capital rationing techniques, which force divisional managers to send only the best projects forward, and intense scrutiny of projects are project-screening techniques that assure only the best projects are accepted for investment.

## II.	SOME "WHAT-IF" QUESTIONS

A.	**Different Possibilities** -- Project cash flows and NPVs may be estimated under different assumptions to improve the decision process.

B. **Sensitivity Analysis**
    1.   Changing a single, specific variable within a range from most likely to optimistic to pessimistic and evaluating the NPVs is called **sensitivity analysis**.
    2.   Sensitivity analysis reveals the significant variables, which, if varied or mis-estimated, would significantly change the NPV and acceptability of the project.
    3.   Sensitivity analysis assumes that the individual variables are independent of each other. This is usually not the case. Sales cannot be varied without significantly affecting certain costs. This interrelationship between variables limits the extent that one variable can be changed without altering another, and thus, narrows the range of the sensitivity analysis.

Sensitivity Analysis (Finefodder's example)

Sensitivity Analysis

	Year 0	Years 1 - 12
Investment	- 5,400	
Sales		16,000
Variable Costs		13,000
Fixed Costs		2,000
Depreciation		450
Pretax profit		550
. Taxes @ 40%		220
Profit after tax		330
Operating cash flow		780
Net Cash Flow	- 5,400	780

NPV= $478

Possible Outcomes

	Range		
Variable	Pessimistic	Expected	Optimistic
Investment(000s)	6,200	5,400	5,000
Sales(000s)	14,000	16,000	18,000
Var Cost (% of sales)	83%	81.25%	80%
Fixed Costs(000s)	2,100	2,000	1,900

95

C. Scenario Analysis
    1.   Like sensitivity analysis, **scenario analysis** involves the same change of variables to see the impact on NPV, but scenario analysis differs from sensitivity analysis in that a particular combination of variables under specific assumptions is compared with another scenario of assumptions.
    2.   Simulation analysis, an extension of scenario analysis, generates many scenarios and, with an estimate of their probability, generates NPV estimates for a wide range of scenarios.

Sensitivity Analysis (Finefodder's example - continued)

NPV Calculations for Pessimistic Investment Scenario

	Year 0	Years 1 - 12
Investment	- 6,200	
Sales		16,000
Variable Costs		13,000
Fixed Costs		2,000
Depreciation		450
Pretax profit		550
. Taxes @ 40%		220
Profit after tax		330
Operating cash flow		780
Net Cash Flow	- 6,200	780

NPV= ($121)

NPV Possibilities

	NPV (000s)		
Variable	Pessimistic	Expected	Optimistic
Investment(000s)	- 121	478	778
Sales(000s)	- 1,218	478	2,174
Var Cost (% of sales)	- 788	478	1,382
Fixed Costs(000s)	26	478	930

III. BREAK EVEN ANALYSIS

A. Break-Even Analysis
1. In any business venture forecast, **break-even analysis**, or an estimate of the sales point where total revenue equals total expenses is an important focus point for managerial analysis.
2. Estimating the accounting break-even point level of sales of a project requires identifying the level of fixed costs involved in the project and the variable cost/sales ratio related to the project.

Break-Even Analysis (Trinova Airliner example)

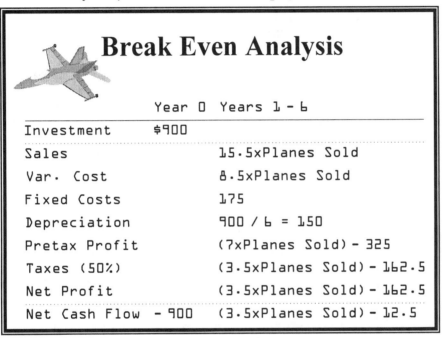

Break Even Analysis

	Year 0	Years 1 - 6
Investment	$900	
Sales		15.5xPlanes Sold
Var. Cost		8.5xPlanes Sold
Fixed Costs		175
Depreciation		900 / 6 = 150
Pretax Profit		(7xPlanes Sold) - 325
Taxes (50%)		(3.5xPlanes Sold) - 162.5
Net Profit		(3.5xPlanes Sold) - 162.5
Net Cash Flow	- 900	(3.5xPlanes Sold) - 12.5

B. Accounting Break-Even Analysis
1. The sales break-even point is estimated to be the fixed costs including depreciation divided by the percentage of sales contribution margin, or the fixed costs including depreciation divided by one minus the variable cost to sales ratio:

$$\text{BEP Sales} = \frac{\text{Fixed costs inc. depr.}}{\text{Added profit for each unit sold}}$$

$$= \frac{\text{Fixed costs inc. depr.}}{\text{Price - variable cost/unit (contr. margin)}}$$

$$= \frac{\text{Fixed costs inc. depr.}}{1 - \text{variable costs/sales or \% contribution}}$$

2.   A project that *just* breaks even in accounting income terms will have a negative NPV.

Answer

The break even point, is the # of Planes Sold that generates a NPV=$0.

The present value annuity factor of a 6 year cash flow at 10% is 4.355

Thus,

`NPV = -900 + 4.355(3.5xPlanes Sold - 12.5)`

C.   NPV Break-Even Analysis

1.   NPV break-even analysis calculates the level of sales that generates an NPV of zero or an internal rate of return that equals the opportunity rate of return of investors.

2.   With the cost of the project = the present value of cash flows = NPV of zero, the level of sales that generates the periodic cash flows needed to generate the given present value is the unknown.

3.   The PV of cash flows = annuity factor (periods/opportunity rate) x (depreciation per period) + [(1 - tax rate)(sales x contribution margin - fixed cost and depreciation)]. The bracketed quantity represents net income plus depreciation or the after-tax cash flows. Sales higher than the zero NPV sales will produce positive NPV.

4.   The sales level that produces an NPV of zero is always *higher* than the sales level for the accounting break-even point.

Break-Even Analysis (Trinova Airliner example - continued)

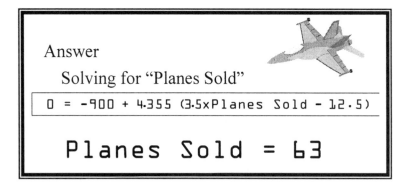

Answer

Solving for "Planes Sold"

```
0 = -900 + 4.355 (3.5xPlanes Sold - 12.5)
```

Planes Sold = 63

D.   Operating Leverage

1.   The accounting break-even point depends upon the level of **fixed costs**, or the costs incurred regardless of the level of output, associated with the project and the variable cost/sales ratio or the profit on each extra sale. **Variable costs** are costs that vary directly with sales.

2.   Projects with a high proportion of fixed costs generate higher NPVs when sales are high than projects with low proportions of fixed costs (high proportions of variable costs). The contribution to fixed cost, sales less variable costs, contributes to fixed cost until the break-even point and thereafter contributes to profit/cash flows. The high fixed cost project will have a high contribution to profit for each higher level of sales.

3.   A project with fixed costs is said to have **operating leverage**. The extent of

$$DOL = \frac{\text{\% change in profits}}{\text{\% change in sales}}$$

operating leverage or the extent of fixed costs versus variable costs/sales is called the **degree of operating leverage** (DOL).

4.   The degree of operating leverage is the percentage change in profits

$$DOL = 1 + \frac{\text{fixed costs}}{\text{profits}}$$

given a one percent change in sales, or:
5.   Arithmetically, the DOL is one plus the fixed costs/profit ratio, measured at a specific level of sales, or:
6.   The risk of a project, or the variability of the realizable NPV, is directly related to the degree of operating leverage of the project. The higher the fixed costs, the greater the variation in cash flows given a change from estimated sales.

IV.   FLEXIBILITY IN CAPITAL BUDGETING

A.   The Rationale
1.   In addition to reviewing all variations of possible cash flows associated with a project, selecting projects with a high degree of flexibility provides managers with the opportunity to adjust to future, unknown, competitive and economic factors associated with the project.
2.   Decision trees assist in measuring the value of management options to vary a future course of action associated with a project with sequential decisions.

B.   Decision Trees
1.   A **decision tree** diagrams alternative sequential decisions and possible outcomes.
2.   Expected cash flow outcomes and the probability of the outcome provide the opportunity to calculate a conditional probability expected NPV of all future cash flow possibilities.
3.   The NPV becomes the discounted, at the opportunity rate of return, expected value payoff of alternative outcomes.

C.   The Option to Expand
1.   Projects which develop in stages, or are developed with future flexibility in mind, provide managers with options to expand at each stage or to change the nature of the project in the future in response to market forces.
2.   The cost of the option is the opportunity costs of not doing the entire project now.

D.   **Abandonment Options** -- Managers must recognize and evaluate the option to abandon a project at every point after they make the initial investment.

E. **Flexible Production Facilities**
   1. Building in an option to change its production or raw material mix provides future flexibility for the manager.
   2. The cost of the option is the flexibility changes built into the project compared to a single purpose design of the project.

F. **Investment Timing Options**
   1. Any project proposal provides the manager the option to invest or accept the project.
   2. The option to invest can be exercised now or later.
   3. One must weigh the value of cash flows lost by delaying the project versus the possibility of adding new information about the future cash flows or possible success of the project if it is postponed for a time.

COMPLETION QUESTIONS

1. The list of planned investment projects for a firm is called the (*capital/cash*) budget.

2. Estimating the effect of changes in the forecasts of key variables such as sales and costs is called (*scenario/sensitivity*) analysis.

3. (*Scenario/Sensitivity*) analysis employs a set of assumptions for interrelated variables.

4. When a computer is used to calculate outcomes from hundreds or thousands of possible combinations of variables, it is called (*financial/simulation*) analysis.

5. Break-even analysis determines the level of (*profits/sales*) needed to achieve zero profits.

6. When the cash flows from operations equal the initial investment, the NPV will be (*negative/zero*).

7. The determination of revenues needed to make the present value of inflows equal to the present value of outflows is done in a (*NPV/future*) value break-even analysis.

8. Fixed costs (*do/do not*) vary with different levels of sales.

9. Variable costs (*are constant/rise*) as output increases.

10. Labor and material costs are (*fixed/variable*).

11. The higher the proportion of fixed costs the (*higher/lower*) the break-even point.

12. The lower the level of fixed costs the (*higher/lower*) will be the operating leverage.

13. The degree of operating leverage is equal to the percentage change in (*costs/profits*) divided by the percentage change in (*costs/sales*).

14. A diagram of alternative sequential decisions and possible outcomes from those decisions is called a _____ _____.

15. Estimation of the probabilities of different possible outcomes from an investment project is called _____ analysis.

16. The closing down of a nuclear generating station is an example of (*negative/positive*) abandonment value.

17. Flexibility in production facilities and multiple sources of raw materials is appropriate because the future is (*certain/uncertain*).

PROBLEMS

1. Last year the AA Division of Long Life, Inc. produced 10 million batteries at a total cost of $0.60 per unit. The chief financial officer estimates they could double production this year without having to add additional fixed costs. The total costs would grow to $10 million. What are the variable costs per unit?

2. How much are the fixed costs in problem 1?

3. Louisville Loopers expects to make baseball bats for labor and materials of $7 per unit. They will wholesale them for $14 each. Investment in depreciable plant and equipment will be $15 million which is to be allocated over the useful life of 15 years. Annual fixed charges for all other costs are $600,000. What is the accounting break-even point?

4. What is the net present value break-even point in problem 3 if the tax rate is 40 percent and the cost of capital is 10 percent?

5. What is the lowest degree of operating leverage for a profitable company with no fixed costs?

6. A manufacturer of memory chips estimates $200 million of sales with a 10 percent profit margin for the coming year. The degree of operating leverage is 8. What will be its profits if it only achieves 90 percent of its sales forecast?

7. Suppose the manufacturer in problem 5 has a banner year with sales reaching 110 percent of projections. What will be the profits?

8. A group of investors is contemplating backing a new Broadway musical that will cost $10 million to produce. There is a 50 percent chance that the show will be successful and return a present value of $15 million. However, there is an equal probability that the show will be a financial failure and result in a present value of inflows of $5 million. They believe if they pay an extra $4 million to hire superstars "Marvelous Marilyn" and "Rugged Ron" that they will assure a successful outcome. Should they hire MM and RR?

9. Given a project with a fixed cost of $10,000, depreciation of $6,000 per year, a selling price for the product of $3.00 per unit, and an 8,000 unit break-even point, what is the variable cost per unit?

ANSWERS TO COMPLETION QUESTIONS

1. capital
2. sensitivity
3. Scenario
4. simulation
5. sales
6. negative
7. NPV
8. do not
9. rise
10. variable
11. higher
12. lower
13. profits, sales
14. decision tree
15. simulation
16. negative
17. uncertain

SOLUTIONS TO PROBLEMS

1. Last year the total costs for the 10 million batteries at a cost of $0.60 per unit were 10 × $0.60 or $6 million. This year the added production was 10 million units for an incremental cost of $10 - $6 or $4 million. On a cost per unit basis this would be $4/10 or $0.40 for each battery.

2. Remember that total costs equal variable costs plus fixed costs. In problem 1 the variable costs last year were 10 million units × the variable cost per unit of $0.40 or $4 million. Subtracting this from the total cost of $6 million yields a fixed cost of $2 million. As a check we can compute the fixed costs in the latest year as the difference between the total costs of $10 million and the variable costs of 20 million units × the variable cost per unit of $0.40. This equals $2 million which is the same fixed cost as for the prior year. This should be the case because the problem states that production could be increased without having to incur any additional fixed costs.

3. The break-even point is where revenues minus costs equals zero. (It is important to note that taxes do not enter into the calculation because they are based on having a profit to tax--no profit, no tax). Depreciation = $15 million/ 15 = $1 million per year. So fixed costs = $400,000 + $1,000,000 = $1,400,000. This must be covered by the contribution margin on the sales. In other words, each unit sold contributes to the coverage of fixed costs. In this case each bat contributes $14 - $7 or $7 so the break-even point will be $1,400,000/$7 or 200,000 bats per year.

4. To compute the present value break-even point, cash flows are needed. Here we are seeking the sales volume that generates cash inflows that are sufficient to offset the cash outflows using present values. The cash inflows are profits after taxes plus the depreciation tax shield. The present value of these cash flows will equal the investment outlay at the break-even volume. Remember the annual depreciation is $1,000,000 so the tax shield will be .4 × $1,000,000 or $400,000 per year. The present value factor for a 15-year annuity at 10 percent is 7.606. Using the tax rate of 40 percent and letting Q equal the break-even volume, the equation becomes:
$$\$15,000,000 = [\{\$14Q - (\$7Q + \$1,400,000)\} \times (1 - .4) + \$400,000] \times 7.606$$
$$Q = 574,316 \text{ bats per year}$$

5. Recall that the degree of operating leverage is one plus the ratio of the fixed costs to profits. In the case of a profitable firm with no fixed costs, the degree of operating leverage is one. This is the lowest degree of operating leverage.

6. The percentage change in profits equals the percentage change in sales × the degree of operating leverage. In this case a sales decline of 10 percent would result in a drop in profits of 10 × 8 or 80 percent. Profits at the projected level would have been 10

percent of sales of $200 million or $20 million. If sales were only 90 percent of the forecast, profits would decline by 80 percent or by $16 million. In other words, a 10 percent shortfall in sales causes profits to fall to $4 million.

7. Profits would increase by the increase in sales × the degree of operating leverage. This would be 10 × 8 or 80 percent. Expressed on an absolute basis profits would rise from the original forecast level of $20 million to $36 million. (The increase is 80 percent or $20 million of $16 million.)

8. In the worst case scenario, the expected net present value is - $10 million + $5 million or a loss of $5 million. They should hire the players for $4 million to avoid the 50 percent chance of the $5 million loss.

9. The profit margin is ($10,000 + $6,000)/8,000 or $2.00 per unit. The variable cost is the difference between the selling price and the profit margin or $3 - $2 = $1 per unit.

INTRODUCTION TO RISK, RETURN, AND THE OPPORTUNITY COST OF CAPITAL

INTRODUCTION

While this is the beginning of a new section related to the discussion of risk and return, it is really a "bridging" section between the asset investment materials of the last section and the financing section which follows this one. The past and prospective investment projects of a business establish a risk profile which determines the opportunity rate of return. There is no cost of capital, required rate of return, nor opportunity rate of return *independent* of where the funds are invested. This connection or bridge of financing and financial markets to the capital budgeting process is an important concept to understand when taking your finance course, because it ties the chapters and course together. This chapter introduces risk concepts, historical rates of return, and the opportunity rate concept. In the next chapter these concepts are inserted in the capital budgeting process. Risk, an important factor in the valuation theme, is focused on financial risk, related to the variability of returns. Your prior experience with risk is with pure risk, the risk of real assets, where the "tail" is single-sided. It is the risk of a loss to something you now have. What is the risk of someone looting your apartment when you are in class? Few students will return to their "digs" to find it cleaned and refurnished, a proxy for the upside return occurrence or second "tail" of possible occurrences or positive benefit. One tail on pure risk and two tails for investment returns! Students often define investment risk as the risk of loss, bringing in their pure risk focus. Investment risk has two tails (as in a normal curve) with an expected average in the middle, and lower and higher to the left and right of the average (mean).

LEARNING CHECKLIST

After preparing this chapter, you should be able to:

_____1. Estimate the opportunity cost of capital for an-average-risk" project.

_____2. Calculate the standard deviation of returns for individual common stocks or a stock portfolio.

_____3. Understand how and why diversification reduces total risk.

_____4. Distinguish between unique risk, which can be diversified away, and market risk, which cannot.

SOURCES OF BUSINESS INFORMATION

Standard and Poor's Stock Reports. When you are researching a specific corporation, two reference works are useful and will provide considerable information to you about the company. The first is the Standard and Poor's Stock Reports, a twelve-volume work referencing both exchange-traded and over-the-counter, dealer-traded stocks. The Standard and Poor's Stock and Bond Guide provides detailed information about companies' stock and bond issues that are outstanding. Find out when dividends or interest is paid, or when the bond matures or is callable.

Wall Street Research Net (WSRN.com). WSRN consists of over 140,000 links to help investors and students find company information. The "Research A Company" search engine provides one a whole page of links to thousands of public companies. From SEC Filings via EDGAR, company home page, the site provides several stock graphs, company news, and access to several research reports on the company. This is a great starting point for students starting to do company research. The site also has an extensive linkage to current economic reports provided by governmental and private sources. Want to find what day of the month that the Consumer Price Index information is released, check here?

CHAPTER OUTLINE, KEY CONCEPTS AND TERMS

I. **RATES OF RETURN: A REVIEW**

    A.   Security return, either stock or bonds, are a combination of dividend or interest payments plus any capital gain or loss.

    B.   The annual percentage return on investment is:

$$\text{Percentage Return} = \frac{\text{Capital Gain} + \text{Dividend}}{\text{Initial Share Price}}$$

    C.   The above return is a nominal return, reflecting how much more money one has at the end of the year.

$$\text{Dividend Yield} = \frac{\text{Dividend}}{\text{Initial Share Price}}$$

D.   The same percentage return or total return is the sum of the dividend yield (annual dividends/initial share price) plus the capital gain yield (annual

capital gain/initial share price).

$$\text{Capital Gain Yield} = \frac{\text{Capital Gain}}{\text{Initial Share Price}}$$

E.   The real rate of return is the nominal rate adjusted for the inflation rate in the period or the additional purchasing power one has with the investment return:

$$1 + \text{real ror} = \frac{1 + \text{nominal ror}}{1 + \text{inflation rate}}$$

II.   SEVENTY-THREE YEARS OF CAPITAL MARKET HISTORY
A.   **Principles**
1.   Managers must estimate current and future opportunity rates of return for investment evaluation. Estimating the opportunity rate begins with a study of historical rates of return on varying risk investments.
2.   The level of risk and required rate of return are directly related. Investors require higher rates of return for increased risk.

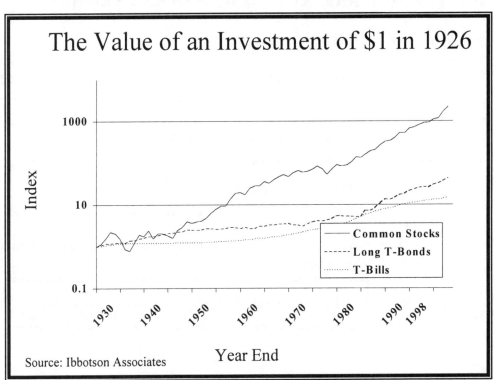

The Value of an Investment of $1 in 1926

Source: Ibbotson Associates

B. **Market Indexes**
   1. Several **market indexes** measure the investment performance of the overall market.
   2. The **Dow Jones Industrial Average** is an equal share index of thirty industrial stocks. It is an index of important but few firms, independently of how many shares each company has outstanding.
   3. The **Standard and Poor's Composite Index** is a share-weighted index of 500 firms, covering about 70 percent of the value of stocks traded. Compared to the Dow, the S&P 500 is a broader index and is adjusted for the relative number of shares available to investors.
   4. The Wilshire 5000, the Nikkei Index (Tokyo), and the Financial Times Index (London) are just a few other market performance indices.

C. **The Historical Record**
   1. The historical returns of Treasury bills, long-term Treasury bonds, corporate bonds, and common stock are compared in Figures 9.1 and 9.2.
   2. With Treasury bills' average returns at the low end of the risk scale, a **maturity premium** is added for long-term Treasury bond returns.
   3. The return differentials between risk-free Treasury bills and corporate bonds and common stock returns is a **risk premium**, or the added return required by investors to invest in risky securities.
   4. Long-term average returns are a starting point in estimating required rates of return for the future, and the opportunity rate of return used in the capital budgeting process.
   5. The riskier securities had wider fluctuations in their yearly returns over the 69 years studied.

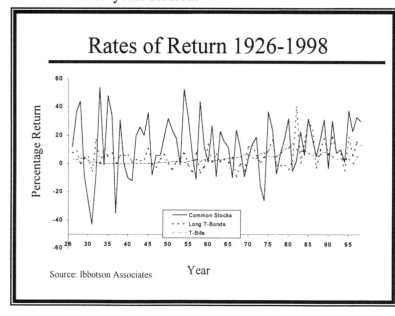

D. **Using Historical Evidence to Estimate Today's Cost of Capital**
   1. The opportunity rate of return given up to invest in the projects of a business are equivalent to the returns on a market portfolio of common stocks.
   2. Estimated stock returns fluctuate yearly (9.3 % average risk premium) around the Treasury bill rate. This assumes that there is a normal, stable risk premium on the market portfolio and that past returns are reliable predictors of future returns.
   3. Historical returns provide benchmark for estimating current and future required rates of return. The market portfolio returns, assumed to be stable and similar to historical returns, may serve as proxy for average-risk project opportunity rates of return.

III. MEASURING RISK

A. **Historical variation**
   1. Variation around a central tendency or mean may be presented visually by constructing a histogram (Figure 9.3) and studying the dispersion or spread of possible outcomes.
   2. Another method is calculating a measure of variation used as a proxy for measuring risk, such as the variance or standard deviation. Risk relates to the variability of future returns.

B. Variance and Standard Deviation
   1. The **variance** statistic is the average value of squared deviations from the mean. The **standard deviation** is the square root of the variance.
   2. The *greater* the variance or standard deviation, the *greater* the dispersion, volatility, or variability of returns, and the *greater* the risk. See this table for the calculation of the variance and standard deviation.

Coin Toss Game-calculating variance and standard deviation

(1) Percent Rate of Return	(2) Deviation from Mean	(3) Squared Deviation
+ 40	+ 30	900
+ 10	0	0
+ 10	0	0
- 20	- 30	900

Variance = average of squared deviations = 1800 / 4 = 450

Standard deviation = square of root variance = $\sqrt{450}$ = 21.2%

C. **Measuring the Variation in Stock Returns**
1. Calculating historical average investment returns and the variability of those returns, the comparison of average returns and volatility indicates that historical risk and return are directly related.
2. Higher risk is associated with higher average returns.
3. One might assume that historical returns and variability (long period) would extend into the future for estimating investor-required or opportunity rates of return.
4. Investors will expect a higher rate of return, risk premium over the Treasury bill rate, with higher standard deviation of returns.

IV. RISK AND DIVERSIFICATION

A. Portfolios
1. Our measures of variation apply to groupings of securities or portfolios as well as single securities.
2. The variability or risk of a portfolio, or a market portfolio such as the S&P 500, is *not* the simple average of the individual stock variability. The portfolio risk is *less* than the average risk of the individual securities.

B. **Diversification**
1. The reduced risk of the portfolio is caused by **diversification** effects of spreading the portfolio across many investments.
2. Portfolio diversification works because prices of different stocks do not move exactly together or are not perfectly correlated (+1). Diversification works best, or the risk-reducing effects of diversification works best, when the stock returns are negatively correlated. Diversification reduces the variability of returns on the portfolio compared to the average variability of the individual stocks.

C. **Asset versus Portfolio Risk**
1. While historical returns on individual securities are good proxies for estimating future returns on individual securities, historical standard deviations of returns are *not* good risk proxies for stocks held in a portfolio.
2. Since stocks and other securities are usually held in portfolios, because of the diversification effect, the relevant risk of a stock to be added to the portfolio is the impact of the added stock on the portfolio variability or risk. The incremental risk of a stock added to a portfolio depends on how the stock varies compared to the portfolio variation. If the historical correlation between the stock and portfolio are high positive (+1), there is no diversification effect of the added stock. If

the relationship is negative, zero or low positive, the addition of the stock lowers the portfolio variance or standard deviation or risk.

3.   Incremental risk does not depend upon the added stock's variability; it depends upon how the stock affects the portfolio's variability when it is added to the portfolio.

D.   Market Risk versus Unique Risk

1.   The diversification effect or the reduction in portfolio risk takes place with the addition of added securities until about 20 or 30 are included in the portfolio. Beyond that, the diversification effect of added securities is minimal.

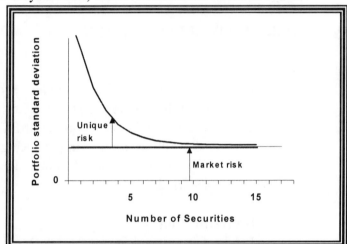

2.   While diversification eliminates the **unique risk** of individual securities, one cannot eliminate the **market risk** or systematic risk, the risks that affect the entire stock market.

3.   For a diversified portfolio, only the market risk matters. When one discusses securities investment or investors, it is assumed that the security is held in a diversified portfolio and the relevant risk is market risk.

V.   THINKING ABOUT RISK

A.   *Three* added risk concepts are presented below.

Message 1: Some Risks Look Big and Dangerous But Really Are Diversifiable

1.   Individual project risk may not be as high when the project is part of a portfolio of business investments. As in the discussion above, the relevant risk is the incremental risk effect on the investment portfolio or the impact on the total business effort.

Message 2: Market Risks Are Macro Risks

2.   Investors holding diversified portfolios are concerned with macroeconomic risks, or the impact of business cycle, exchange rates,

etc., on investor decisions related to investment and disinvestment in financial markets. Specific or unique risk is not relevant.

3. Managers must deal with unique risk exposure in addition to market risk, but only market risk affects the opportunity rate of return of the firm.

Message 3: Risk Can Be Measured

4. The risk, measured by the variance or standard deviation, of individual stocks can be easily measured, but when diversification is assumed for investors, only the incremental risk effects of adding a security to a portfolio is relevant.

5. In the next chapter this relevant risk, or the individual stock's relationship with fluctuations in the market portfolio, is discussed and measured.

COMPLETION QUESTIONS

1. Returns from stocks come from (*dividends/interest*) and _____ gains or losses.

2. (*Nominal/Real*) returns indicate buying power.

3. A measure of the investment performance of the overall market is a (*industry/market*) index.

4. The Dow Jones Industrial Average includes (*less/more*) stocks than the Standard and Poor's Composite Index.

5. Short-term Treasury bills are (*less/more*) risky than long-term Treasury bonds.

6. Corporate bonds are (*less/more*) risky than common stocks.

7. The extra average return from investing in long-term versus short-term Treasury securities is known as the _____ premium.

8. On an historic basis, the higher the risk the (*higher/lower*) the return.

9. The expected market return is equal to the interest rate on Treasury bills plus the (*normal/real*) risk premium.

10. The opportunity cost of capital for (*safe/risky*) projects is the rate of return offered by Treasury bills.

11. Measures of dispersion are used to measure (*return/risk*).

12. A measure of volatility that is the average value of squared deviation from the mean is called _____ .

13. Another measure of risk is the square root of variance which is also called the _____ _____ .

14. The (*expected/historical*) return is equal to the probability-weighted average of possible outcomes.

15. Common stocks as a group have a (*higher/lower*) standard deviation compared to corporate bonds.

16. Diversification (*increases/reduces*) variability because prices of different stocks (*do/do not*) move exactly together.

17. Counter cyclical stocks do well when others do (*poorly/well*).

18. _____ risk refers to risk factors affecting only a particular firm. It is also called (*diversifiable/non-diversifiable*) risk.

19. Another name for systematic risk is _____ risk.

20. Systematic risk (*can/cannot*) be eliminated.

21. Drilling for oil and fire insurance are examples of (*diversifiable/market*) risk.

22. Grocery chains have (*less/more*) market risk compared to automobile manufacturers.

PROBLEMS

1. Tim purchased a stock for $25 per share and sold it one year later for $30 after having received dividends of $1 per share. What was his rate of return?

2. If the inflation rate during the year Tim had the stock described in the preceding problem was 8 percent, what was his real rate of return?

3. Using the DJIA method and starting at 100, construct a measure of price changes in the stock market from a sample of the 3 stocks as shown in the table below:

STOCK PRICE IN $ PER SHARE			
PERIOD	A	B	C
1	15	25	80
2	20	23	86
3	17	28	69

4. If the average annual compound rate of return for all large U.S. common stocks between 1926 and 1992 was 12.4 percent and the risk-free return averaged 3.8 percent, what was the average risk premium (excess rate of return)?

5. In one year when inflation was 12 percent, the real return on long-term bonds was -3 percent. What was the nominal return that year? Why did investors accept the negative real return? What could they have done about it?

6. Suppose a stock is projected to sell for $30 per share in a year from now. What price would you pay today for that stock if it was expected to pay a dividend this coming year of $4 per share and if you required a return of 12 percent?

7. What would be the value of the stock described in problem 6 if instead you required a return of 18 percent?

8. Suppose you own stock in a company that is widely expected to be acquired by another firm but antitrust consideration might block the merger. If the deal fails to go through the price will fall from the present $50 per share to $40. If the combination is approved your shares will increase to $60. The probability of a positive outcome within the next year is 0.7 with a 0.3 chance that the acquisition will not occur. What is your expected return?

ANSWERS TO COMPLETION QUESTIONS

1. dividends, capital
2. Real
3. market
4. less
5. less
6. less
7. maturity
8. higher

9. normal
10. safe
11. risk
12. variance
13. standard deviation
14. expected
15. higher
16. reduces
17. poorly
18. Unique, diversifiable
19. market
20. cannot
21. diversifiable
22. less

SOLUTIONS TO PROBLEMS

1. The only returns from common stock are in the form of dividends and capital gains or losses based on the difference between the price paid and the price at which the shares are sold.

$$\text{Rate of return} = \frac{\text{dividends} + \text{capital gains}}{\text{initial price}}$$

$$= \frac{\$1 + (30 - 25)}{\$25}$$

$$= .24 \text{ or } 24\%$$

2.

$$\text{Real return} = \frac{1 + \text{nominal rate}}{1 + \text{inflation rate}} - 1$$

$$= .148 \text{ or } 14.8\%$$

3.

PERIOD	AVE. PRICE, $	% CHANGE	CALCULATED AVE.
1	40	-	100
2	43	7.5	107.5
3	38	-11.6	95.0

4. The actual return minus the risk-free rate equals the risk premium:
$$12.4 - 3.8 = 8.6\%$$

5. Recall that the approximate real return equals the nominal rate minus the rate of inflation. This means the nominal rate is about equal to the real rate plus the inflation rate. In this case the nominal rate = -3 + 12 = 9 percent.

Investors did not expect inflation would be so high or they never would have accepted a 9 percent return. They were hurt by having inflation exceed their fixed return but there was nothing they could do about it. They did make up for the loss of purchasing power by requiring higher nominal rates later.

6. The return on a share of stock over one year is equal to the dividend plus the capital gain or loss divided by the initial price. Expressed in symbols this is:

$$k = \frac{D + (P_1 - P_0)}{P_0}$$

solving this equation for P_0

$$P_0 = \frac{D + P_1}{k + 1}$$

$$= \$30.36$$

7. This is a case of becoming less optimistic about the future which translates into higher risk. The higher risk means a higher required return. If nothing else changed, the maximum price you would pay would be:

$$P_0 = \frac{\$4 + \$30}{1 + .18}$$

$$= \$28.81$$

This is one explanation why stock prices fall when investors become more conservative in their view of the future. The way they can achieve the higher required returns is to decrease their valuation of stocks which means they will not pay as much for shares. The weakened demand will result in a drop in share prices.

8.   The expected stock price is the sum of the products of the possible prices multiplied by the likelihood of their occurrence. The price would be:

$$60x0.7 + 40X0.3 = \$54$$

$$\frac{\$60 - \$54}{\$50}$$

The expected return would be:

$$= .12 \text{ or } 12\%$$

RISK, RETURN, AND CAPITAL BUDGETING

CHAPTER IN PERSPECTIVE

This chapter continues to build the bridge between asset investment, capital budgeting, and financial markets. This chapter continues our study of risk measurement, starting with calculation of beta, the variability of an investment's return relative to fluctuations of the market portfolio. Beta is a relative risk measure; the risk of a company's stock relative a broad-based market portfolio of stocks. Students with their new financial/statistical calculator should be able to crank out a regression line. Try the text example.

The concepts of risk and return have been building slowly in the text and now are concluded in this chapter. Later in the chapter, risk and capital budgeting concepts are combined in a short but important discussion of the project cost of capital. The last section in the chapter is the connecting link of CAPM to the asset side of the balance sheet.

LEARNING CHECKLIST

After preparing this chapter you should be able to:

_____1. Measure and interpret the market risk, or beta, of a stock. What does beta measure?

_____2. Relate the market risk of a security to the rate of return that investors demand.

_____3. Calculate the opportunity cost of capital for a specific project.

SOURCES OF BUSINESS INFORMATION

Standard & Poor's Outlook. Another important source of investment information is the Standard & Poor's Outlook, a weekly publication about the global world of investments. Each issue of the Outlook includes articles, charts, graphs, statistical data, projections, and Standard & Poor's predictions. This is an excellent reference when beginning an investment project or for those who want to learn the practical side of investing.

Bloomberg Online. As one of the most used source of financial and economic information, Bloomberg's net version is a great place for business students to see the variety of financial and business, and economic data that are used in business decision making. Bloomberg Online provides a variety of links to financial resources on the web, access to Hoover's Company Research Directory, a great place to research companies, and links to Money and Capital Markets. Bloomberg sponsors an investment game that students should check out. Finally, in the personal finance area, Bloomberg provides a mortgage calculator and, for students who have children, or think they may want children, take a look at Bloomberg's "Expected Future Education Cost Calculator.

CHAPTER OUTLINE, KEY CONCEPTS, AND TERMS

I. **MEASURING MARKET RISK**

A. **Concepts**
1. Only "macro" events affect the value of the **market portfolio**, or a portfolio of all assets in the economy.
2. A broad market base, such as the S&P Composite, is often used as a proxy for the market portfolio.
3. Firm specific or unique risk are averaged out or diversified away when considering the market portfolio.
4. A measure of a stock's risk relative to the risk of the market portfolio is called the stock's **beta**, and is expressed as the Greek letter β.

B. **Measuring Beta**
1. Investors with diversified portfolios are not concerned about the specific or unique risk of a stock, only the impact of the stock on the risk of the entire portfolio.
2. The relative risk of the stock compared to the portfolio risk or beta is the relevant risk to consider when a new stock is added to the portfolio.
3. Defensive stocks historically tend to vary less than the market portfolio; aggressive stocks have a history of more variation relative to the market portfolio.
4. Beta is the slope of the regression line of the individual stock returns relative to the market portfolio returns. If the slope indicates a change

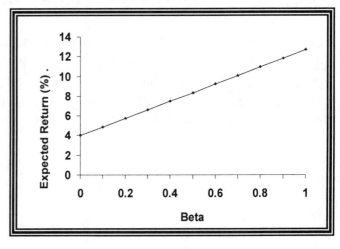

120

in historical stock returns *similar* to the market (-1 to +1), the beta has a value of 1. If the variations in the stock return, given a 1 percent variation in the market returns, is less than the market variation, the beta is *less than* 1 and the stock is noted as a "defensive" stock. If the slope of the line through the points found by plotting the stock's returns relative to a 1 percent change in the market portfolio is *greater than* 1, the beta has a value greater than 1.

5.   Any stock's return is comprised of two parts. The first is explained by the macro events in the market or the market rate of return. The second part of the return is related to the specific or unique risk of the stock relative to the market rate of return, or the stock beta.

6.   The beta is calculated by 1) observing monthly rates of return for the stock and the market; 2) plotting the observations as in Figure 10.1; and, 3) fitting a regression line showing the average returns to the stock (dependent variable) at different market returns (independent variable). The slope of the line, beta, relates the change in stock returns, given a change in market return.

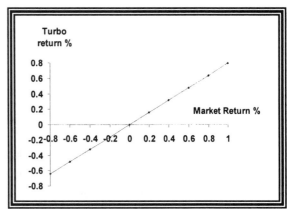

C.   Betas for MCI WorldCom and Exxon

1.   Betas for MCI and Exxon are calculated in Figure 10.2. Sixty months' return of the stocks and market are plotted and a regression line is calculated and drawn.

2.   The beta is the "b" in the (a + bx) function of the straight line drawn or the slope of the line. It indicates the change in the stock return, given a change in the market rate of return.

3.   MCI had a beta of 1.3, or a stock variation 30% higher than the market variability over the period. Exxon tended to vary less than the market in the same period (beta of .61).

4.   Table 10.1 is a table listing popular stocks and their betas for a specific period.

D.   **Portfolio Betas**
   1.   Diversification decreases the variability from unique risk but not from market risk.
   2.   The beta of a portfolio is an average of the stock betas weighted by the investment in each security. One may construct a higher risk than the market average portfolio (portfolio beta greater than one), or a portfolio with an average risk less than the market (portfolio beta less than one).
   3.   A large portfolio of diversified stocks would approximate the market index and have a portfolio beta around one. An index mutual fund is a "market portfolio" of stocks with a beta close to the value of one.

II.   RISK AND RETURN

A.   **Calculations**
   1.   U.S. Treasury bills have very low risk and a beta of zero, or no relationship with the variations of the market stock portfolio which has a beta of 1.0.
   2.   The difference between the return on the market and the T-bill rate is called the **market risk premium**, or the risk premium demanded by investors to hold the market portfolio rather than T-bills.
   3.   Over the past 73 years, the market risk premium has averaged over 9.0 percent per year.
   4.   The expected rate of return on any portfolio combining T-bills and the market portfolio lies on a straight line between *all* T-bills (5%) and *all* stocks of the market portfolio (14%).
   5.   The risk premium is proportional to the portfolio beta. A portfolio with one-half T-bills and one-half the market portfolio of stocks would have a beta of .5, and a risk premium of one-half the market portfolio risk premium.
   6.   The market risk premium is the market return *less* the return on T-bills.
   7.   Beta measures risk of the stock relative to the market. The expected risk premium on an individual stock is the stock return less the risk-free rate or beta *times* the market risk premium.
   8.   The total expected return on a stock is the risk-free rate plus the risk premium of the stock.
       Expected Return on stock = risk-free rate + risk premium.

$$\text{Market risk premium} = r_m - r_f$$
$$\text{Risk premium on any asset} = r - r_f$$
$$\text{Expected Return} = r_f + B(r_m - r_f)$$

9. The above formula relating the expected return as the sum of the risk-free rate plus the risk premium is called the **capital asset pricing model (CAPM)**. The rate of return on an individual stock is dependent upon the risk-free rate and the risk premium which is related to the market risk premium and the risk of the stock relative to the market risk premium, its beta.

B. **Why the CAPM Works**

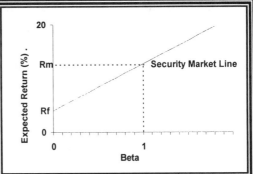

1. The CAPM assumes well-diversified investors; market risk is the only relevant risk.
2. The expected return on a portfolio is equal to the risk-free interest rate plus the expected portfolio risk premium.

C. **The Security Market Line**
   1. A plot of expected rates of return of varied risk (beta) portfolios is called the **security market line**. This is illustrated in Figure 10.5.
   2. According to the CAPM, expected rates of return for all securities and all portfolios lie on this line.
   3. The required risk premium for any investment is given by the security market line.
   4. A stock with a given beta that is expected to earn a return higher than that on the security market line will be purchased by investors, bidding up the stock price and lowering the expected rate of return to the security market line. Investors keep expected returns on the security market line.
   5. The security market line is the risk-return trade-off of investors.
   6. The CAPM states that the expected risk premium on an investment should be proportional to its beta.
   7. The CAPM explains the risk-return trade-off well in the period 1931 to 1991, thought the SML tends to understate low risk returns and overstate high beta portfolios. In the period 1966-1991, however, there is little relationship between portfolio betas and the return on the portfolio. Other variables outside the simplified CAPM are involved in establishing returns besides beta.
   8. The CAPM, though not the only model of the risk-return trade-off, is a good practical rule of thumb. It presents a simplified approach noting that extra required returns are required by investors to take added risk, and investors are primarily concerned with market risk that cannot be diversified away.

D.   Using the CAPM to Estimate Expected Returns
1.   To estimate expected investor returns for a selected stock, *three* numbers are needed: 1) the risk-free rate of interest, 2) the expected market risk premium, and 3) the beta of the stock, or the historical variation in stock risk premium relative to the market risk premium.
2.   The CAPM may also be used to estimate the discount rate for new capital investments when calculating net present value. The security market line provides a standard for investment project acceptance. If the internal rate of return on a project exceeds the opportunity rate of return (investor returns in a portfolio of equal risk securities), the firm should make the investment.
3.   For any risk level or beta, project returns below the security market line are unacceptable and have negative NPV's.

III.   CAPITAL BUDGETING AND PROJECT RISK

A.   **Concept**--Before the CAPM, financial manager's intuition indicated that riskier projects are less desirable than safe projects and that riskier investments must have higher expected rates of return relative to safe projects.

B.   **Company versus Project Risk**
1.   The estimated required rate of return of investors on a firm's securities is called the **company cost of capital**. The cost of capital is the discount rate used in calculating the NPV of investment projects and is the minimum acceptable rate of return when compared to the internal rate of return (IRR).
2.   The cost of capital is determined by average risk of a company's assets and operations. The cost of capital is applicable as a discount rate only on projects with the average risk of the business.
3.   The **project cost of capital** is a risk-adjusted minimum acceptable rate of return used as a discount rate on a specific project. The project cost of capital depends on project risk, not the company cost of capital, representing an average risk project.

C.   **Determinants of Project Risk**
1.   Project risk is usually assumed to be associated with the variability of cash flow of the project itself, but what matters is the relationship between the project's cash flows and the total firm (portfolio) variability or the project's beta.
2.   Projects that tend to have high operating leverage (high fixed costs) tend to have high project betas.

D. **Don't Add Fudge Factors to Discount Rates**
   1. Concern over the downside features of risk encourages managers to add risk premiums to discount rates in project analyses, thus forsaking many value-creating projects.
   2. Special risk factors should be incorporated into the cash flow estimation, not the discount rate. Special risks are often unique risks which are diversified away with other projects.

COMPLETION QUESTIONS

1. Macro risk (*can/cannot*) be eliminated by diversification.

2. _____ risk is measured by the sensitivity of an investment's returns as related to fluctuations in the market.

3. The market portfolio is represented by the (*Dow Jones Industrial Average/Standard and Poor's Composite Index*).

4. The sensitivity of a particular stock's return to the return from the market portfolio is measured by _____.

5. Defensive stocks have (*high/low*) betas.

6. The returns from aggressive stocks will vary (*less/more*) than the market return.

7. Aggressive stocks will have betas that are (*less/more*) than 1.0.

8. If the returns from the market were expected to increase by 10 percent, a stock with a beta of 0.9 would be expected to return an extra _____ percent.

9. An attraction of (*over-the-counter stocks/mutual funds*) is that they offer small investors diversification at low cost.

10. An (*index/mutual*) fund is expected to track the market as a whole. Such as fund has (*considerable/extremely small*) unique risk.

11. The difference between the return on the market and the return on risk-free Treasury bills is termed the _____ _____ _____ .

12. The beta for Treasury bills is (*0/1.0*).

13. The _____ _____ _____ _____ states that the expected return on any security is equal to the risk-free return plus the security's beta multiplied by the market risk premium.

14. When the Treasury bill return is 5 percent and the market risk premium is 10 percent, a portfolio with a beta of 1.2 will be expected to return (*12/17*) percent according to CAPM.

15. The _____ _____ _____ shows the relationship between expected return and beta.

16. Investors expect a (*penalty/reward*) for both waiting and worrying. (THIS IS A FUNDAMENTAL PRINCIPLE OF FINANCE--think carefully about its meaning).

17. CAPM can be used to estimate the (*discount rate/internal rate of return*) for capital budgeting projects.

18. For capital budgeting projects with high risks beta should be (*decreased/increased*).

19. The expected rate of return by investors in a company is determined by the average (*return/risk*) from the company's assets and operations.

20. The discount rate that is the minimum acceptable expected return on a project given its risk is known as the project _____ _____ _____ .

21. Projects involving revenues that are strongly dependent on the state of the economy tend to have (high/low) betas and a (high/low) cost of capital.

22. Projects that have (high/low) fixed costs will tend to have high betas.

23. Discount rates for high risk projects (should/should not) reflect the market risk of the project and (should/should not) be adjusted to offset errors in the cash flow forecast.

PROBLEMS

1. What is the capital asset pricing model (CAPM)? Explain the concept and express the model as an equation.

2. What will be the beta for a Myranda's portfolio that is invested 40 percent in Treasury bills and 60 percent in a group of stocks that track returns from the Standard & Poor's 500 Composite Index?

3. Suppose that in a year of strong economic growth, an airline stock is expected to provide a return of 30 percent and the market return is expected to be 20 percent. On the other hand when the economy is stagnant, the expectations are for returns of 4 percent for the airline and 8 percent for the market. Estimate the beta for the airline stock.

4. What will be the expected return from the portfolio specified in problem 2 if the risk-free rate is 6 percent and the expected market return is 14 percent?

5. Compare the return expected for the airline stock in problem 3 when the market return is expected to be 12 percent and 18 percent. The Treasury bill rate in both cases can be assumed to be 7 percent.

6. What conclusions can be drawn from the returns estimated for the airline stock in problem 5?

7. What is the standard deviation of a well-diversified portfolio with a beta of 0.9 when the standard deviation of the market returns is 30 percent?

8. When the market return increases by 2 percent, stock M averages increases of returns of 4 percent. What is stock M's beta?

9. For a project having a beta of 0.8, what is the appropriate discount rate for evaluating its potential investments if the market risk premium is 10 percent and the Treasury bill rate is 7 percent?

10. Suppose the internal rate of return on the potential project described in problem 9 is 20 percent. Should the firm make the investment proposed?

11. For a company having a beta of 1.1, a current stock price of $40 per share, and an expected dividend this coming year of $2.80 per share, what is the projected stock price one year from today? (Assume the market risk premium is 12 percent and the risk-free rate is 6 percent).

12. A company is considering an investment that offers a net cash flow of $100,000 per year for the indefinite future. The risk of this project is felt to be the same as the average for all stocks. If the Treasury bill rate is 8 percent and the market return is expected to be 14 percent, what is the maximum investment outlay that should be made?

ANSWERS TO COMPLETION QUESTIONS

1. cannot
2. market
3. Standard & Poor's Composite Index
4. beta
5. low
6. more
7. more
8. 9
9. mutual funds
10. index, extremely small
11. market risk premium
12. 0
13. capital asset pricing model
14. 17
15. security market line
16. reward
17. discount rate
18. increased
19. risk
20. cost of capital
21. high, high
22. high, high
23. should, should not

SOLUTIONS TO PROBLEMS

1. CAPM is a model that helps explain the trade-off between risk and return for a security. Risk is measured for a particular security relative to the variation of returns for the overall market. The expected return (r) is based on the expected return for the overall market (r_m) and the current risk-free rate (r_f). CAPM states that the expected return for a particular security is equal to the risk-free rate plus a premium. This premium is the product of the premium return for the overall market and the riskiness of the individual security (β). In symbols the CAPM is expressed as:

$$r = r_f + \beta(r_m - r_f)$$

2. The portfolio beta will be the weighted average of the securities comprising the portfolio. Remember that the beta for Treasury bills, which are risk-free, is zero and, by definition, the beta for the market is 1.0. The portfolio beta is thus:
$$0 \times 0.4 + 1.0 \times 0.6 = 0.6$$

3. The beta can be estimated by dividing the change in the return for a particular stock by the

$$\frac{30 - 4}{20 - 8} = 2.17$$

change in the return for the overall market. In this case beta for the airline is:

4. According to the CAPM:
$$r = r_f + \beta(r_m - r_f)$$

$$r = 6 + 0.6 \times (14 - 6) = 10.8\%$$

5. When the market return is 12 percent, CAPM predicts the airline stock return will be:
$$= 7 + 1.6 \times (12 - 7)$$
$$= 15\%$$
When the market return is 18 percent, the airline stock return is expected to be:
$$= 7 + 1.6 \times (18 - 7)$$
$$= 24.7\%$$

6. The high degree of sensitivity of returns for the airline stock compared to the market is caused by the high beta. The conclusion is that if one expects the market to increase it is advisable to be invested in stocks with betas above one. In other words, if a bull market is forecast, high beta stocks should be chosen. Of course if the market is weak, the high beta

stocks will experience an even poorer performance. Also the sensitivity of a stock to the market is a general relationship that does not always hold true.

7. The standard deviation for a well-diversified portfolio is related to the market which, by definition, is fully diversified through beta as:
$$beta_{portfolio} = 0.9 \times 30 = 27\%$$

8. Beta is a measure of sensitivity of the returns from a particular security, or portfolio of securities, to changes in returns from the overall market. In this case when the market return increases by 2 percent, stock M increases by twice as much. Therefore its beta is 2.0.

9. The appropriate discount rate is the required return calculated from CAPM as:
$$r = 7 + 0.8 \times 10 = 15\%$$

10. The IRR of 20 percent means the NPV is zero at that discount rate. At lower discount rates the NPV will be positive. Since the appropriate discount rate for this project is 15 percent, the calculation will result in a positive NPV so the project should be <u>accepted</u>.

11. First we need to calculate the required rate of return:
$$r = r_f + \beta(r_m - r_f)$$
$$r = 6 + (1.1 \times 12)$$
$$r = 19.2\%$$
The next step is to recognize that the required rate of return is also equal to the dividend

$$r = \frac{\$2.80}{\$40} + \frac{P_1 - \$40}{\$40}$$

yield plus the capital gain or:
$$P_1 = (.192 - .07 + 1) \times \$40 = \$44.88$$

12. According to the CAPM, the required rate of return is:
$$= 8 + 1.0 \times (14 - 6)$$
$$= 16\%$$
For a perpetuity, the value is:
$$= \$100,000/.16 = \$625,000$$
This is the maximum price that should be paid to provide a 16 percent return. If the outlay is less, the return will be higher.

THE COST OF CAPITAL

INTRODUCTION

This chapter, like the entire section, continues to bridge the relationship between investor concerns and minimum required returns and the internal decision-making processes of a business. The cost of capital or required rate of return concepts are covered in this chapter. While the opportunity rate of return concept was introduced generally several chapters ago, the specific theory and processes involved in estimating the cost of capital are covered in this chapter.

The opportunity cost of capital is used in the NPV and IRR evaluation of investment opportunities. This shareholder involvement or perspective in the investment process says that if the cost of capital return is generated as the return on investment, shareholders will receive their minimally acceptable rate of return. If they receive less, they are likely to sell the stock and move to investments that provide competitive rates of return relative to risk assumed. What if returns higher than the opportunity cost of capital are earned on investments? More investors will be attracted to the stock, the current stock owners will be pleased and will want to buy more stock, and the stock price is likely to increase.

What determines this opportunity rate of return? The market determines the cost of capital; management only estimates what it will be, based on a current evaluation. This market determined rate of return required on one business is the rate forgone on similar investments of similar risk (opportunity cost). Like the NPVs and IRRs in the capital budgeting chapters, reasonable accuracy of the estimate is a function of the quality of inputs. Like the cash flow estimates in capital budgeting, estimating the required rate of return today and over the life of the investment requires considerable insight in addition to technique. Remember, there is no cost of capital independent of where funds are invested. Note the relationship between capital budgeting and financial markets. Finally, do not get mired in the details and fail to keep a broad perspective. This is a chapter where the "trees" can keep you from seeing the "forest."

LEARNING CHECKLIST
After studying this chapter you should be able to:

_____1. Select the balance accounts representing a company's capital structure.

_____2. Estimate the current, required rates of return on the securities issued by the firm in the past.

_____3. Calculate the weighted average cost of capital.

_____4. Understand when the weighted average cost of capital is or is not the appropriate discount rate for a new project. Note how this "financing" chapter ties loosely with "investing."

SOURCES OF BUSINESS INFORMATION

Mutual Fund Information. Mutual funds have been very popular in the last several years. They provide the small investor a chance to invest in a portfolio of securities, attaining both diversification and professional management of their savings. There are several good references to use when one wants to learn more about mutual funds or pick one for your IRA or 401k pension investment in a few years. The Mutual Funds Profiles, published by Standard & Poor's/Lipper offers monthly data and statistics on all major mutual funds. The Lipper (Dow Jones, Inc.) data is also published daily in The Wall Street Journal, with quarterly performance analyses in both The Wall Street Journal and Barron's. Business Week, published by McGraw-Hill, Inc., publishes an Annual Guide to Mutual Funds. COA/Wiesenberger's Mutual Funds Update is an excellent monthly analysis and summary, while the Morningstar publications have become very popular with investors. There are many more, but check with what services your library carries. Your pension will be invested by **you** over the next forty years, and mutual funds are a likely investment choice for many. No matter what your major is, **you** now have a personal interest in the concepts of risk and return and investing.

Mutual Funds On The Web. Mutual funds are likely to be a part of your retirement nest egg in the years to come. While taking a finance course and learning investment basics, take the time to look over several web sites related to what might be called mutual funds "search engines," such as http://www.morningstar.com provide connections to education, ratings, mutual funds evaluation concepts, and access to the many mutual fund families such as Vanguard or Fidelity, or specific mutual funds. This site also has a large number of sites which focus on personal financial decision-making related to investments. Vanguard's "Investor Education," available through their home page (http://www.vanguard.com) provides a series of educational modules for anyone new to mutual funds. Mutual Funds Interactive (http:www.brill.com) is another great mutual funds site. From daily information and chat rooms, their "library" section is a great place to start a research paper on this topic. Mutual funds have attracted billions of dollars from investors in the last few years. Buying and selling funds is available online from several sources and the internet has become a popular place for learning about mutual funds. You are likely to have mutual funds as part of your retirement portfolio in the years to come. This course is a great starting point for this life long venture.

CHAPTER OUTLINE, KEY TERMS, AND CONCEPTS

I. THE COST OF CAPITAL

A.   The cost of capital for an all-equity financed firm is the required return on the firm's assets. Owning all the stock is the same as owning all the assets and the expected return on the stock is the expected return on the assets.

B.   Note the following identities:
1.   Value of business = value of stock
2.   Risk of business = risk of stock
3.   Rate of return on business = rate of return on stock
4.   Investor's required return = investor's required return from business from stock

C.   The **capital structure**, or the market value mix of debt and equity securities, features the sources of financing as a portfolio of financing funding a portfolio of assets.

D.   The cost of capital is the weighted average of returns (weighted by market value) on debt and equity which is equal to the expected rate of return on the portfolio of assets.

E.   The cost of capital is the discount rate for evaluating new, similar risk asset investments.

Cost of Capital Example (Geothermal)

> *Geothermal Inc. has the following structure. Given that geothermal pays 8% for debt and 14% for equity, what is the Company Cost of Capital?*

Market Value Debt	$194	30%
Market Value Equity	$453	70%
Total Firm Value	$647	100%

$$WACC = (.3 \times 5.2\%) + (.7 \times 14\%) = 11.4\%$$

II.   CALCULATING THE WEIGHTED AVERAGE COST OF CAPITAL

A.   **General Principles**

1.   The cost of capital is the opportunity cost of capital for the firm's existing assets. The cost of capital is used to assess or value new assets with risks similar to existing assets.

2.   In the following sections, cost of capital concepts are discussed as is the weighted average cost of capital (WACC), a method for estimating the company cost of capital when debt capital is present, and an after-tax cost of debt capital must be calculated.

B.   **Calculating Company Cost of Capital as a Weighted Average**

1.   When only equity is financing a business, the CAPM may be used to calculate the company cost of capital.

2.   When debt securities finance a portion of assets, the cost of capital is a weighted average of the returns demanded on the debt and equity securities. It is the expected return on the portfolio of all the firm's securities, which in turn is driven by the expected return on the business assets, or $V = D + E$.

3.   The cost of capital is the expected return on assets, r_{assets}/V, which is equal to the expected income returns to the debt portion of total assets, $(DV \times r_{debt})$, plus the expected income returns to equity portion of total assets, $(EV \times r_{equity})$.

$$r_{assets} = \frac{\text{total income}}{\text{value of investments}}$$

$$r_{assets} = \frac{(D \times r_{debt}) + (E \times r_{equity})}{V}$$

$$r_{assets} = \left(\frac{D}{V} \times r_{debt}\right) + \left(\frac{E}{V} \times r_{equity}\right)$$

C.   **Three Steps in Calculating Cost of Capital**

1.   Calculate the market value of each security as a proportion of the firm's total value.

2.   Determine the current required rate of return on each security.

3.   Calculate a weighted average of the required returns.

D. **Market versus Book Weights**
1. The cost of capital is the expected rate of return that investors require on the business assets, based on the market value of the securities of the firm.
2. The market value of securities versus book values should be used as weights when calculating the weighted average cost of capital.

E. **Taxes and the Weighted-Average Cost of Capital**
1. Taxes are important considerations in the cost of capital calculation because interest payments on debt are deductible. At a 35% tax rate, the after-tax cost of $1 of interest paid is $1 \times (1-.35)$ or $.65. This interest tax shield of $1 x 35% or $.35 on $1 reduces the pre-tax cost of debt by (1- tax rate). The after-tax cost of debt with a required pre-tax return of 8% is $8\% \times (1-.35) = 5.2\%$.
2. The after-tax version of the company cost of capital is called the **weighted average cost of capital**, which is the expected rate of return on a portfolio of all the securities of the firm and the discount rate for the NPV evaluation of new investments of similar risk.

F. **Wrapping Up Geothermal**
1. The use of lower cost, tax-deductible debt lowers Geothermal's cost of capital below that of an all-equity firm.
2. The WACC is the minimum acceptable rate of return on Geothermal's investment. The expected internal rate of return (IRR) exceeds the WACC and the NPV analysis indicates that the new project will add $9.5 million to the net wealth of Geothermal's owners.

$$ WACC = \left[\tfrac{D}{V} \times (1 - Tc) r_{debt} \right] + \left[\tfrac{E}{V} \times r_{equity} \right] $$

G. **Checking Our Logic**
1. If Geothermal earns the cost of capital on assets, 11.4%, the debt security holders will earn their required rate of return, 8%, and shareholders will earn their required rate of return of 14%.
2. If Geothermal earns an IRR greater than (less than) the cost of capital, shareholders will earn a return higher (lower) than their required rate of return of 14%. Creditors will earn only their fixed rate, required rate of return of 8% in all periods.
3. Projects with actual NPVs greater than zero will earn shareholders a return greater than the required rate of return on equity. Projects earning IRRs less than the cost of capital will produce actual NPVs less than zero and returns to equity below the required rate of return.

III. MEASURING CAPITAL STRUCTURE

A. Some of the practical problems involved in measuring the cost of capital include 1) identifying market values, and 2) determining the current market value of securities.

B. Market value weights are preferred over book value weights. Publicly traded share prices may be listed in newspapers. Market value estimates may be calculated by finding the present value of future cash flows discounted at the current interest rates.

C. The market value of equity may be estimated by multiplying the share price by the number of shares outstanding.

IV. CALCULATING REQUIRED RATES OF RETURN

A. Estimate the current, required rate of return on each security the firm has outstanding. For bonds, the current yield to maturity is a good proxy; for stocks, estimates using the CAPM or dividend discount model are reasonable numbers.

B. **The Expected Return on Bonds** -- The yield to maturity, or the yield calculated to equate future cash flows with the price of the bond, is a good proxy for expected bond returns for healthy firms.

C. **The Expected Return on Common Stock**
   1. The cost of equity capital may be estimated using the CAPM, where the expected return on equity is equal to the sum of the risk-free, T-bill rate plus the firm's beta times the market risk premium.
   2. The dividend discount model may be used to estimate the required rate of return on equity, $P_o = DIV_1/(r_{equity} - g)$, where P_o is the current price, DIV_1 is the expected first year's dividend, and g is the expected growth rate. Solving for r_{equity}, the equation is transformed into the sum of the dividend yield plus the dividend growth rate or:

$$ r_e = \frac{Div_1}{P_0} + g $$

D. The Expected Return on Preferred Stock
   1. The estimated market value of preferred stock is found by dividing the constant dividend by the current required rate of return on similar risk preferred stock in the market. The price is equal to expected annual

$$ r_{preferred} = \frac{Div_1}{P_0} $$

dividend divided by r_{pfd}.

2. Solving for the required rate of return on the preferred, use the following estimates:

V. BIG OIL'S THE WEIGHTED AVERAGE COST OF CAPITAL

A. The weighted average cost of capital is the weighted sum of the after-tax cost of debt plus the cost of equity.

B. This section provides you with a simple example of the math involved in such calculations.

VI. INTERPRETING THE WEIGHTED AVERAGE COST OF CAPITAL

A. **When You Can and Can't Use WACC**
1. The WACC is the rate of return that the business must expect to earn on its average-risk investments in order to provide the opportunity rate of return to all its investors, debt and equity.
2. Investment projects under consideration with higher or lower risk than average business risk should be discounted with rates above or below the WACC.

B. Some Mistakes People Make Using the WACC
1. Because debt is tax deductible and its after-tax cost is far less than the cost of equity, one may reason that funding the project with increased proportions of debt will lower the WACC.
2. As the debt ratio increases, the incremental cost of debt, both explicit interest rates and implicitly through increases in the cost of equity capital, raises the WACC.

C. How Changing Capital Structure Affects Expected Returns
1. If there are no corporate taxes, a change in the capital structure does not affect the WACC, though it does affect the incremental cost of each component of the capital structure.
2. The shareholder's required rate of return adjusts to the changing capital structure and its component parts in order to keep the WACC the same.

VII. Flotation Costs And The Cost Of Capital

A. Flotation Costs Represent The Costs Of Issuing Or "Floating" New Securities.
   1. Flotation costs increase the cost outlay of investment projects and lower NPV's.
   2. Recognizing flotation costs as an upward adjustment in the cost of capital is not as practical or as logical as including flotation costs as a negative cash flow outlay.

B. The Cost of Capital Depends Only On The Risk Of The Project
   1. Flotation costs should be treated as a negative, incremental cash flow.
   2. Flotation costs do not increase the required rate of return.

COMPLETION QUESTIONS

1. When a firm has no debt, all its assets are financed with _____.

2. When a firm has (*considerable/no*) debt its value is equal to the value of its stock.

3. The (*capital/financial*) structure is the mix of debt and equity.

4. The company _____ of _____ is the weighted average of the returns required by debt and equity investors.

5. The weighting factors for debt and equity are based on (*book/market*) values.

6. The inclusion of income taxes will lower the cost of (*debt/equity*) capital.

7. The cost of equity is (*raised/unaffected*) by the existence of income taxes.

8. A project with a zero NPV will generate (*excess/sufficient*) funds for investor requirements.

9. The stock price for a firm having a market value of $200 million and 5 million shares outstanding must be _____ per share.

10. According to the CAPM, the cost of equity capital is (*higher/lower*) for high beta stocks.

11. According to the CAPM, when the market risk premium decreases, the cost of equity capital for all firms will (*decrease/increase*).

12. According to the dividend discount model, the cost of equity is higher for (*faster/slower*) growing firms.

13. The cost of preferred stock is (*higher/lower*) for higher dividends.

14. If income tax rates were increased, the cost of debt would (*decrease/increase*).

15. The weighted average cost of capital is adjusted (*downward/upward*) when evaluating above average risk projects.

16. As more financing for assets comes from debt, the cost of equity will (*decrease/increase*).

17. The market risk of a firm's projects is known as the (*asset/liability*) beta.

18. The cost of debt is (*greater/less*) than the cost of equity.

ANSWERS TO COMPLETION QUESTIONS

1. equity
2. no
3. capital
4. cost, capital
5. market
6. debt
7. unaffected
8. sufficient
9. $40
10. higher
11. decrease
12. faster
13. higher
14. decrease
15. upward
16. increase
17. asset
18. less

PROBLEMS

1. Allequity Corporation is a manufacturing firm with an equity beta of 1.1. Currently Treasury Bill rates are 5% and the market-risk premium is estimated at 8%. What is the required rate of return by the shareholders of Allequity Corporation? What is Allequity's cost of capital? What is the minimum acceptable rate of return on new investments?

2. Bryon Corp. issued 20 year bonds two years ago when rates were 7%. The $1000 face value bonds are now selling at $940. What is the current required rate of return on Bryon Corp. bonds?

3. With marginal tax rates of 40%, what is the current after-tax cost of capital for Bryon Corp. bonds? See problem 2.

4. Bryon Corp. estimates the market value of its equity to be $20 million and its debt, $10 million. The total assets listed on the balance sheet are $30 million. If equity investors now require an 18% rate of return on equity, what is the estimated weighted average cost of capital (WACC) for Bryon Corp? See problems 2 and 3 above. If Bryon Corp. recently evaluated an investment project with a positive NPV, what is the approximate rate of return on the investment?

5. Akron Tire issued preferred stock several years ago with a face value of $100, paying a dividend of 9%. Recently the preferred was trading at $105. What is the approximate required rate of return on preferred if Akron Tire decided to sell an issue of preferred stock?

6. Buchtel Industries has the following capital structure. If the corporate tax rate is 40%, what is the WACC for Buchtel Industries?

Security	Market Value	Required rate of return
Debt	$5 million	10%
Preferred stock	$3 million	12%
Common stock	$8 million	18%

7. Buchtel Industries above is evaluating a project which is expected to generate a $50,000 cash flow for 5 years with a salvage value in the 5th year of $25,000. What is the maximum amount that Buchtel Industries should pay for the project? If they pay this amount, what is the expected NPV of the project?

8. What is the expected rate of return on a project with a NPV of zero, financed with equal amount of debt costing 12% and equity with an opportunity rate of return of 20%? What is the WACC, assuming no taxes paid. If the firm is considering financing with 52% debt, how would the IRR on the project and the company's WACC change?

9. Monitor Software has a WACC of 14%. Its stock sells for $8, currently pays a dividend of $.50, and has a growth rate of 8%. If the debt outstanding is priced to yield to 10%, what are the proportions of debt and equity? Assume no taxes.

10. A business with 40% debt, yielding 10% before a tax rate of 40%, and the rest equity with an opportunity cost of capital of 20%, is contemplating an investment with an NPV of zero. Calculate the WACC, listing the steps involved in calculating the WACC.

11. In problem 10 , should the business make the investment?

12. If the stock of Geothermal, pp. 275-6 in the chapter, is selling at $24 and the equity required rate of return is 20%, what is the WACC of Geothermal?

13. In problem 12 , would you recommend that Geothermal make the expansion?

14. In problem 12, what annual amount must Geothermal earn on the investment to provide bondholders and stockholders their required rate of return?

SOLUTIONS TO PROBLEMS

1. The required rate of return (RRR) is the risk-free rate plus the beta times the market-risk premium (required return on the market portfolio minus the risk-free rate) or:
$$RRR = .05 + 1.1(.08) = 13.8\%$$

Since Allequity has no debt, the required return on the stock is the cost of capital and the <u>minimum</u> acceptable return on any new investments.

2. The recent yield to maturity is a proxy of the pre-tax required rate of return on bonds of Bryon Corp. At a price of 94% of face value or $940 with annual coupon payments of 7% of $1000 or $70 for 18 years with a final cash flow of $1000 at maturity,

Financial calculator: $940 PV, $1000 FV, $70 PMT, 18 N
$$I = 7.62\% \text{ yield to maturity}$$

The approximate market rate of return on Bryon Corp.'s long-term debt is 7.62%.

3.   The after-tax cost of debt is the pre-tax rate of 7.62% times one minus the marginal tax rate of 40% or:

After-tax cost of debt = 7.62%(1 - .4) = 4.57%

4.   The WACC for Bryon Corp., using the market value of debt and equity as weights is:

WACC = (10/30).0457 + (20/30).18 = 13.52%

If a recent investment proposal had a positive NPV after discounting the expected cash flows at the cost of capital, 13.5%, the rate of return of the project is greater than 13.5%.

5.   The required rate of return (RRR) on the preferred stock of Akron Tire is the yield now demanded by the market or,

RRR = $9 dividend/$105 price = 8.57%

6.   Buchtel Industries has a total market value of $16 million and an after-tax cost of debt of 10%(1 - .4) = 6%.

WACC = 5/16 × .06 + 3/16 × .12 + 8/16 × .18 = 13%

7.   Using the WACC calculated in problem 6 above, discount the 5 year, $50,000 annuity and single cash flow (5th year) value of $25,000 at 13 percent:

PV = $50,000(3.517) + $25,000(.543) = $189,425

The present value or maximum investment of $189,425 would generate an internal rate of return of 13%, yielding the sources of funding, including equity, their required rate of return.

8.   WACC = .5(.12) + .5(.20) = 16%

If the project cash flows discounted at the WACC of 16% yields a NPV = 0, the expected IRR on the project equals the WACC of 16%. Any variation in the funding mix should not affect the expected return on the project, but just divide the cash flow earnings among the sources of funding.

9.   This problem works back from the WACC of 14% to determine the debt/total value and equity/total value ratios. Using the constant growth estimate of price as the expected dividend in period one, $.50(1.08) = $.54, divided by the difference between the required rate of return on equity and the growth rate or:

$$r = \frac{Div_1}{P} + g$$

$r = \$.54/\$8 + .08$

$r = .1475\%$

Let x = Debt/total value ratio
$1 - x$ = Equity/total value ratio

WACC = $.10x + .1475(1 - x) = .14$

$x = 15.8\%$ debt proportion
$1 - x = 84.2\%$ equity proportion

10.   The after-tax cost of debt is $10\%(1 - .4) = 6\%$

WACC = $.06 (.4) + .20 (.6) = .144$ or 14.4%

   1.   Calculate the proportional weights of each source of capital, using market values.
   2.   Determine the required rate of return today of each security.
   3.   Calculate the WACC.

11.   If the project has an NPV of zero calculated by discounting expected cash flows at the 14.4% WACC, the IRR on the project equals 14.4% and will provide the required rate of return to each source of capital. Assume a $100,000 investment invested at 14.4%, the WACC, generating $14,400 each year and available for interest on the debt and returns to equity. Forty percent or $40,000 of the $100,000 investment is financed by debt; sixty percent or $60,000 is financed by equity.

$ 14,400   14.4% return on $100,000
- 2,400 $40,000 debt @ 10% cost of debt(1-.4)
$ 12,000   Available for $60,000 equity contribution or

$12,000/$60,000 = 20%$ return on equity

Both debt and equity will receive their required rate of return if the investment is invested at the WACC or if the NPV on an investment equals zero.

If the project earns an IRR greater than the WACC, or if the NPV is greater than zero, the shareholders will receive a return greater than their RRR. For example, if the investment earns a 20% return, the returns to equity on the $60,000 of contributed equity is:

$20,000 ($100,000 x 20%)
 -2,400 after-tax cost of debt (does not change)
$17,600 earnings available for common

$17,600/$60,000 equity or a 29.3% rate of return on equity. The expected rates of return (IRR) on equity on positive NPV projects exceed the WACC.

12.   If Geothermal's stock were priced at $24, the market value capital structure would be:

Debt $194.0 million (26.3%)
Equity 543.6 million (73.7%)
      $737.6 million 100.0%

WACC = .263(.08) + .737(.2) = .168 or 16.8%

The market value of the assets is the same as the value of the securities, $737.6 million. The increased proportion of equity and recent higher required rates of return (now 18%) increased the WACC to 16.8%.

13.   The expected IRR on the project of 15% is less than the WACC of 16.8%. Jo Ann would recommend that the project be rejected because the IRR is less than the WACC.

14.   The investment must earn the WACC or 16.8% to earn the required rate of return for shareholders.

$5,040,000   (16.8% return on $30 million)
- 631,000   (.263 x $30 million x .08 cost of debt)
$4,409,000 (Available for common investment of .737 x $30 million or
            $22,110,000)

$4,409,000/$22,110,000 = .20 or 20%

The project is expected to only earn 15% per year or .15 x $30 million = $4.5 million, less than the $5.04 million (above) needed to compensate investors at their RRR. The proof is:

$4,500,000 (15% return on $30 million)
- 631,000 (cost of debt)
$3,869,000   return on $22,110,000 equity.

The ROE is $3,869,000/$22,110,000 = .175 or 17.5%. The 15% project return would earn shareholders 17.5% which is less than the 20% needed to retain investors in the stock at $24. If the investment is made, selling pressure on the stock is likely to drop the price to provide the RRR of 20%.

CORPORATE FINANCING AND THE LESSONS OF MARKET EFFICIENCY

INTRODUCTION

This is the first of three chapters related to financing in financial markets. An earlier section reviewed asset investment, followed by the last section covering concepts bridging asset investment and financial markets (financing). To understand the variables and the process of making financing decisions, one must first consider a few assumptions related to the financial markets and investors. These are covered in this chapter.

The first section of the chapter covers the efficient market hypothesis in a very readable, practical presentation. Varying degrees of efficiency are covered as are classic issues such as timing and other issues related to less than efficient markets. Your former experiences with efficient markets was in your microeconomics course. Comparing the pure competitive model of economics with the efficient markets discussion with multiple period decision periods and variability of results of decisions (risk) will help you make the transition from prior knowledge to this chapter.

LEARNING CHECKLIST

This is challenging concepts chapter. Read and study to grasp the concepts and be able to:

____1. Show how competition among investors leads to efficient markets.

____2. Cite evidence that supports the hypothesis that security markets are efficient, or evidence that financial markets are less than efficient.

____3. Understand the implications and impact of market efficiency on business financing decisions.

SOURCES OF BUSINESS INFORMATION

Moody's Manuals. One of the most popular sources of business information are Moody's <u>Manuals</u>, including the <u>Industrials, Public Utility, Bank & Finance, International, Municipal and Government, OTC,</u> and <u>Transportation</u> manuals. The <u>Bank & Finance Manual</u> is a four-volume, comprehensive reference work related to financial institutions. It offers financial statements for the largest, publicly-traded commercial banks and bank holding companies (Vol. 1), insurance companies (Vol. 2), and unit investment trusts (Vol. 3 and 4), which are fixed investment pools that issue securities to investors.

Company Information Via the Web. Moody's Manuals, discussed above have been one of the classic sources of financial information on companies in the library. Moody's also has an online service to their information via a subscription fee. Other free sources include **Invest Quest** (http://www.investquest.com) which provides financial information (SEC Reports of 10K, 10Q, and proxy information) for the last three years for over 10,000 U.S. and Canadian companies. Invest Quest provides an industry classification index for the student studying a specific industry.

CHAPTER OUTLINE, KEY CONCEPTS AND TERMS

I. DIFFERENCES BETWEEN INVESTMENT AND FINANCING DECISIONS

    A.   Financing decisions are more complicated than investment decisions for the variety of securities to sell is large and continually expanding, the number of financial institutions providing financing is extensive, and the market is very competitive.

    B.   In some ways financing decisions are easier than investment decisions. Financial decisions may be reversed more easily than investment decisions. The level of competition in financial markets is extensive so it is hard to make an incorrect financial decision. All prices, rates, and terms are fair, or are true values, and unlike investment decisions which usually provide positive net present values, financing decisions usually provide fairly priced, zero NPVs.

    C.   Funds are raised, or securities are sold in efficient capital markets, or markets where security prices rapidly reflect all relevant information, currently available, about asset values.

    D.   In efficient markets all securities are fairly priced, so financing is always a zero NPV transaction.

    E.   The rest of the chapter discusses the efficient market hypothesis, providing a background of the idea, its logic, and several tests of market efficiency.

II. WHAT IS AN EFFICIENT MARKET?

    A.   **A Startling Discovery: Price Changes Are Random**
        1.   Research by Maurice Kendall indicated that security market price changes were unrelated to prior price changes with no predictable trends or patterns or that the prices tended to be a **random walk** over time. See Figure 12.1.

2. Support of the efficient market theory is indicated in the scatter diagram of daily price changes of the stock of Weyerhaeuser during a thirty-year period. The dots are evenly distributed in the four quadrants, indicating no recurring pattern of price changes, or that price changes are random.

3. Another test of the efficient market theory is to review the level of correlation between daily price changes. Much research has indicated little correlation or low correlation coefficients (close to zero). New information is random; prices react accordingly.

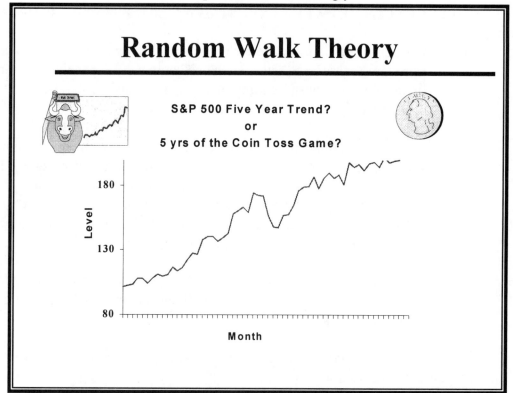

4. **Technical analysts** attempt to find patterns in security price movements and trade accordingly. Their trading tends to quickly offset any price trend and keep the markets efficient.

B. **Three Forms of the Efficient-Market Theory**
1. The first form of market efficiency is **weak-form efficiency** which is a situation in which market prices rapidly reflect all information contained in the history of past prices. Past price movements are random; the past cannot predict future price changes.

2. **Fundamental analysts** attempt to find under- or over-valued securities by analyzing "fundamental" information, such as earnings, asset values, etc., to uncover yet undiscovered information about the future of a business. They look ahead trying to forecast future information; technical analysts are studying past prices, looking for predictable patterns. New

information is quickly reflected in the price of the stock, and investors were not able to earn superior returns by buying or selling after the announcement date.

3. A second form of market efficiency, **semi-strong form efficiency**, is a market situation in which market prices reflect all publicly available information.

4. A third form of market efficiency, **strong-form efficiency**, is a situation in which prices rapidly reflect *all* information that could be used to determine true value. In this market pricing situation, all prices would always be fairly priced and no investor would be able to make superior, accurate forecasts of future price changes. Even professional portfolio managers do not consistently outperform the market, thus supporting the creation of "index" portfolios, assembled to match popular market indices.

5. The efficient market theory implies that security market prices represent fair value. Some argue this cannot be for prices go up and down, and that fair value should change very little. Fair market value changes with new information about the future cash flows associated with a security.

6. The efficient-market theory implies that portfolio managers work in a very competitive market with little or no added advantage over the next portfolio manager. They make few extraordinary returns, not because they are incompetent, but because the markets are so competitive and there are few easy profits.

C. **No Theory is Perfect**

1. Though the efficient markets hypothesis is well supported by research, there are a few unexplained events and exceptions.

2. One exception is the evidence that managers have made consistently

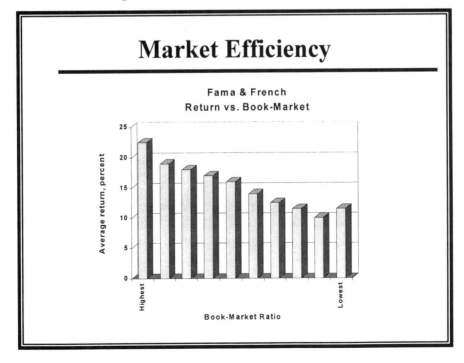

149

superior profits trading their own company's stock, probably with good insider information, but testing the strong-form efficiency theory. The managers know more about the company's opportunities than other market participants.

3. Small firm stocks have consistently outperformed large firm stocks, especially in January, questioning even the weak-form efficiency hypothesis. The fact that other yet-explained variables are involved is the likely answer.

D. **The Crash of 1987**

1. The 20% decline in the S&P 500 on Monday, October 19, 1987, led many to question the efficient-market theory. Critics assumed the market had no new information, that prices were irrationally high before the crash, or irrationally low after the crash.

2. A slight drop in market growth prospects could have produced the decline.

3. The challenge related to studying common stock valuation has *two* implications:

    a   Investors value stocks related to yesterday's price, which is assumed to be correct. When the prior price is deemed to be incorrect, an adjustment is made to find the fair value of the market.

    b   The assumption that yesterday's price was the true fair value is difficult to verify. Price adjustments of significant magnitude may be plausible if adjustments are explained on a relative basis.

III. LESSONS OF MARKET EFFICIENCY

A. **Markets Have No Memory**

1. Even though the efficient-markets theory assumes that past prices contain no information about future prices, or that prices are a random walk, financial managers often act as if they did not accept such a hypothesis:

    a   Managers are reluctant to issue stock after a decline, waiting for a rebound.

    b   Managers favor the issuance of equity over debt after an increase in equity values. They are attempting to sell when the stock is high, reducing the dilution of EPS.

    c   Managers are reluctant to sell equity if favorable announcements are to be made in the future, but inside information has nothing to do with past prices, only the future of the firm.

B. **There Are No Financial Illusions**
1. Investors are not concerned with accounting income and its measurement or timing, only cash flows.
2. Creative accounting is an invisible curtain to analysts, but managers feel others benefit with their "smoke and mirrors" accounting methods.
3. Research indicates that such creative announcements produce no long-term value, and that only information related to future cash flows are "value relevant" information to the market.

C. **There Are No Free Lunches on Wall Street**
1. Trust market prices in an efficient market. There is no better deal tomorrow.
2. Term structure differences in interest rates offer no deal for today or tomorrow. The markets' expectations of future interest rates determine the rate differences over time. Choosing short or long-term rates for financing or investment will likely yield or cost the same over the long term.

COMPLETION QUESTIONS

1. Competition in financial markets is (*less/more*) thorough than in most product markets.

2. Financial markets in which security prices rapidly reflect all relevant information about asset values are called _____ capital markets.

3. Prices that are equally likely to rise or fall on any particular day, regardless of price movements on previous days, are said to follow a _____ _____ .

4. With remarkable unanimity statistical researchers have concluded that there is (*little/much*) useful information in the sequence of stock prices.

5. _____ analysts are persons who attempt to find patterns in security price movements.

6. According to (*strong-/weak-*) form efficiency, market prices rapidly reflect all information contained in the history of past prices.

7. _____ analysts are persons who attempt to value securities by examining information about the firms's earnings, assets, and business prospects.

8. In semi-strong-form efficiency investors (*can/cannot*) make superior profits by using information that is publicly available.

9. The strong-form efficiency means that people having private information (*can/cannot*) consistently outperform the market after taking account of differences in risk.

10. Investors who agree with strong-form efficiency would be more likely to buy (*index funds/individual stocks*).

11. Stock prices (*do/do not*) represent fair values because they do rise and fall.

12. According to (*strong-/weak-*) form efficiency, approximately half of a group of professional portfolio managers will outperform the market in any particular year.

13. If stock prices were consistently more volatile in one month compared to all other months, this would be (*consistent/inconsistent*) with weak-form efficiency.

14. Small company stocks have significantly (*higher/lower*) returns in January, compared to larger firms.

15. The "January Effect" (*is/is not*) consistent with weak-form market efficiency.

16. Sudden downturns in the stock market, like the crash of 1987, can be explained by a sudden (*decrease/increase*) in investor expectations about the future growth rate in dividends.

17. The belief that markets have (*considerable/no*) memory and that prices follow a random walk is another way of stating the (*strong/weak*)-form efficient market theory.

18. Researchers have shown that investors (*are/are not*) mislead by accounting changes designed to (*deflate/inflate*) earnings.

19. If a company splits its stock two-for-one and has no changes to report in its future prospects, its stock price will (*fall by one-half/stay the same*).

20. If interest rates are lower on 2-year bonds in comparison with those on 1-year bonds, the market is forecasting a (*decrease/increase*) in short-term interest rates.

PROBLEMS

1. Bill Begee, head of Korrison-Minudsen, has instructed his chief accounting officer to employ the most aggressive accounting practices that are legal so as to report the highest possible earnings for the company. What likely effect will this action have on K-M's stock price?

2. If security markets are truly efficient, explain why all stocks don't provide the same return to investors?

3. "According to the strong-form of the efficient markets hypothesis (EMH), there are no surprises in security markets." Explain why this is not a true statement.

4. Professional investors should be able to outperform the market. Explain why this statement is true or false according to the EMH.

5. Chief financial officers of companies are well-advised to time their security offerings. Explain whether or not this is the case according to the EMH.

6. What does a downward sloping yield curve indicate that investors are expecting to happen to long-term interest rates?

ANSWERS TO COMPLETION QUESTIONS

1. more
2. efficient
3. random walk
4. little
5. Technical
6. weak
7. Fundamental
8. cannot
9. cannot
10. index funds
11. do
12. strong
13. consistent
14. higher
15. is not
16. decrease
17. no, weak
18. are not, inflate
19. fall by one-half
20. decrease

SOLUTIONS TO PROBLEMS

1. The effect will be nothing substantial either in the short- or long-run. This is because investors are very savvy and are typically not fooled by manipulation of financial statements. Creative accounting does not succeed in distorting underlying values that are reflected in stock prices.

2. All stocks don't provide the same returns to investors because different stocks have different risks. The expected returns reflect these perceived risks. Investors will only purchase higher risk stocks <u>if</u> they expect to be rewarded accordingly. On the other hand, investors will accept lower returns if they believe the risk of realizing those returns is lower.

3. The quoted statement in this problem is simply not an accurate interpretation of the efficient markets hypothesis (EMH). The EMH does not hold that investors know the future. Investors are not perfect forecasters. Rather the EMH states that security prices reflect information that is currently available. No one knows exactly what will happen tomorrow. Investors act on what is known today and their actions result in prices that are based on this information. Surprises certainly do occur but investors expect future returns that match their risk assessments.

4. There is a level of anticipated risk in the market. Investors expect to receive rewards corresponding to that level. But these returns have occurred on average for many cases over long periods of time. A similar generalization can be made for professional investors who are seeking undervalued stocks relative to the value determined by perceived riskiness. Thus over the long-run and for numerous instances, the returns will indeed have higher average amounts. Professional investors tend to do this. They are in the market for long periods of time and are making hundreds and hundreds of investments. If they undertake higher than average risks, they will tend to have higher than average returns and thus "beat the market". But many of these professionals will fail to meet the averages from time to time, especially those who are consistently taking the higher risks. Some analysts tend to make more insightful use of available information which also helps them to realize superior returns from time to time.

5. No one without special knowledge that will have a predictable effect on values will be able to consistently earn higher returns than expected, given the level of perceived risk. Financial managers may be able to make more informed judgements about the future potential performance of their firm. However. the marketplace is the ultimate determiner of value. Even the insider doesn't know what will happen to other firms, to the economy, or to the stock market. Furthermore, company executives may be overly optimistic or super-aggressive as was hinted in problem 1. The most obvious example of the folly of believing that financial managers should be able to wisely time the security market actions is in the case of interest rates. Statistical analyses of historical interest rate patterns cast overwhelming doubt on those who claim to be able to know what will happen to interest rates.

6. When the yield curve is downward sloping, short-term rates are higher than long-term rates. This situation is an indication that investors expect a decline in long-term rates. When this is the case, investors try to lock-in the current long-term rates by buying long-term bonds. This tends to drive their price up resulting in lower yields. Also investors will be shifting out of short-term debt which tends to force the short-term debt prices down resulting in higher short-term yields. These actions cause the downward slope in the yield curve.

AN OVERVIEW OF CORPORATE FINANCING

INTRODUCTION

This is the second chapter on business financing. It covers the many varieties of financing alternatives available in financial markets. There is an in-depth discussion of common stock, preferred stock, and debt securities. Much of the discussion focuses on the standard terms of common stock, etc., that most of you learned in accounting. Here, try to focus on the risk/return considerations of each of the characteristics, features, or covenants discussed. Each feature affects the future cash flows, their timing, and variability. Keep this valuation theme in your mind as you study the details. At the end of the chapter is a section related to historical patterns of corporate financing. This section provides a good historical perspective for understanding today and, important to you, the future.

LEARNING CHECKLIST

After studying this chapter, you should be able to:

____1. Be able to compare and contrast the three major securities discussed, common stock, preferred stock, and bonds as to maturity, claims on income, claims on assets in case of liquidation, and voice in management of the firm.

____2. Name and discuss variations of the above securities and special terms or covenants that increase or decrease the risk/return potential for investors and the issuing business.

____3. Summarize recent trends in the use made by firms of different sources of financing.

SOURCES OF BUSINESS INFORMATION

A.M. Best's Insurance Reports. One of the most popular sources of information about insurance companies that you may buy from or work for is Best's Insurance Reports Life-Health and Insurance Reports Property-Casualty. They offer a complete, thorough analysis of domestic life, health, and property-casualty (auto, liability, homeowner's) companies. Best gives a risk rating for each company. Life insurance companies are major pension fund managers and sell long-term retirement annuities.

The Insurance Forum. Professor Joseph M. Belth is the editor and publisher of this consumer oriented publication. The Insurance Forum bills itself as the "unfettered exchange of ideas about insurance." More than just a forum, here you will find some of the most provocative investigative reporting in the insurance industry. The special ratings issue (published once a year) is a must for anyone researching life insurance carriers. The Insurance Forum attempts to maintain its objectivity by adhering to a strict policy of not accepting advertising. To find out more visit http://www.insuranceforum.com

CHAPTER OUTLINE, KEY CONCEPTS AND TERMS

I. COMMON STOCK

A. Terminology
1. Corporations issue common shares of ownership. Shareholders or stockholders own the shares and may trade the shares.
2. Common stock has several classifications or "sets" of shares. The total possible number of shares that the company may issue are the shares **authorized** by a vote of the common stock. Of the authorized, usually a large proportion are **issued**, and the rest are authorized, not issued. Of the issued, most are **outstanding**, except the **treasury** shares which have been repurchased by the company.
3. The number of outstanding shares are used to calculate dividends and earnings per share.
4. When a share is issued or sold it is recorded or "booked" usually at a nominal, low **par value**. If sold above par, the remainder is recorded in the **paid-in capital** or capital surplus account of the general ledger.
5. Cumulative earnings, not paid out in dividends, but reinvested in the firm, are accounted for in the **retained earnings** account.
6. Net common stockholders equity is the sum of the common stock account recorded at par value, the paid-in surplus, and the retained earnings, less the amount of repurchased or treasury stock. The amount represents the historical value of money raised from the sale of stock plus earnings retained over the past, less the amount of shares repurchased.

B. Book Value versus Market Value
1. Net common stockholders equity is recorded at original, historical book value.
2. The market value of common equity is the product of the number of shares *outstanding* times the current market value per share.
3. The market value is determined in the market based on the prospects of future cash flows, their timing, and the riskiness of the cash flow.
4. Market value is usually greater than book value if the managers have been investing in positive, added value creating, net present value investments. If actual NPVs are negative for the business over time, the economic or market value will be less than the accounting or book value.

Book Value vs. Market Value Example (Heinz)

Common Stock

Example - H.J. Heinz Book Value vs. Market Value (4/99)

Total Shares outstanding = 358 million

Common Shares ($.25 par)	108
Additional paid in capital	278
Retained earnings	4,380
Treasury shares at cost	- 2,435
Accumulated losses	- 527
Net common equity (Book Value)	1,803

April 1999 Market price =	$49/sh
# of shares	x 358
Market Value	$17.5 billion

C. **Dividends**
1. The board of directors declare dividends. They are not contractual like interest payments to creditors.
2. Unlike interest expense, dividends are deemed a return of capital by the Internal Revenue Service, and are not a *deductible* expense.

D. **Stockholders' Rights**
1. Stockholders, as owners of the corporation, have ultimate responsibility for the actions of the company.
2. Shareholders delegate most decisions to the board of directors they elect, and the management which is appointed by the board. Some decisions related to the number of authorized shares, mergers, etc., are retained by shareholders.

3.   The board, comprised of insiders, (corporate officers), and outside directors appoints top managers and provides an overview of managerial activities and performance for the shareholders.

E.   **Voting Procedures**
1.   Shareholders vote for members of the board of directors, using one of two voting methods.
2.   When each vacant board seat is voted upon *one at a time*, with one vote per share, a majority vote is needed for election. Under this **majority** voting method, a dominant shareholder group, electing one board member at a time, can usually elect their candidates to all positions.
3.   Under the **cumulative** voting procedure all directors are elected in one vote. Minority group shareholders may cumulate their votes (number of shares times directors elected) and cast a block of votes. The largest block of votes appoints the first director and so on.
4.   Shareholders may delegate or proxy their vote to others, usually management-oriented shareholders or dissident shareholder groups. A **proxy contest** occurs when shareholder groups compete with existing management for control of the board and the corporation.

F.   **Classes of Stock**
1.   While a single class of common stock is prevalent, some corporations have "A" or "B" stock, restricting the voting rights or dividend rights of one of the classes.

G.   **Corporate Governance in the United States and Elsewhere**
1.   The separation between ownership (principals) and management (agents) may create a potential conflict of interest between owners and managers. The study of this conflict and resolutions is called agency theory.
2.   The Japanese structure of holding companies and interlocking directorships and share ownership is called a *kiretsu*. The combination of industrial and financial firms provides for less "public" borrowing or financing and a better focus on long-term versus short-term performance.

II.   PREFERRED STOCK

A.   The terms of **preferred stock**, especially the priority of claims on the declared dividend pool and the claim on assets in case of liquidation, are ahead of those of common stock.

B.   In exchange for the above preferred treatment, preferred stockholders usually waive their full voting rights and accept a limited dividend return.

C.   The **net worth** of a corporation is the sum of the common and preferred stockholders equity accounts. When no preferred is outstanding, net worth and common stockholders equity are the same.

D.   Preferred dividends, like common dividends, are not tax deductible. Preferred dividend income, if received by a corporation like State Farm or Allstate Insurance through their investment in preferred stock, has a generous tax sheltering feature. In order to prevent triple taxation (corporation, corporation, shareholder), only 30 percent of preferred dividends received by a corporation are taxable.

E.   If declared, preferred dividends are paid before common dividends are paid, and usually are cumulative. Cumulative preferred is very common and requires that if dividends are passed in one period (common would have been passed also), the averages will be paid in the future before any common dividends are paid.

F.   Some preferred stock are **floating-rate preferred** with their dividend varying or floating with the change in a specific index or interest rate level.

III.   CORPORATE DEBT

A. **Concepts**
   1.   Common and preferred stock represent ownership and voting control in a corporation; corporate borrowings are non-ownership contractual obligations to receive amounts of capital for corporate investment projects, pay a usually fixed cost interest rate on the debt, and repay the principal at maturity or in payments (sinking fund).
   2.   Interest expense on debt is tax deductible, unlike common and preferred dividends. A company with a 34 percent tax rate would effectively pay (1-.34) or 66 cents on any dollar of interest expense.

B. **Debt Comes in Many Forms**
   1.   There are many variations of interest rates, terms, repayment provisions, seniority of claims in case of liquidation, collateral, and risk.
   2.   The interest rate paid, or coupon rate, is the going market rate at the time the money is borrowed. Some bonds are zero coupon, discount bonds; others have rates that are adjustable. The bank **prime rate** or *LIBOR* varies with market interest rates.
   3.   **Funded debt** is debt payable after one year; unfunded debt is short-term bank loans, a current liability. Funded debt such as bonds often have long maturities.
   4.   Debt comes due! Repayment may be at maturity, but more commonly is paid-off in installments or payments. A **sinking fund** is an arrangement

for periodic payments to a fund, or to reduce the amount outstanding (buy back bonds).

5. **Callable bonds** are able to be paid-off early, the price stipulated in the contract, at the discretion of the borrower. Firms are more likely to call bonds when interest rates have fallen or when their investments have generated high levels of cash flows.

6. Some unsecured, general creditors may, for a higher interest rate, be positioned as **subordinated debt**, which means if the firm defaults the senior general creditors are paid-off from the dissolution of assets before the subordinated creditors.

7. If collateral, such as plant and equipment, railroad cars, or land is pledged backing the debt obligation, the bonds are **secured bonds**.

8. Funded debt may, at the corporation's option, be *rated* by rating services such as Moody's or Standard and Poor's. If the securities have minimum default risk, they will be awarded an **investment grade**. Below investment grade, securities have the infamous title of **junk bonds**.

9. Securities may be issued in specific currency denominations, such as **Eurodollar**, dollar denominated short-term deposits held in foreign banks. A bond that is sold internationally is called a **eurobond**.

10. Securities may be sold to the broad general public class of investors called a **public offering**, or "placed" with a small group of investors, usually financial institutions, called a **private placement**. The publicly offered, and later publicly traded, securities are more likely to have a ready market in case investors wish to sell the securities.

11. Lenders impose a number of conditions on borrowing companies, called **protective covenants**.

12. Variations of debt, such as a **lease**, are common. Instead of borrowing and buying a productive asset, such as machinery, the business may lease, not own, paying lease payments instead of debt installments.

C. **An Example: The Terms of Heniz's Bond Issue** -- See Table 13.3 for a description of Heinz's bond issue. Note the above mentioned terminology and characteristics of the bonds. Look up its market price in **Barron's** or **The Wall Street Journal.**.

D. **Innovation in the Debt Market**
  1. As conditions and needs of investors and corporations change, new types of funding contracts arise.
  2. In areas, such as South America, where inflation is often high, price level **indexed bonds** are often sold. Other bonds' return may be indexed to the price or value of a commodity or interest rate, such as Treasury rates.
  3. **Reverse floaters** are variable rate bonds that pay a higher rate when other interest rates fall, and vice versa.
  4. **Pay in kind bonds (PIK)** pay interest and, in the early years, some other form of return (commodity or product), thus giving the issuer or borrower more flexibility in case cash flows lag for a time.

IV. **CONVERTIBLE SECURITIES** -- Some bonds may be issued with options that grant the investor the right to *buy* shares of common stock (**warrants**) or the option to *trade* the bond for a stated number of shares of common stock (**convertible**).

V. **PATTERNS OF CORPORATE FINANCING**

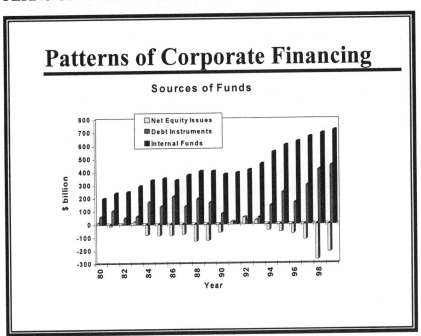

A. **Choices**
  1. Funds for investment may be raised from external (debt or equity security issues) or internal sources, such as cash flows from operations.
  2. **Internally generated funds**, derived mostly from net income retained in the period plus non-cash depreciation expenses (cash flow from operations) are a major source of funds for both U.S. corporations and businesses of other countries.

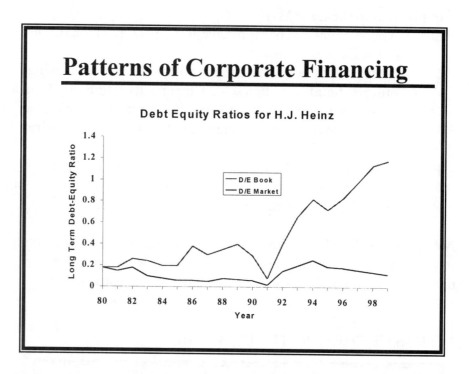

Patterns of Corporate Financing

Debt Equity Ratios for H.J. Heinz

B.   **Do Firms Rely Too Heavily on Internal Funds?**
1.   Research by Gordon Donaldson indicates that a business' growth or investment growth rate is determined by the growth rate of internally generated funds, rather than the quantity of positive NPV investments.
2.   Managers that do not wish to be critically assessed or monitored by the financial markets and financial institutions when financing externally might follow this strategy.
3.   The costs of financing externally is avoided when internally generated funds are used as is the possible downward movement in stock prices when a new equity issue is announced. Investors feel managers "signal" lower expected profits when new equity is issued, rather than a debt issue announcement where expectations are for higher profits in the future.

C.   **External Sources of Capital**
1.   The financing trends of the 1980s reveals that debt issues were popular and stock buy-backs were popular.

COMPLETION QUESTIONS

1. Sources of finance are classified as _____ or _____.

2. Equity has a (*priority/residual*) claim on the firm.

3. Shares that are held by the company that have been issued but are not outstanding are called _____ stock.

4. (*Book/Par*) value is the value of stock shown on the certificate.

5. Another name for additional paid-in-capital is capital _____.

6. Earnings not paid out as (*dividends/interest*) are retained earnings.

7. Book value is a (*backward/forward*) looking measure.

8. _____ value is usually greater than book value because of inflation and capital investments in projects with present values that exceed initial costs.

9. On most matters shareholder control is exercised through voting on (*boards of directors/ company officers*).

10. The voting system in which all the votes of a shareholder can be cast for one board candidate is known as _____ voting.

11. The process in which outsiders compete with existing management for shareholders' votes is called a _____ contest.

12. A firm may have two or more classes of common stock which differ in their right to _____ and/or to receive _____.

13. Preferred stock has priority over (*bondholder/common stockholders*).

14. Net worth or _____ value (*does/does not*) include preferred stock.

15. If a firm goes out of business, preferred stockholders claims are (*behind/ahead of*) those of bondholders.

16. Preferred dividends (*are/are not*) deductible from taxable income.

17. (*30/70*) percent of dividends received by one corporation from another corporation are treated as taxable income.

18. Preferred stock paying dividends that vary with short-term interest rates are called _____-_____ preferred.

19. The deductibility of interest means, in effect, that the government (*discourages/subsidizes*) the use of debt.

20. _____-rate loans are tied to variations in the prime rate or the London _____ _____ _____ _____ (LIBOR).

21. Debt that is repayable more than one-year from the date of issue is called _____ debt.

22. A (*floating/sinking*) fund is established to retire debt before maturity.

23. A (*callable/secured*) bond may be repurchased by the firm before maturity at a specified price.

24. The call and sinking fund provisions (*do/do not*) effectively place a limit on capital gains for the investor.

25. A bond that is subordinated has claims that are junior to some other (*creditors/share- holders*).

26. Secured debtholders have claims on specified collateral that are (*junior/senior*).

27. _____ bonds have unusually high risks and high expected returns.

28. Eurodollars are dollar deposits held (*by foreigners/in banks outside the U.S.*).

29. Bonds that are sold throughout the world are called _____.

30. Private individuals (*do/do not*) usually buy private placements.

31. A protective covenant is a restriction placed on (*borrowers/lenders*).

32. A lease is similar to (*debt/preferred stock*).

33. Bonds having payments that are tied to some measure of prices are called_____ bonds.

34. Pay in kind bonds (PIKs) allow the issuer to pay interest with (<u>commodities/more bonds</u>).

35. The right to buy shares from a firm at a specified price before a set date is called a _____.

36. A convertible bond has a provision that allows the (*investor/issuer*) to exchange the bond for a predetermined number of shares.

37. Internally generated funds equals profits not paid out as dividends plus _____.

38. The cost of internally generated funds is (*less/more*) than the cost of money raised from a new stock issue.

39. Debt ratios in the U.S. are (*higher/lower*) than those found in most developing nations.

PROBLEMS

1. Bonnie's Boleros, Inc. (BBI) has authorized 1 million shares of common stock. How many shares are outstanding if the shareholders' equity portion of the balance sheet is:

ACCOUNT	$THOUSANDS
Common stock ($1 par)	200
Paid in surplus	400
Retained earnings	2000
Common equity	2600
Treasury stock	100
Net common equity	2500

2. If the treasury shares in problem were purchased on the open market for $5 per share, how many share of BBI are currently outstanding?

3. If BBI sold 50,000 shares of authorized but unissued stock for $10 per share, how would the shareholders' equity accounts change?

4. Suppose BBI issued 50,000 shares of preferred stock at $10 per share. How would this affect the shareholders' equity accounts shown in problem 1?

5. Suppose a company has 8 directors being nominated for re-election by the owners of 1 million outstanding shares. How many shares would need to be controlled in order to elect at least one director if the cumulative voting process was in place?

6. How many votes does the owner of 100 shares have to cast in the election described in the preceding problem?

7. How many shares would be needed to elect at least one director in the situation outlined in problem 5 if majority voting procedures were in effect instead of cumulative voting?

8. What would be the likely explanation for a case where Kali Company bonds are selling at a price that offers a yield to maturity of 9 percent when its preferred stock is yielding 8 percent? (Assume a 40 percent tax rate applies).

9. Using the data from problem 8, explain why the majority of preferred stock is not owned by individual investors.

10. Which of the following will tend to increase the cost of debt for a firm?
    a. Subordination clause
    b. Convertibility feature
    c. Debenture classification

ANSWERS TO COMPLETION QUESTIONS

1   debt, equity
2. residual
3. treasury
4. Par
5. surplus
6. dividends
7. backward
8. Market
9. board of directors
10. cumulative
11. proxy
12. vote, dividends
13. common stockholders
14. book, does
15. behind
16. are not
17. 30
18. floating, rate
19. subsidizes
20. Floating, Inter-bank, Offered Rate
21. funded
22. sinking
23. callable
24. do

25. creditors
26. senior
27. Junk
28. in banks outside the U.S.
29. Eurobonds
30. do not
31. borrowers
32. debt
33. indexed
34. more bonds
35. warrant
36. investor
37. depreciation
38. less
39. lower

SOLUTIONS TO PROBLEMS

1. The par value per share multiplied by the shares issued equals the dollars of common stock entered on the balance sheet. So the shares issued must be:
$$\$200,000/\$1 = 200,000$$

2. Since $5 per share was paid with a total outlay of $100,000, the number of treasury shares must be:
$$\$100,000/\$5 = 20,000$$
The number of shares outstanding equals the shares issued minus any treasury shares or:
$$200,000 - 20,000 = 180,000$$

3. BBI would receive $10 for each of the 50,000 shares sold or a total of $500,000. This would be accounted for by adding the product of the 50,000 shares and the $1 per share par value to the par value account and 50,000 times the remaining $9 per share or $450,000 to the paid in surplus account.

4. There will be no effect on any of the shareholders' equity accounts because each of those shown in problem 1 pertained only to the common equity. While preferred stock is an equity security, it is limited as to claim and does not impact on the common stockholder for balance sheet entries.

5. There will be 8 votes for each share held. This means a total of 8×1 million or 8 million votes eligible to be cast in this election with the positions going to the top 8 vote-getters. Therefore,

the minimum number of votes needed to elect one director is 1 million. This is equivalent to 1 million/8 or 125,000 shares.

6. Shareholders receive 8 votes for each share held so the owner of 100 shares would have 800 votes. These could be spread evenly or allocated to one or more of the nominees.

7. Under majority voting, the majority rules. This means that one share more that one half of the outstanding number of shares is needed to elect the directors. In this case it would be 500,001 shares. In most elections the number of shares actually voted is less than the number that are outstanding so as a practical matter it takes somewhat less than half of the outstanding shares to control the election. The important point is that one more than half the votes cast will elect all of the directors. No Directors can be elected by the under 50 percent minority.

8. Taxes are the likely explanation. Companies (but not individuals) that receive dividends from another company only pay taxes on 30 percent of the dividends received. Companies (and individuals) must pay taxes on all interest received from corporate bonds they hold. For example, firms that pay taxes at the rate of 40 percent would have after-tax yields of $(1 - .4) \times 9$ or 5.4 percent on the bonds. The after-tax yield on the preferred stock is:
$\{1 - (.3 \times .4)\} \times 8 = 7.04$ percent. The after-tax figures are in line with the risk and return relationship which says that preferred stock is always riskier than the bonds issued by the same company.

9. Remember that individuals pay taxes on all interest and dividends received from corporate securities they own. (Only in the case of municipal bonds are they exempt from taxation on the interest). This means there is a bias against individual owning preferred shares. Note that most individuals pay federal, state, and perhaps local income taxes that are at least 40 percent. At that rate their after-tax yield on the bonds is $(1 - .4) \times 9$ or 5.4 percent. This is the same as for the companies in the problem. But an individual's after-tax yield on the preferred stock is $(1 - .4) \times 8$ or 4.8 percent. This is lower than the return on the bonds which are less risky. The tax laws discourage ownership of preferred stock by individuals.

10. a. The subordination clause will increase the yield that firms must offer to investors because some other debt will be senior to the subordinated issue. This adds to the riskiness of that issue so investors will require a higher rate of return.
    b. The convertibility feature is a significant addition to the desirability of a bond. Investors therefore will not require as high a coupon as they would if the bond was not convertible.
    c. A debenture bond is not backed by any pledge of specific assets. This means in the case of trouble, they will have no preference over other creditors. The higher risk translates into higher expected returns.

HOW CORPORATIONS ISSUE SECURITIES

INTRODUCTION

For most students this section is one of the most interesting and exciting, and this chapter is most exciting. Why? The initial public offering (IPO) is where all the sweat-equity of a business cumulates in riches. Mr. Bell, of Taco Bell, sold his taco stands to the public and eventually to Pepsico with a combination secondary and IPO and took home millions. In this chapter the process of going public, the role of investment banking, and a discussion of venture capitalists are presented. There are always a number of interesting current events from The Wall Street Journal and other sources to enrich this well-written chapter. Look for the large "tombstone" ads in the third section of the WSJ, or stop in at a local brokerage office in town and ask for copies of offering prospectus, which are given to investors thinking of buying newly issued securities.

LEARNING CHECKLIST

After studying this chapter you should be able to:

_____1. Understand how venture capital firms design successful deals and how they obtain their return on their investment.

_____2. Understand the process of making an initial public offering (IPO) and the costs of an IPO. Who receives the "costs" of going public?

_____3. Know the process and terms associated with a new security offering by an established firm (not an IPO), both a public cash offering and a private placement. Who are the parties involved?

_____4. Explain the role and services of the underwriter in an issue of securities.

SOURCES OF BUSINESS INFORMATION

Barron's. One very important weekly "investing" related publication is Barron's, published by Dow Jones, Inc. Like The Wall Street Journal, Dow Jones makes half-priced subscriptions available to students. Ask your professor. Barron's is really comprised of two parts. The first is the "magazine" section, and the second is a pull-out statistical section. The first section leads with a classic, well-written, often-caustic, column by Alan Abelson. Following the Abelson column are several in depth articles related to "investing." Interviews with top-rated investment managers are common. One can learn a lifetime of good common sense investment ideas from Barron's. Look at one in the library, then find a finance professor at the beginning of the term to get your half-priced subscription started. Remember, you will have to manage your pension funds in the years to come!

Wall Street City. Wall Street City (http://www.wallstreetcity.com/home.asp), like Barron's above, is a source of considerable investment information. One can quickly get a quote on a stock or slowly walk through a "Learn About Investing" tutorial. Featuring the top recent investment news stories, the site also has updates on the current stock market mood and commentaries from top stock analysts. Wall Street City is the gateway to hundreds of web sites related to news, quotes and graphs, financial reports on companies, search engines, and recent stock performance from a variety of sites listed "Best & Worst Lists." For the technical analyst, who believes that the stock market move in a predictable pattern, there are several sites for you. Of course if you are an investor, Wall Street City will provide additional services for a subscription fee. But for the student new to investments, this one of the better starting points.

IPOs Online. IPO home.com (http://www.ipo-fund.com/) offers a comprehensive site on upcoming IPOs. They provide news, commentary and analysis on a variety of IPOs, as well as simple to understand education on the mechanics of initial public offerings. Since nothing is ever too good to be true, the company behind the web site, Renaissance Capital, uses the site to offer their commercial wares. This combination of free service and value added product sales is a growing trend with web based information providers.

CHAPTER OUTLINE, KEY CONCEPTS AND TERMS

I. **VENTURE CAPITAL**

      A.   Equity capital provided to a promising new business is called **venture capital**. Venture capital is provided by wealthy individuals, investment companies, and some pension funds.

Venture Capital

First Stage Market Value Balance Sheet ($mil)

Assets		Liabilities and Equity	
Cash from new equity	0.5	New equity from venture capital	0.5
Other assets	0.5	Your original equity	0.5
Value	1.0	Value	1.0

B.	The success of the new business is directly related to the entrepreneur who originated the business.

C.	The growing business generates the entrepreneur's capital along with capital contributed by venture capitalists.

D.	The big payoff for the entrepreneur and venture capitalist is when the firm goes public.

Venture Capital

Second Stage Market Value Balance Sheet ($mil)

Assets		Liabilities and Equity	
Cash from new equity	1.0	New equity from 2nd stage	1.0
Other assets	2.0	Equity from 1st stage	1.0
		Your original equity	1.0
Value	3.0	Value	3.0

## II.	THE INITIAL PUBLIC OFFERING

A.	**Definition**
1.	If the developing business is going well, it is time for the original investors to cash in by selling stock to the investing public for the first time, called an **initial public offering (IPO)**.
2.	When newly issued shares are sold to the investor public, it is called a primary issue (money raised by the firm). When original shareholders sell a number of their shares in an IPO, it is called a secondary offering (money raised goes to the selling stockholders).

B.	**Arranging a Public Issue**
1.	Before the IPO, an **underwriter** is selected to assist in arranging the procedural requirements, to buy the issue from the firm, and finally, to sell the issue to the investor public.
2.	Under a firm commitment, the underwriter pays a fixed price to the firm for the stock then sells the stock to the public for, hopefully, a higher amount. The difference is called the **spread**. If it is too risky to offer a firm commitment, the underwriter may sell the stock for the firm at the best price, called a best efforts underwriting.
3.	Before a public offering is made, the firm must be in compliance with federal laws enforced by the Securities and Exchange Commission (SEC). A registration statement detailing the facts of the company

and issue is filed with the SEC. A summary of the registration statement called a **prospectus**, both a preliminary, "red herring" (from red writing on the side) or final copy after all terms are finalized, is given to all investors considering the investment. Each state has its own securities registration requirements, often called "blue-sky laws."

4. In order to sell all the stock quickly, **underpricing** or selling the securities below the true value of the security, is practiced by the underwriter. Averaging about 16 percent, underpricing is a significant cost of a stock underwriting. Other costs of the underwriting include administrative (legal, accounting) costs and the spread taken by the underwriter. The underwriter gets the spread, the public investor the underpricing, the professionals get their take, and the firm gets the remaining cash.

Average Expenses on 1767 IPOs from 1990-1994			
Value of Issues ($mil)	Direct Costs (%)	Avg First Day Return (%)	Total Costs (%)
2 - 9.99	16.96	16.36	25.16
10 - 19.99	11.63	9.65	18.15
20 - 39.99	9.7	12.48	18.18
40 - 59.99	8.72	13.65	17.95
60 - 79.99	8.2	11.31	16.35
80 - 99.99	7.91	8.91	14.14
100 - 199.99	7.06	7.16	12.78
200 - 499.99	6.53	5.70	11.10
500 and up	5.72	7.53	10.36
All Issues	11.00	12.05	18.69

III. THE UNDERWRITERS

A. **Role**
    1. The underwriter has *three* functions: providing advice (pricing and timing), buying the issue from the company (risk taking), and selling the issue to the public.
    2. A group of underwriters, or a syndicate, is usually formed to share the risk of buying the issue. A larger selling group of underwriters and broker/dealers is formed to sell the issue quickly. The spread is split among the lead underwriter, syndicate, and selling group.

B. **Who Are the Underwriters?**
    1. Underwriters comprise the large investment banking firms listed in Table 14.2 and thousands of other investment banks, brokers, dealers located domestically, and increasingly, internationally.

2.   Most underwriting involve a negotiated price with the firm and in a few utility holding companies and governmental bodies, competitive bidding determines which investment banker and what price/yield will be paid.

Top U.S. Underwriters in 1998 ($bil of total issues)	
Merrill Lynch	$304
Saloman Brothers	225
Morgan Stanley Dean Witter	203
Goldman Sachs	192
Lehman Brothers	147
CS/First Boston	127
JPMorgan	89
Bear Stearns	83
Chase Manhattan	71
Donaldson Lufkin Jenrette	61
All Underwriters	$1,820

IV.   GENERAL CASH OFFERS BY PUBLIC COMPANIES
A.   Rights Offering
1.   After the IPO, additional common stock issues may be sold by businesses seeking financing. This is called a **seasoned offering**. The stock may be offered to existing shareholders, called a **rights issue**, or sold to the general public.
2.   In a rights issue, shareholders would be able to purchase additional shares at a price below current market price. A 25 percent increase in shares would entitle a shareholder to buy one share at the lower price for every four that they own.
3.   Rights issues are less common in the U.S. than in other countries.

B.   General Cash Offers and Shelf Registration
1.   If a rights issue is not elected, additional stock may be sold to the general investing public, called a **general cash offer**.
2.   Under SEC **Rule 415** a firm may file a single registration statement for continuous security offerings over a period of time. This process, called a **shelf registration**, enables the firm to quickly respond to financing needs or financing opportunities, to issue small amounts

with inordinate costs, and still have underwriting firms courting its business.

C. **Costs of the General Cash Offer**
1. The costs of an underwriting includes the underpricing of the issue, the spread to the underwriters, and the administrative costs.
2. From Figure 14.1, the costs of underwriting common stock as a percent of the proceeds, has averaged about 6 percent, has been around 14-15 percent for small issues and decreases to around 4 percent for large issues.
3. Issue costs are lower for debt securities than for equity, often around 1 percent for large firm bond issues.

D. **Market Reaction to Stock Issues**
1. Does adding more shares depress stock prices below true value and decrease the motivation to sell stock? The answer is no. If a stock price were to drop just because of added supply, the yield on the stock would be higher than alternative risk investment, and investors would bid the stock price back up the investor required rate of return.
2. Research indicates that prices do drop slightly (3 percent) after the announcement of a stock offering, and that is a considerable amount of funds each year for business. If it cannot be added to supply alone which causes the market to depreciate the stock, what is it? Investors are signaled by the announcement of stock issue that management feels the stock is overpriced by the market and are rushing in to sell stock. If they thought the stock were undervalued, they would probably sell debt or forgo the investment, rather than drop the stock price to investors by an announcement of a stock offer.

E. **The Dilution Fallacy**
1. Is selling stock priced below book value wise, since it causes dilution of book value? If the "value" was higher before the stock sale and was expected by all to drop after issue, who would buy it? The stock price is not determined by the historical accounting value or book value, but by future prospects of the business.
2. A stock price below book indicates that actual NPVs of completed projects and current projects have been judged by the market to be less than zero.
3. Stock should be sold below book if expected NPVs are positive and should, if correct, eventually cause more investors to buy the stock and bid up the price. If announced uses of capital do not have the prospects of positive NPVs by investors, the stock price of the firm will fall.

V. THE PRIVATE PLACEMENT

A. Instead of a public offering of securities, a firm may negotiate a **private placement** of the securities with a small number of investors, such as an insurance company.

B. Since the general public is not involved, federal security laws do not require registration, prospectus, etc. The issue may be placed quickly and at a lower cost of financing.

C. Since the investor has purchased a security with little or no marketability, the yield demanded by the investor will likely be higher.

D. The usually small and medium firms and investors can custom tailor the issue so that both are satisfied.

COMPLETION QUESTIONS

1. The money invested to finance a new firm is called (*bank loans/venture capital*).

2. In an initial public offering a firm sells its (*bonds/stock*) to raise funds.

3. In an underwriting a firm (*guarantees/makes its best effort*) to provide a company with new money.

4. The difference between the offering price of a security and the price received by the issuer is called the _____.

5. The document that provides information to potential investors in a security offering is called a _____.

6. Underwriters typically (*over/under*) price initial public offerings.

7. The larger the offering the (*higher/lower*) the costs, expressed as a percentage of funds raised, of going public.

8. The role of (*brokers/underwriters*) in a new issue includes advising on the terms, buying the new issue, and reselling it to the public.

9. With large issues, underwriters may form a (*corporation/syndicate*) to handle the sale.

10. Underwriters may sell the new issue at (*above/below*) its stated offering price.

11. Utility holding companies are required to choose their investment bankers by _____ bids.

12. In a few cases, companies offer new shares only to their existing shareholders through a _____ issue.

13. In the vast majority of instances, already-public companies needing additional funds do so through a (*general/tender*) offer.

14. Rule 415 allows companies to make a filing with the SEC that permits issues to be quickly offered any time during a period in a process known as a _____ registration.

15. Costs to the issuer are (*higher/lower*) for bonds compared to common stocks.

16. A new issue of common stock in already-public firms will typically cause a slight (*decline/increase*) in the price of the stock after the announcement.

17. When a public corporation sells more stock the price of existing shares (*will/will not*) fall if the firm does not earn an adequate return on the money raised.

18. A company that earns an adequate return on new investments (*will/will not*) experience a dilution in book value if the new shares are sold below book value.

19. Shares bought in a private placement (*can/can not*) be re-sold to individual investors.

20. Firms that sell bonds in a private placement will usually pay a slightly (*higher/lower*) rate.

PROBLEMS

1. Explain how a rights issue can be used to enhance a stock offering.

2. Chelsea's Classics Inc., a publicly-held firm, recently announced plans to raise new equity funds for expansion. They will have a rights offering at a subscription price of $20 per share with 10 rights necessary to buy each new share. The 1 million shares currently outstanding are trading for $25 per share. How much new money will be raised through this offering?

3. What will be the expected stock price after the rights issue described in problem 2?

4. If flotation costs are expressed as a percentage of the dollar amount of a new offering, rank the following from the highest to the lowest.

a. $50 million bond
b. $100 million bond
c. $50 million stock
d. $100 million stock

5. Which offering will return the most money to the issuing company:
   a. a $50 million 9 percent, 20-year bond that is sold to the public with an underwriting fee of 1 percent and other expenses of $100,000 or
   b. a $50 million 20-year, 9.2 percent coupon bond privately place for total fees of $100,000?

6. Which bond described in problem 5 is actually cheaper for the issuer?

7. What other factors might influence the decision to choose a method for the proposed offering as described in problem 5?

8. Tressa Corporation plans to sell 80,000 shares of stock at the current market price of $50 per share. The firm has 200,000 shares already outstanding with a book value of $60 per share. What will be the new book value immediately after the new stock is issued?

9. What will be the likely market price immediately after the stock issue as described in problem 8?

10. Use the calculations is problems 8 and 9 to explain the dilution fallacy.

ANSWERS TO COMPLETION QUESTIONS

1. venture capital
2. stock
3. guarantees
4. spread
5. prospectus
6. under
7. lower
8. underwriters
9. yndicate
10. below
11. competitive
12. rights

13. general
14. shelf
15. lower
16. decline
17. will
18. will not
19. can not
20. higher

SOLUTIONS TO PROBLEMS

1. Rights are used as sweeteners to make a stock offering more attractive to existing shareholders. Most uses of this vehicle occur because the firm's by-laws require it whenever new stock is sold to the public. The concept is to allow existing shareholders to buy new shares at a discount from the currently quoted market price. In actuality, the total value of each shareholder's stake will be unchanged after the offering is completed. The market price per share will decline after the offering so that the total value of the outstanding shares equals the pre-offering value plus the amount of new money which is invested in the new shares. Market value is not created by a rights offering--only other changes in the market cause total shareholder value to change. See problem 2 for an illustration of the rights offering process.

2. Since 10 rights are needed for each new share and there are 1 million shares outstanding, the number of new shares is 1,000,000/10 or 100,000. Each new share will provide $20 to the company so the total funds raised will be 100,000 × $20 or $2 million.

3. The market value of the firm before the issue is 1 million shares times the market price of $25 per share or $25 million. This will increase by the amount of new money added ($2 million as shown in problem 2) so the total shareholder wealth is $27 million. This can be understood by reasoning that the shareholders had cash before the offering and they allocated a total of $2 million of it to the investment in College Classics. The $27 million is wealth that will not be changed during the process of the rights offering. The share price of the 1 million original shares plus the 100,000 new shares will be $27 million/1.1 million or $24.55.

4. The $50 million stock offering is the highest because stock issues cost more than bond issues and smaller offerings are relatively more expensive compared to larger offerings. This means the ranking for the other issues will be the $100 million stock, then the $50 million bond, and the $100 million bond offering will be the lowest.

178

5.   a. The costs of the public offering will be the $300,000 expense plus the underwriting fee of 1 percent of the $50 million or $500,000 for a total of $800,000. The net proceeds will be $50,000,000 - $800,000 = $49,200,000.

b. The private placement will yield net proceeds of $50,000,000 - $100,000 = $49,900,000.

6.   This problem requires the use of present value calculations to determine if it is worth paying more for the fund raising in order to save interest costs during the life of the bond. From the solution to problem 5 we know that it costs $800,000 - $100,000 or $700,000 more to make a public offering. The annual interest costs would be $50,000,000 × .09 = $4,500,000. The annual interest costs for the privately placed issue would be $50,000,000 × .092 = $4,600,000. The savings with the public offering would be $4.6 - $4.5 or $100,000 for each of the 20 years that the bonds will be outstanding. The appropriate discount rate is 9 percent since the comparison base is the public offering. The present value of the interest savings is $100,000 × 9.129 = $912,900. This is greater than the initial added cost of $700,000 so the public offering should be chosen.

7.   Even though the present value analysis in problem 6 favored the public offering, a private placement could be selected because it provides the potential for greater flexibility. When the negotiations are being conducted at the outset, it is possible that the privately placed issue will have fewer restrictions placed on the company. Later, during the life of the bond, there is a higher likelihood that the original terms can be modified because it is much easier to negotiate with the small number of investors involved in a private placement. The more flexible nature of the situation with a private placement can offset the higher costs.

8.   The company is selling 80,000 shares at $50 per share for a total of $4,000,000. This will be added to the existing book value of 200,000 shares at $60 per share or $12,000,000. This amount plus the new funds of $4,000,000 will provide a total book value of $16,000,000. (The typical accounts affected are the par value of the common stock and the paid in surplus). The book value of each of the 280,000 shares outstanding after the new issue will be $16,000,000/280,000 or $57.14.

9.   The market price after the offering will likely be unchanged at $50 per share. Only if investors feel the new money will be invested for a positive present value will the share price increase.

10. Dilution refers to the decline in book value per share when new stock is sold at below the current book value. As shown in problem 8, the book value per share in those circumstances will indeed fall. (In that case the book value declined from $60 per share

to $57.14). However, investors base their valuations on the earning power of the firm. This is what influences the stock price and not the book value. The fallacy is in thinking that the drop in book value per share (that will always occur when new stock is sold below book value) will cause a decline in market value.

THE CAPITAL STRUCTURE DECISION

INTRODUCTION

Does capital structure and dividend policy affect the value of the business? Such has been the discussion in finance for years. What are the conditions in which debt and dividend policy does not impact the value of the business? Modigliani and Miller were presented the Nobel Prize for their work in this area. The authors feel that the MM argument provides a good start for this section on capital structure.

Just as the pure competitive model provides us a look at market conditions where price is minimized and quantity maximized, an early review of the MM thesis is an important start before looking at an economy *with* taxes, agency costs, bankruptcy, etc. As the simplistic assumptions are relaxed, we find that capital structure mix and dividend policy *does affect* investor cash flows, required rates of return, and value. While some finance texts are reluctant to mention the MM thesis, these authors introduce and explain the MM ideas with ease. Discussing the MM ideas here provides a connection to early chapters (value is in assets), provides conditions necessary where capital structure is irrelevant or does not impact value, and finally links the contributing factors that may affect value: investment, debt, and maybe dividend decisions.

Some of the most important ideas of this course are presented in this chapter. Your understanding of these concepts should tie the course together to this point and provide you the concepts necessary to proceed to the coming chapters.

LEARNING CHECKLIST This is an important concepts chapter and after preparing the chapter you should be able to:

____1. Analyze the effect of debt finance on the risk and required return of equity holders.

____2. Understand the advantages and disadvantages of debt and how increasing debt affects the value of the business.

____3. Discuss the various costs of financial distress that is associated with increased debt levels.

____4. Explain why the debt-equity mix varies across firms and across industries.

SOURCES OF BUSINESS INFORMATION

Business Week. One of the best business news weekly magazines published today is <u>Business Week</u>, published by McGraw-Hill, Inc. <u>Business Week</u> is also available at one-half subscription price through your professor. <u>Business Week</u> provides an excellent coverage and in depth analysis of the business news of the prior week. In addition, there is always a cover story related to a current business development. Weekly section topics include "International Business," "Economic Analysis," "Government," "Industries," "Marketing," "Finance," "The Corporation," "Information Processing," "Legal Affairs," "Science & Technology," and "Personal Business." That list looks like your business core course offering and can provide you, at half-price, a weekly course in current and future-oriented business ideas. An "Investment Figures of the Week" page at the end of the magazine provides current economic and financial statistics. Book reviews and editorials provide an opportunity to test your opinions and feelings related to current issues.

Business News On The Web. There are a number of business/financial news services available on the web. Go to any search engine homepage and there will be links to business news. From CNNfn, always a leader in breaking business and economic news, the Reuters Headline News site, available directly or listed in the Wall Street City directory under "News," feeds their breaking stories from their worldwide network of wire services. Other business periodicals, such as Fortune, Forbes, The Wall Street Journal Online, and others have in-depth business, finance and economic news.

CHAPTER OUTLINE, KEY CONCEPTS AND TERMS

I. **HOW BORROWING AFFECTS COMPANY VALUES IN A TAX-FREE ECONOMY**

      A.   Capital Structure and Value

          1.   The value of business assets, assuming there is no tax deductibility of interest, is not affected by the capital structure mix of debt and equity.

          2.   The present value of the cash flows from assets, the value of assets, is equal to the value of securities issued by the business. Changing the mix of securities does not affect the value of the assets.

          3.   The right-hand side of the balance sheet, assets, determines the *size* of the pizza; the mix of securities on the left-hand side of the balance sheet determines *how* the pizza is sliced. The only way to increase the amount of pizza is to increase the value of assets (pizza), not slicing (financing) in a new combination of slices.

          4.   This theory or idea won Franco Modigliani and Merton Miller (MM) a Nobel Prize.

II.   MM's Argument

A.   The value of business asset is not affected by the capital structure mix. This is known as MM's proposition I (debt irrelevance proposition). Debt policy should not matter to shareholders. It is the assets that count for value.

B.   Why should leveraging, or substituting debt for equity in the capital structure, affect the value of assets? Investors do not need businesses to add leverage to their investment portfolio. Financial institutions will lend investors money if they want, so adding debt to the business capital structure is no big thing, or certainly nothing of value to investors.

River Cruises - All Equity Financed

Data

Number of shares	100,000
Price per share	$10
Market Value of Shares	$1 million

Outcome	State of the Economy		
	Slump	Expected	Boom
Operating Income	$75,000	125,000	175,000
Earnings per share	$.75	1.25	1.75
Return on shares	7.5%	12.5%	17.5%

C.   **How Borrowing Affects Earnings Per Share**
1.   The existence of debt can impact the earnings of a company in two important ways. The first is by reducing earnings available to shareholders. The second is by reducing the need for equity capital.
2.   Tables 15.3 and 15.4 show how the inclusion of debt into a firm's capital structure can alter the earnings per share. For now, we will assume the change is cosmetic in nature and represents mathematical gymnastics. The impact on risk is coming right up!

D. **How Borrowing Affects Risk and Return**
1. Increasing the amount of debt versus equity, called **restructuring**, *does* increase shareholder's expected return. If leverage is favorable with the return on assets exceeding the cost of debt, earnings and returns to shareholders will increase.
2. These higher expected returns are not without a cost. The cost is increased risk to the shareholders, for now with debt, there is a prior claim (creditors) on their income stream and assets, in case of failure.
3. Shareholders, with debt above them, have prospects for higher returns, but added risk. The net effect in the valuation process is that the expected future cash flows have gone up, with the use of debt, but so has the shareholder required rate of return. The increased cash flows in the valuation function have increased, but are offset by the increased discount rate. There is no change in the value of the assets or the stock of the shareholders.
4. The **operating risk** or **business risk**, or the risk or variability of the operating income or earnings before interest and taxes (earnings before distributions are made to sources of funds) is not affected by the capital structure mix.
5. While the operating risk is not affected by increased proportions of debt or use of **financial leverage**, the **financial risk**, or risk (variability or returns) to shareholders has increased with increased use of debt. With increased financial leverage and increased financial risk, shareholder required rates of return increase. The higher expected value from the use of debt are canceled out by the higher discount rate applied to the higher cash flows. The value of the assets are left unchanged or are not affected by changing the mix of debt and equity.

E. *Debt and the Cost of Capital*
1. The weighted average cost of capital (WACC) is the expected return on the assets, and correspondingly, the securities of a business and is the required rate of return on any new average risk investment project.
2. In an all equity business the WACC = $r_{assets} = r_{equity}$, or the expected return on assets equals the expected rate of return on equity.
3. When debt is added or the capital structure mix changed, the cost of debt, and equity, must be weighted by their relative market value proportions so that:

$$\text{WACC} = r_{assets} = r_{debt}[D/(D+E)] + r_{equity}[E/(D+E)]$$

4. The WACC or the r_{assets} does not change as debt is added to the capital structure. This concept is **MM's proposition II** which states that the expected return on the common stock increases as the

debt/equity ratio increases. Why doesn't the WACC change? As more low cost debt is added to the capital structure, the required rate of return on equity increases to offset the advantage of low cost debt. The WACC does not change; the market value of the firm does not change. Debt does not matter in this situation where the deductibility of interest is not a factor.

5. Debt has an explicit cost in the form of an interest rate, and an incidental, implicit cost impact on the required rate of return on equity as debt is added to the capital structure. Debt is no "cheaper" than equity and the use of debt does not affect the WACC, nor the value of the firm.

6. Figure 15.3 shows the offsetting effects of lower cost debt, even if risk-free, added to the capital structure relative to the increasing required rate of return of equity of greater financial leverage. One offsets the other and the expected return on assets, r_{assets}, is not affected by changing the capital structure mix.

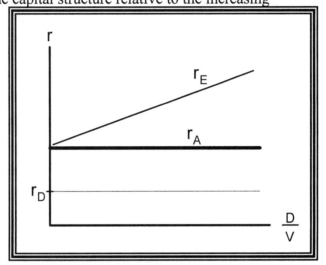

7. Adding a bit of reality does not change the conclusion. In Figure 15.4 risky debt is considered, where with increases in the debt/equity ratio, the cost of debt increases as creditors get edgy about sharing the income stream, and the rate of increase in the shareholder's required rate of return begins to slow as bondholders begin to bear a greater share of the risk. The conclusion is the same: the WACC or expected return on assets or the cost of the package of debt and equity (WACC) does not change. Debt does not affect the value of the assets!

III.   CAPITAL STRUCTURE AND CORPORATE TAXES

A.   Impacts
1.   Reality says that financial managers are concerned about finding that "right" mix of capital structure that produces the lowest or optimal cost of capital. This indicates that there are other factors working beyond MM's assumptions.
2.   The presence of taxes, bankruptcy costs, potential conflicts of interests between creditors and shareholders, and ways that financial decisions could affect investment decisions *do* affect the value of assets.
3.   If this is true, what is the value of the MM propositions? How did they win a Nobel Prize with a theory with such limiting assumptions? Their propositions provided the foundation upon which we study reality or the real-world situation as it exists. Just as the pure competitive model studied in microeconomics was used as a basis for evaluating existing market structure, MM's basic theories provide a basis for explaining how these other variables affect asset or business values.

B.   **Debt and Taxes at River Cruises**
1.   Interest expense is deductible against taxable income, which means that the combined income of debt and equity holders is increased with the use of debt. See Table 15.5.
2.   The added value is the **interest tax shield**, or the tax savings resulting from the deductibility of interest payments.
3.   The annual interest tax shield is the product of the interest paid, (r_{debt} x D), times the tax rate, T_c. Since the creditors or bond holders receive their same interest payment and no more, the added annual value of the tax shield accrues to shareholders.
4.   Assuming a constant level of debt, the value over time of the tax shield is the annual tax shield capitalized or divided by the current cost of debt capital, or, another way, is the product of the amount of debt, D, times the corporate tax rate, T_c:

$$\text{PV of Tax Shield} = \frac{D \times r_D \times Tc}{r_D} = D \times Tc$$

(assume perpetuity)

186

C.	How Interest Tax Shields Contribute to the Value of Stockholder's Equity
   1.	There are three claims on the operating income of business: creditors, shareholders, and government.
   2.	The deductibility of interest is a tax shield that diverts government taxes to the shareholders. Thus the tax shield increases the value of an all-equity business by the amount equal to the value of the tax shield, T_cD, or:

Value of levered firm = value if all-equity financed + T_cD
See Figure 15.5.

D.	**Corporate Taxes and the Weighted-Average Cost of Capital**
   1.	The value of the corporate tax shield is represented in the lower after-tax cost of debt. Lower after-tax costs of debt lowers the WACC and increases the present value of stream of asset cash flows.
   2.	The value of the tax shield is represented in the value of the assets.

E.	**The Implications of Corporate Taxes For Capital Structure**
   1.	If the value of the tax shield increases as the debt/equity ratio increases, as in Figure 15.5, why doesn't all business borrow as much as they can?
   2.	There are other factors, such as the increased costs of possible financial distress that offsets the value of the tax shield at high debt/equity ratios.

IV.	**COSTS OF FINANCIAL DISTRESS**

A.	**General**
   1.	As the debt/equity increases, the **costs of financial distress**, or the costs of possible bankruptcy, increases.
   2.	The market value of the business is equal to the value of an all-equity business *plus* the present value of the tax shield *less* the present value of financial distress.
   3.	The added costs of financial distress overtakes the added value of the tax shield at some point and may lower the value of the firm at some high debt/equity ratio. See Figure 15.7.
   4.	The theoretical optimum capital structure is the debt/equity level in which the PV of the tax shield is just offset by the PV costs of financial distress. This debt/equity level will maximize market value of the business.

B.	**Bankruptcy Costs**
   1.	Bankruptcy occurs as the value of a business declines. Bankruptcy does not cause the value of a business to decrease. It is a court-

directed legal process that occurs when the value or the financial conditions of a business deteriorate to the point where the bills are not paid or the value of the equity is zero.

2.   If bankruptcy occurs the costs are deducted from the remaining value of the business and shareholders are the last in line for any proceeds. Shareholders are likely to lose their investment in this situation.

C.   **Evidence on Bankruptcy Costs** -- Research indicates that the costs of bankruptcy for large firms is a relatively small proportion of the value of the securities.

D.   **Direct Versus Indirect Costs of Bankruptcy** -- While direct bankruptcy costs are relatively small, the indirect costs associated with bankruptcy related to managerial limitations and efforts to correct the economic problems may be significant.

E.   **Financial Distress Without Bankruptcy**
1.   As long as bills are paid, a firm in financial distress may avoid bankruptcy, reduce costs, and begin a turnaround.
2.   Often a valueless firm may take added risk to bet on a turnaround, or linger for a significantly long time before an interest payment is missed or some bankruptcy act occurs.

F.   **What the Games Cost**
1.   Until bankruptcy occurs, owners still control investment and operating strategy. With little remaining to lose, managers/owners may bet the creditor's money in a risk turnaround venture, thus increasing the costs of financial distress.
2.   Added equity invested in a financial distressed situation for a reasonable project may reward creditors, not reward owners, and the project may be ignored.

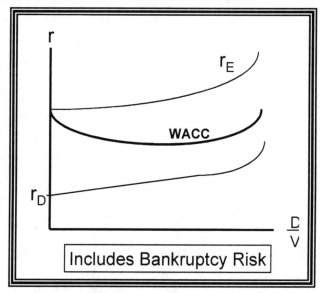

3.   Positive NPV projects that tend to be in the creditors' interest and not shareholders may be avoided, especially if close to bankruptcy. Shareholders may

be interested in getting their money out, not putting more into the business that may go to creditors.

4.   It is in stockholders' interest to avoid high-debt situations where "betting games" may occur because stockholders generally lose. Borrowing contracts are generally in favor of creditors if problems should occur. Thus owners' required rates of return for investment in high-debt firms may keep debt/equity ratios in the moderate range.

G.   **Costs of Distress Vary With Type of Asset**
1.   Real asset firms tend to lose less value in bankruptcy than firms with significant intangible assets, such as research and development firms who depend upon human capital.
2.   From the arguments above, companies with safe, tangible assets such as real estate and high taxable income should have high debt ratios, while people-oriented firms with little or no taxable income should have low debt ratios.

V.   EXPLAINING FINANCING CHOICES

A.   **The Trade-off Theory**
1.   The theory that there is an optimum debt/ratio that maximizes market value, offsetting the benefits of the tax shield against the increasing costs of financial distress is called the **trade-off theory**.
2.   The support of the trade-off theory is evidenced by a wide variety of debt/equity ratios between industries and companies, but with some consistent with the trade-off theory and some operating inconsistently with the theory.
3.   Utilities and retailers tend to borrow heavily and their assets are tangible and relatively safe, but the most successful companies, such as Merck, with very high taxable profits, tend to forgo the tax shield advantage of debt.

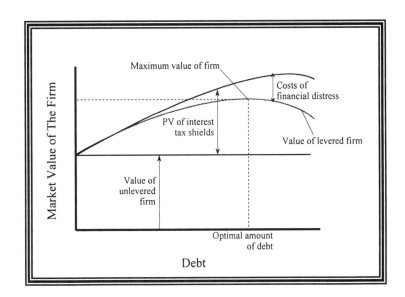

B.   **A Pecking Order Theory**

    1.   Research has shown that stock sales announcements tend to drive stock prices down, indicating that investors think managers feel the stock price is overvalued if they attempt to sell equity.

    2.   Likewise, the announcement of a debt issue has little or no affect upon equity prices.

    3.   The above observations indicate a pecking order theory of capital structure alternative ways to fund investment.

    4.   Businesses prefer to issue debt rather than equity if internally generated cash flow is insufficient. Use of internally generated funds does not have the signaling effect, positively or negatively, that external funding does.

    5.   If external funds must be raised, equity will be used reluctantly, reserved as the residual in the financing pecking order.

    6.   Under the pecking order theory there is no target debt/equity ratio because there are two kinds of equity: internally generated earnings retained and external stock sales. Internal equity is the first choice for financing ahead of debt, and finally, external equity funding.

    7.   Profitable firms have sufficient internally generated capital to fund their high NPV investments. Hence, they have all equity or low debt ratios.

    8.   Less profitable firms tend to issue more debt as they run out of internally generated funds quickly and turn to debt as the next source of funding in the pecking order.

COMPLETION QUESTIONS

1.   Firms try to use the particular combination of debt and (*assets/equity*) that will maximize their overall market value.

2.   The mix of a firm's financing sources is known as its _____ _____.

3.   According to reasoning of Modigliani and Miller's (MM) proposition I, financial managers (*can/cannot*) increase value by changing the mix of securities used to finance a company.

4.   Restructuring is the process of changing a firm's capital structure (*by/without*) changing its assets.

5.   If the return on assets is greater than the cost debt the return to shareholders will be (*decreased/increased*) by borrowing.

6.   Business risk is associated with variations in operating (*costs/income*).

7. Risk to shareholders resulting from the use of debt is known as _____ risk.

8. Financial leverage (*decreases/increases*) the variability of shareholders returns.

9. The weighted average cost of capital is equal to the expected return on (*assets/debt*).

10. MM's proposition II states that the required rate of return on equity increases as the firm's debt-to-equity ratio (*decreases/increases*).

11. The (*explicit/implicit*) cost of debt is interest and the (*explicit/implicit*) cost is the higher return demanded by shareholders.

12. Another way of expressing MM's proposition II is to say that the expected return on (*assets/equity*) does not change no matter what the level of borrowing is.

13. The existence of income taxes results in a cost advantage for (*debt/equity*) because (*dividends/interest*) is deductible for companies.

14. The interest tax shield is equal to the corporate tax rate (*divided/multiplied*) by the dollar amount of interest paid.

15. The modified MM proposition I states that the value of the leveraged firm is equal to the firm's value with all equity financing (*minus/plus*) the present value of the tax shield.

16. A tax-related disadvantage to borrowing recognizes that some returns to (*debtholders /stockholders*) come as capital gains which may be deferred and eventually taxed at a lower rate.

17. (*Benefits/Costs*) of financial distress arise from bankruptcy or near bankruptcy.

18. In the case of bankruptcy, the _____ become the new owners.

19. The (*direct/indirect*) costs of bankruptcy are measured by legal and administrative fees.

20. For companies in financial distress but not yet in bankruptcy there is a strong temptation to bet the future on (*creditors'/shareholders'*) money.

21. Firms facing bankruptcy often (*do/do not*) have difficulty attracting new equity capital because returns on the new investment (*will/will not*) have to be shared with creditors.

22. A theory of capital structure states that there is a _____ between the interest tax shield and the distress costs of debt.

23. According to the pecking order theory of capital structure, firms prefer to issue (*debt/equity*) if internally generated funds are insufficient.

PROBLEMS

1. Refer to Table 15.2 of the textbook and suppose that River Cruises offers a $300,000 bond issue with a 10 percent coupon. Assume it uses the entire proceeds to repurchase stock on the open market at its current price of $10 per share. If you ignore any impact of the restructuring on stock price and use an income tax rate of 40 percent, what would be the expected earnings per share given a normal state of the economy?

2. Recompute earnings per share for the situation prescribed in problem 1 if no debt was issued and the tax rate was 40 percent.

3. What conclusion can be drawn from the calculations in problems 1 and 2?

4. If the beta of River Cruises as described in the problem was 1.2, what must be the beta on River Cruises' assets?

5. Leverage, Inc. has $100,000 of capital including $30,000 of debt at an interest rate of 9 percent. If shareholders expect a return of 20 percent, what is the expected return on total assets? (Ignore taxes).

6. Suppose Leverage, Inc. decided to restructure its balance sheet by issuing enough debt to repurchase stock to bring the debt/equity ratio to 1.0. Assuming its debt is default-free, what would be:
    a. The expected return on assets?
    b. The expected return on equity?

7. No Growth, Inc. (NGI) has EBIT of $100,000. If it has no debt financing, what will be the value of the firm if it indeed does not expect to grow, it pays taxes of 40 percent, and a discount rate of 12 percent is appropriate?

8. What is meant by the term "interest tax shield"?

9. What is the present value of the interest tax shield for a firm with $1 million of a 7 percent perpetual debt issue, if the tax rate is 40 percent and the discount rate is 10 percent?

10. What would the present value of the interest tax shield change in problem 9 if:
    a. The debt issue had a 10-year maturity? and
    b. The WACC was 15 percent?

ANSWERS TO COMPLETION QUESTIONS

1. equity
2. capital structure
3. cannot
4. without
5. increased
6. income
7. financial
8. increases
9. assets
10. increases
11. explicit, implicit
12. assets
13. debt, interest
14. multiplied
15. plus
16. stockholders
17. Costs
18. creditors
19. direct
20. creditors'
21. do, will
22. trade-off
23. debt

SOLUTIONS TO PROBLEMS

1. The debt issue will provide funds to repurchase $300,000/$10 per share or 30,000 shares. After this occurs, the number of outstanding shares will be reduced from 50,000 to 20,000. The interest on the new debt will be 10 percent of $300,000 or $30,000 per year. This lowers taxable income from $125,000 to $95,000. The after-tax income will be (1 - 0.4) × $95,000 or $57,000. The earnings per share will be $57,000/20,000 or $2.85.

2. The taxable income was $125,000. The after-tax income would be (1 - 0.4) × $125,000 or $75,000. The earnings per share in this case would have been $75,000/50,000 or $1.50.

3.	The use of leverage is profitable for the shareholders. Earnings per share increased from $1.25 to $2.85 by borrowing and using the proceeds to repurchase some of the shares outstanding. This is made possible because the after-tax interest cost incurred is more than offset by the reduction in the number of shares outstanding. The positive or negative aspect of leverage depends on the level of pre-tax profits. If the company encountered a downturn in profitability, the use of debt financing would exacerbate the problem just as it helped make the firm even more profitable in the situation where the restructuring occurred.

4.	Since the beta for debt is zero, the beta for the total assets must be 70 percent of the equity or $0.7 \times 1.2 = 0.84$

5.	The firm must earn $0.09 \times \$30,000$ or $\$2,700$ for the debt. For the equity it must earn $0.20 \times \$70,000$ or $\$14,000$. The total earnings must then be $\$16,700$. The return on assets will be $\$16,700/\$100,000$ or 16.7 percent.

6.	a. The return on assets, given the default-free assumption, will be unchanged by the restructuring so it will remain at 16.7 percent. There will be a higher return expected on the equity to offset the higher cost of interest payments as shown in part b below.
	b. A debt/equity ratio of 1 means the proportions of debt and equity are equal. The total return on assets for the new financing structure will be:
$$0.5 \times r_{equity} + 0.5 \times .09 = .167$$
$$r_{equity} = .244 \text{ or } 24.4 \text{ percent}$$

7.	The value of the firm will be equal to the present value of all future earnings. The after-tax earnings are $(1 - 0.4) \times \$100,000$ or $\$60,000$ per year. Recall that a stream of a constant amount has a value of that amount divided by the expected rate of return. (This is the procedure for valuing preferred stock and perpetual bonds). The value of NGI will be $\$60,000/.12$ or $\$500,000$.

8.	The interest tax shield refers to the tax savings resulting from the deductibility of interest payments. It recognizes the "partnership" of government with business by allowing taxes to be lowered by reducing taxable income by payments to debtholders. Remember that dividend payments are not deductible when figuring taxes so there is encouragement for borrowing as a source of funds. The encouragement is the interest tax shield.

9.	The amount of the interest tax shield depends on the amount of interest payments, the tax rate, and the discount rate. In this case the firm will pay $0.07 \times \$1,000,000$ or $\$70,000$ per year. This will reduce taxes by $0.40 \times \$70,000$ or $\$28,000$ annually. In present value terms this is $\$28,000/.10$ or $\$280,000$.

10.　　a. The tax savings are unchanged at $28,000 per year but the present value is of an annuity for 10 years at 10 percent. For each $1 this is 6.145 so the tax shield value is 6.145 × $28,000 or $172,060.

　　b. Just as the value of the tax shield was reduced by shortening the life of the bond, the value will also be reduced by increasing the discount rate. With a 15 percent discount rate for 10 years, the present value will be 5.019 × $28,000 or $140,532.

DIVIDEND POLICY

INTRODUCTION

In finance, we are fairly convinced that investment decisions are the key to value creation. In the last chapter, we saw that the government tax shield adds to this value by the use of debt, but to some limit. In this second of "do capital structure decisions matter?" chapters, you are provided excellent coverage of an area that half your professors do not think is relevant: dividend policy. As in the last chapter, starting with the conditions under which dividends are irrelevant, then adding more realistic assumptions is a proven method for learning the concepts. The valuation theme, and the factors affecting value, connects this chapter with the theme of the text, and adds another piece of the puzzle.

LEARNING CHECKLIST

After studying this chapter you should be able to:

____1. Describe the process by which dividends are paid by a corporation.

____2. Explain why, under special conditions and assumptions as set forth by M&M, dividend policy should not affect the value of a business.

____3. Explain why dividends may be used by managers to signal the prospects of their business.

____4. Show how tax rate differences on cash dividends versus capital gains might affect dividend policy and value.

SOURCES OF BUSINESS INFORMATION

S&P Security Price Index. Want to know a little about the "market index" that we used as a basis for calculating the beta or individual risk measure of a stock in an earlier chapter? The Standard & Poor's Security Price Index is a classic reference for anyone searching for statistics on stock market indices or interest rates from the 1940s to present. The Security Price Index details how S&P calculates the S&P 500 index and many other indices published by Standard & Poor's Corporation. Need to know what government bond rates were in 1981, or the high/low of the Dow Jones Industrial Average in 1955? This is the reference book for you. Studying chemical stocks? Use the S&P Chemical index to measure your company's return relative to all chemical stocks. Stock price indices are presented for many industrial, financial, utility, and retailing segments of business. Stock yields, price-earnings ratios, company earnings averages, are included in this work.

Check The S&P 500 Anytime Online. Many websites provide constant updates as to how the various financial markets are progressing through the day. **Security APL Market Watch** provides information on the major stock market indexes throughout the day. From the Dow Jones, S&P, NASDAQ, New York Stock Exchange, Canadian Exchanges, and other indexes, one is able to follow the movement of many major markets.

CHAPTER OUTLINE, KEY CONCEPTS AND TERMS

I. HOW DIVIDENDS ARE PAID

A. **Cash Dividends**
1. **Cash Dividends**, the payment of cash by the firm to shareholders, are declared by the board of directors on the declaration date.
2. A regular dividend is a level the board hopes to maintain in the future; a dividend payment called a special or extra dividend is viewed as a one-time payment.
3. The dividend is paid on the payment date to all shareholders of record on the record date which is perhaps two weeks before.
4. To be a shareholder of record, and thus receive a dividend, one must have purchased the stock before the **ex-dividend date**, which is five business days before the record date.
5. The stock price should drop by the amount of the dividend on the ex-dividend date.
6. Instead of cash dividends, many companies have automatic reinvestment plans in which additional shares of stock are purchased. The business keeps the cash and shares are given to shareholders.

B. **Some Legal Limitations on Dividends**
  1. Creditors may limit or prevent the payment of dividends until the debt is paid.
  2. States may also limit dividend payment (reduce cash, reduce retained earnings) if the payments would lower capital below the amount of retained earnings, thus impairing original paid in capital.

C. Stock Dividends and Stock Splits
  1. A **stock dividend** is distribution of additional shares to shareholders. The cash is kept in the firm for investment; shareholders receive added shares. A ten percent stock dividend would issue one share per ten owned by stockholders.
  2. A **stock split** is an issuance of added shares to shareholders. No cash is exchanged, only a change in the number of shares issued and the par value.
  3. A stock dividend is a mini-stock split. No cash is involved and the book value of shareholder's equity does not change. They are accounting entries; a recapitalization. With more shares outstanding, the market value *per share* drops because more shares are outstanding, but the *total market value of the firm does not change.*

D. **Stock Repurchase**
  1. A **stock repurchase** occurs when the company buys back stock from shareholders.
  2. A stock repurchase has the same impact of a dividend: The cash account in the business is reduced and the shareholders as a group have more cash. The book value of the equity is reduced in both cases.

Example - Cash dividend versus share repurchase

Assets		*Liabilities & Equity*	
A. Original balance sheet			
Cash	$150,000	Debt	0
Other assets	850,000	Equity	1,000,000
Value of Firm	1,000,000	Value of Firm	1,000,000

Shares outstanding = 100,000

Price per share = $1,000,000 / 100,000 = $10

Example - Cash dividend versus share repurchase

Assets		Liabilities & Equity	
B. After cash dividend			
Cash	$50,000	Debt	0
Other assets	850,000	Equity	900,000
Value of Firm	900,000	Value of Firm	900,000

Shares outstanding = 100,000

Price per share = $900,000 / 100,000 = $9

Example - Cash dividend versus share repurchase

Assets		Liabilities & Equity	
C. After stock repurchase			
Cash	$50,000	Debt	0
Other assets	850,000	Equity	900,000
Value of Firm	900,000	Value of Firm	900,000

Shares outstanding = 90,000

Price per share = $900,000 / 90,000 = $10

II. HOW DO COMPANIES DECIDE ON DIVIDEND PAYMENTS?

A. Survey research of business indicates that dividend payments may be determined a variety of ways:

1. The business may have a predetermined long-run **dividend payout ratio**, which establishes the percentage of earnings to be paid in dividends.
2. Managers tend to focus on dividend *changes* rather than absolute levels.
3. Dividend changes follow shifts in long-run, sustainable levels of earnings, rather than short-run fluctuations in earnings.

4. Managers are reluctant to make changes in dividend payments that are likely to be reversed in the future.

B. A constant payout ratio means that dividends will vary as earnings vary. Companies tend to change dividends steadily in response to a sustainable increase in earnings. Cash dividends per year were more stable than earnings. See Figure 16.2.

C. Future earnings prospects by managers are built into dividend policy. Higher earnings tend to follow higher dividends and lower earnings follow low dividends.

III. WHY DIVIDEND POLICY SHOULD NOT MATTER

A. **Efficiency and Value Arguments**
1. *If markets are efficient*, dividend policy should not affect shareholder value. Assuming that a business' capital budgeting decision (accept all positive NPVs) and borrowing decisions have been made, it then becomes a choice as to *how* to raise equity capital: internally from earnings paying cash common dividends or financing externally from the sale of stock?
2. Dividend policy, with the capital budgeting and debt policy *established*, is then the choice between internal equity or paying dividends and using external equity.
3. This area of dividend policy has a variety of opinions as to how or if dividend policy affects the value of the business. Some are of the opinion that value is affected by dividend policy, some such as the MM proposition in the next paragraph think dividend policy has no effect on value, and finally, some think that dividends cost the shareholders added taxes to the point where dividends may have a negative impact upon value.

B. **Dividend Policy Is Irrelevant in Competitive Markets**
1. If efficient, competitive markets exist, then the **MM dividend-irrelevance** theory is reasonable. Given an investment program and debt policy, the equity portion of the financing may come internally, from retained income, or raised externally and at low cost in equity markets.
2. If earnings exceed the necessary equity funding for the capital budget, the *residual* can be paid in dividends. If the equity capital needed for investment exceeds the internally generated earnings, external equity can be raised inexpensively in financial markets.
3. The existing shareholders' value will remain the same if external debt is sold for they now have their dividends plus the now diluted market value of their shares.
4. If dividends are not paid, how can existing shareholders generate cash if needed? MM's answer for those who need cash is to sell a few shares of

stock in efficient markets. The added value created by positive NPVs and financed with retained earnings, will be represented in higher stock prices. After selling a few shares each period, the investor's total net worth has not changed.

5.   With efficient markets, it does not matter if earnings are retained and, with expected positive NPVs, shareholder value is built up via capital gains, or if dividends are paid out as dividends and the equity needed is raised in financial markets. The investor's net worth (value) is only affected by the prospects of expected NPVs from the new investments. Value comes from assets, not financing, with efficient markets.

Example - Assume ABC Co. has no extra cash, but declares a $1,000 dividend. They also require $1,000 for current investment needs. Using M&M Theory, and given the following balance sheet information, show how the value of the firm is not altered when new shares are issued to pay for the dividend.

Record Date		Pmt Date	**Post Pmt**
Cash	1,000	0	**1,000** (40sh @ $25)
Asset Value	5,000	5,000	**5,000**
Total Value	6,000	5,000	**6,000**
# of Shares	200	200	**240**
price/share	$30	$25	**$25**

NEW SHARES ARE ISSUED

C.   Dividend Irrelevance--An Illustration

1.   The shareholders of Rational Demi-conductor are the same regardless of which dividend policy is followed (pay or not pay dividends).

2.   The investor's value remains the same because, in the case of no dividends, the efficient financial markets are able to provide, via capital gains, shareholders with the added value of expected positive NPV investment funded by retained earnings.

```
Example - continued - Shareholder Value

                    Record        Pmt         Post
Stock               6,000        5,000        6,000
Cash                    0        1,000            0


Total Value         6,000        6,000        6,000

Stock = 240sh @ $25 = 6,000

⮷ Assume stockholders purchase the new issue with the cash
  dividend proceeds.
```

D. **Calculating Share Price**
1. When dividends, which serve as a residual to fund the equity portion of the capital budget, are low or not paid in a period, investors with current cash needs can easily sell appreciated (investments were made in positive NPV investments) shares at a fair price to provide them cash.
2. When dividends are paid, the firm must fund the equity-contributed cash from the sale of new equity providing the funds needed to finance all positive NPV projects. The total value of the firm does not change because of the dividend policy.

IV. THE ASSUMPTION BEHIND DIVIDEND IRRELEVANCE

A. **General Arguments**
1. Given efficient capital markets, MM argues that dividends do not affect the value of the business. In this section, other arguments counter the MM ideas.
2. One argument is that dividends now have added value over capital gain maybe later. Managers can stabilize dividends, but not the market price of the firm's stock. *But*, as long as investment debt policy is held constant, the overall cash flows of the business are the same regardless of the dividend policy. The risks that shareholders bear are related to the investment and debt policies, not the dividend policy. Investors, by themselves with efficient markets, can adjust any riskiness associated with the dividends now, appreciation later argument by altering their investment portfolio between risky common stock and cash assets.
3. An efficient market provides, at fair prices, for transfers in ownership created by shifts in dividend policy all the while the total value of the

business is unaffected by dividend policy, only investment and debt policy through the tax shield.

B. **Why Dividends May Increase Firm Value**
   1. When markets are less than efficient, dividend policy may affect firm value. The impact of dividend policy impact upon firm value then depends on the extent of market inefficiency.
   2. Given high proportional transaction costs on the sale of stock, investors may be better off if the company constantly pays the dividend.

C. **Dividends as Signals**
   1. Firm value is not increased by increased dividends; firm value increases if management's increase in dividends signals the presence of high NPV opportunities.
   2. In markets where there is little information, increased dividends portend increased future cash flows or dividend policy is a form of communications to the market about future prospects.
   3. Just as dividend increases add expectations of favorable future prospects, dividend cuts are assumed by the market as a signal of bad news to come.

V. **WHY DIVIDENDS MAY REDUCE FIRM VALUE**

A. **Supporting logic**
   1. There is an argument that, just as corporate deductibility of interest affects value, differential taxation of cash dividends and capital gains may provide a value edge of one dividend policy (dividends) over another (no dividends, capital gains).
   2. If cash dividends are taxed at a rate higher than capital gains, shareholder's after-tax return is higher if no dividend is paid, earnings are retained and invested, and the return is taken as a capital gain.

B. **Why Pay Any dividends at All?**
   1. If dividends are taxed at a high rate, and they have been in the past, why pay dividends at all?
   2. The IRS would penalize companies that retain all earnings in lieu of dividends as tax evaders.
   3. With the higher tax rate on dividends, firms should attempt to retain earnings and minimize the extent to which they issue stock, as long as all positive NPV investments are being pursued.

C.　**Taxation of Dividends and Capital Gains under Current Tax Law**
   1.　Before 1986 cash dividends were taxed at a higher rate than capital gains.
   2.　The Tax Reform Act of 1986 cut the differential to very little: 28 percent for capital gains, from 31 percent to 39.6 percent for dividends.
   3.　Tax on dividends must be paid immediately; capital gains taxes are paid when the gain is "realized." This delay favors the after-tax, time adjusted capital gain return alternative.
   4.　With the narrowing of the tax rates on dividends and capital gains, pressure for increased dividends has increased on corporations.

	Firm A	Firm B
Next years price	$112.50	$102.50
Dividend	$ 0	$10.00
Total pretax payoff	$112.50	$112.50
Todays stock price	$100	$97.78
Capital gain	$12.50	$4.72
Pretax rate of return (%)	$\frac{12.5}{100}$ = 12.5%	$\frac{14.72}{97.78}$ = 15.05%
Tax on dividend @ 40%	$0	.40 x $10 = $4.00
Tax on capital gain @ 20%	.20 x $12.50 = $2.50	.20 x $4.72 = $.94
Total after tax income (dividend plus capital gains less taxes)	(0 + 12.50) - 2.50 = $10.00	(10.00 + 4.72) - (4.00-.94) = $9.78
Aftertax rate of return (%)	$\frac{10}{100}$ =.10 = 10%	$\frac{9.78}{97.78}$ =.10 = 10%

COMPLETION QUESTIONS

1.　Directors who expect to maintain the same payment in the future declare (*extra/regular*) cash dividends.

2.　The record date always occurs (*after/before*) the payment date.

3.　On the ex-dividend date owners of the stock (*will/will not*) receive dividends that were declared earlier.

4.　(*No/Some*) restrictions apply on the payment of dividends as long as the company has sufficient cash.

5.　Distributions of additional shares to a firm's stockholders is known as a stock _____ or a stock _____ .

6. A stock repurchase had the same effect as a (*cash/stock*) dividend.

7. Dividends divided by (*cash flow/earnings*) equals the dividend payout ratio.

8. Dividends tend to follow (*long/short*) -run shifts in earnings.

9. Changes in dividends (*are/are not*) viewed as forecasts of future earnings.

10. Dividends fluctuate (*less/more*) than earnings.

11. A firm that is planning for a large expansion would likely pay (*high/low*) dividends.

12. _____ policy the trade-off between retaining earnings and paying out cash and issuing new shares.

13. One view of dividend policy is that high dividends bring about high taxes which (*decreases/increases*) the value of the firm.

14. According to Modigliani and Miller (MM), the value of the firm (*is/is not*) affected whether the firm pays any dividends or not.

15. MM's argument for the irrelevance of dividend policy (does/does not) assume a world of certainty; it (*does/does not*) assume efficiency in capital markets.

16. People who believe dividends are "good", because they add value, base their argument on the fact that dividends are a (*risky/safe*) stream of cash instead of the (*certain/uncertain*) future of capital gains and/or some investors prefer spendable income from dividends because they are legally restricted from using capital gains or because dividends are a cheap and convenient way for them to receive cash from a company.

17. Another argument favoring high dividends is based on a firm's ability to convert dividends into (*capital gains/cash flows*) which are taxed at lower rates.

18. The argument for low dividends is based on a firm's ability to convert dividends into (*capital gains/cash flows*) which are taxed at lower rates.

19. The Internal Revenue Service has the authority to prevent companies from disguising (*dividends/interest*) as a stock (*issue/repurchase*).

20. The higher the tax rate paid on dividends received the (*stronger\weaker*) the incentive to pay dividends.

21. Any company receiving a dividend from another company pays income tax on only (*30/70*) percent of the dividends received.

22. A reduction in the capital gains tax rate (*decreases/increases*) the incentive to pay dividends.

PROBLEMS

1. Arrange the following dates in chronological order as they occur during the dividend payout procedure:

> Payment date
> Record date
> With-dividend date
> Declaration date
> Ex-dividend date

2. What is the dividend yield for a firm that recently announced a quarterly dividend of 50 cents per share when its stock is trading at $25 per share?

3. If nothing else happened to affect stock prices when would the dividend payment cause an impact on stock price?

4. What is the payout ratio for a company that is expected to earn $3.20 per share for the current year if its latest quarterly dividend was $0.32 per share?

5. Give an example showing how a stock dividend will affect the price of that stock?

6. Ryan's Rafts Company has 100,000 shares outstanding and declares a 20 percent stock dividend. If the total market value of the shares is $1 million before the stock dividend is paid, what will be the price per share after the dividend is paid, assuming nothing else happens to influence the stock price?

7. Suppose a firm with 50,000 shares outstanding has a market capitalization value of $1 million. If it has declared a dividend of $1 per share and the average tax rate on dividends is 30 percent, what will be the expected price per share on the ex-dividend date?

8. Bonto Ltd., reported earnings of $20 million and dividends of $12 million in its most recent year. The company has 5 million shares outstanding but has just announced plans for a two-for-one stock split. Assuming a current (pre-split) stock price of $80 per share, what are the dividends per share:

a. Before the split?
b. After the split what will the expected annual dividend rate be?

9. What will be the expected stock price of Bonto after the split?

10. What is the market value of Bonto
    a. Before the split?
    b. After the split?

ANSWERS TO COMPLETION QUESTIONS

1. regular
2. before
3. will not
4. Some
5. dividend, split
6. cash
7. earnings
8. long
9. are
10. less
11. low
12. Dividend
13. decreases
14. is not
15. does not, does
16. safe, certain
17. are
18. capital gains
19. dividends, repurchase
20. stronger
21. 30
22. decreases

SOLUTIONS TO PROBLEMS

1. The process of paying dividends involves a set of standardized procedures. First the board of directors meets and **declares** a dividend. They establish a **record** date. By standard agreement this sets the **ex-dividend** date as 4 business days *before* the record date. People who buy the stock on that day or any day thereafter will not be entitled to receive the dividend that was previously declared. The **with-dividend** date is then understood to be the last day before the stock is traded without the right to receive the previously declared dividend. The dividend will actually be **paid** several weeks after the record date. Thus, in chronological order, the dates are: declaration, with-dividend, ex-dividend, record, and finally the payment date.

2. Dividend yields are computed as the total expected annual amount of dividends divided by the current market price for the stock. The $0.50 quarterly payout translates to $2.00 per share for the year. The dividend yield would be $2.00/$50 or 4 percent.

3. From the time after the declaration date through the with-dividend date, the price will only move due to other factors affecting the company or the market in general. On the ex-dividend date purchasers of the stock will not be entitled to receive the previously declared dividend. This is the date that the stock will fall by the amount of the dividend.

4. The payout ratio is the amount of dividends expected to be paid for the year expressed as a percentage of the earnings for that year. The annual dividend for this situation is expected to be $4 \times \$0.32 = \$1.28$ per share. The dividend payout ratio is: $\$1.28/\$3.20 = 0.4$ or 40 percent.

5. Assuming there is no news affecting the stock or the stock market, the individual stock price will fall by the percentage of the stock dividend. Thus for a stock trading at $60 per share which has a 15 percent stock dividend, the new stock price will be $60/1.15 or $52.17 per share.

6. The firm will be sending new shares to its stockholders. But that is all that happens. The company has not received any money, nor has its earning power increased as a result of the transaction. The value of the firm remains unchanged, as does the value of each stockholder's total share holding. After the 20 percent stock dividend there will be $100,000 \times 1.2$ or 120,000 shares outstanding. The share price before the dividend was $1,000,000/100,000 shares or $10 per share. The new price will be $1,000,000/120,000 or $8.33 per share. The increase in the number of shares exactly offsets this decline in stock price. For example, the owner of 100 shares before the dividend had a market value of $10 × 100 or $1,000. After the dividend that person has 120 shares × $8.33 or $1,000 of market value.

7. This problem incorporates the effect of income taxes. The share price before the dividend was $1,000,000/50,000 shares of $20. If we ignore taxes the ex-dividend price will be $20 - $1 or $19 per share. Because the investor pays 30 percent of the dividend in taxes, the net benefit of the $1 dividend is only $1 × (1 - 0.3) or $0.70 per share. So the new stock price will be $20 - $0.70 or $19.30.

8. a. The $12 million of dividends are paid on the 5 million shares so the amount for each share is $12 million/5 million or $2.40.
    b. There will be twice as many shares outstanding after the split or 10 million. Because the company has not indicated that they are increasing the dividend rate, the total amount of dividends will remain the same. This means the expected dividends per share after the split will be $12 million/10 million or $1.20.

9. Because of the two-for-one split the stock price will fall by one half to $40 per share. The value of each individual shareholder's stock will be unchanged. For example, someone who owned 100 shares before the split had a value of 100 × $80 per share or $8,000. After the split that person had 200 shares at $40 per share for a value of $8,000.

10. a. The market value of the 5 million shares of Bonto before the split was 5 million shares × $80 per share or $400 million.
    b. After the split the market value is 10 million shares × $40 per share or $400 million. Market value is not affected by this type of transaction. Only when investors expect a change in basic forces surrounding the company and the market itself will there be a change in the valuation.

FINANCIAL STATEMENT ANALYSIS

INTRODUCTION

This is the first chapter of a three-chapter series covering working capital management topics. Financial analysis is first covered followed by financial planning, and finally, working capital management and short-term financing. Working capital greases the skids for the efficient utilization of capital assets that produce value. Too little working capital (current assets) and production and sales are hindered; too much working capital and the rate of return on capital diminishes. Working capital is justified as long as the incremental rate of return of an added dollar invested in working capital exceeds the opportunity rate of return of capital.

This chapter categorizes the scope of financial ratio analysis into *five* areas: 1) leverage, 2) liquidity, 3) efficiency or turnover, 4) profitability, and 5) market value. Several ratios are covered for each area, including an explanation of why the ratio is a good proxy for the concept. You studied ratio analysis in your second accounting course. Focus your thoughts on how each of the five areas, and their ratio measures, affects the value of a business. This "value" orientation is the main focus of finance, so be sure to carry the theme into this chapter. Table 17.8 presents a variety of ratios for several industries.

LEARNING CHECKLIST

After studying this chapter you should be able to:

____1. Calculate and interpret ratio measures of leverage, liquidity, profitability, asset management, and market valuation for a business.

____2. Use the Du Pont formula to understand the components of profitability measures such as return on assets and return on equity.

____3. Evaluate the potential pitfalls of ratios based on accounting data.

SOURCES OF BUSINESS INFORMATION

Dun & Bradstreet Financial Information. For this financial ratio analysis chapter, we should observe several published sources of industry financial ratios. The most frequently cited work is Dun & Bradstreet, Industry Norms & Key Business Ratios. Dun & Bradstreet uses Standard Industrial Codes (SIC) to organize nine broad industry classifications. This annual work provides both operating data and financial ratio averages. Approximately fifteen financial ratios are provided, including most of the ratios discussed in this chapter. Other industry ratios sources are discussed in the next few chapters of the study guide.

Financial Data Finder. One of the better collections of finance, economics, government and business web sites is published and maintained by the Finance Department at Ohio State University. Search OSU's College of Business for the Finance Department. This is just one of their better sites. The Financial Data Finder is an alphabetical listing of hundreds of sites with a short description of each. From the Australian Stock Market to the ZZ's site, one can find a connection to any type of economic and financial information. Check it out today!

CHAPTER OUTLINE, KEY CONCEPTS AND TERMS

I. FINANCIAL RATIOS

    A. **Principles**
       1.   Financial ratios are used to summarize financial information about a company. Information from the **income statement**, a listing of revenue, expenses, and profits over a period of time, and the **balance sheet**, a listing of assets, liabilities, and net worth at a point in time, are used to calculate financial ratios related to the performance and risk level of a business.
       2.   A balance sheet and income statement is often calculated as a **common-size** statement by dividing the balance sheet ledger items by total assets, and income statement items by total revenue.
       3.   Five types of risk/return areas are studied in this chapter, using financial ratios as proxies to measure each risk.

    B. **Leverage Ratios**
       1.   The use of fixed cost financing, either debt or preferred stock, is called financial leverage. Financial leverage presents a risk/return opportunity. Shareholders may magnify their earnings/returns by the use of fixed cost financing but, on the other hand, debt is a fixed cost, contractual commitment to pay regardless of the asset earning rate.
       2.   Creditors, owners, and suppliers are interested in the extent to which a firm has sought the tax shielded benefits from financial leverage producing debt.
       3.   Leverage ratios are of two types: balance sheet ratios comparing leverage capital to total capitalization (long-term debt and equity) or total assets, and coverage ratios which measure the earnings or cash-flow times coverage of fixed cost obligations.
       4.   The long-term debt ratio measures the proportion of the capital structure that is made up of debt and lease obligations:

          Long-term debt ratio = long-term debt ÷ (long-term debt + equity)

The higher the ratio the greater the use of financial leverage, posing an increased risk/return situation for investors.

5. The debt to equity ratio measures the amount of long-term debt to equity or the amount of leverage capital in relation to the equity cushion under the debt:

    Debt-equity ratio = long-term debt ÷ equity

6. The total debt ratio measures total liabilities, current and long-term, relative to total assets or the proportion of assets financed by debt:

    Total debt ratio = total liabilities ÷ total assets

7. A coverage ratio, such as the times interest earned ratio, measures an amount available relative to amount owed. How many times is the obligation covered?

    Times interest earned = EBIT ÷ interest expense

    One may include principal payments necessary per period in the denominator to review the ability of operating earnings to cover the total debt obligation of principal and interest.

8. The cash coverage ratio broadens the numerator to cash flow from operations relative to the interest expenses:

    Cash coverage ratio = (EBIT + depreciation) ÷ interest expense

C. Liquidity Ratios

1. Liquidity ratios attempt to measure the ability to pay obligations such as current liabilities and the pool of assets available to cover the obligations. **Liquidity** is the ability of an asset to be converted to cash quickly at low cost. Converting an asset to cash occurs in one of two ways. Sell the asset, hoping it has reasonable liquidity, or in the case of a financial asset, like accounts receivable or Treasury bill, maturity brings cash. Working capital circulates from inventory to accounts receivable to cash, etc. Accounting value estimates of liquid assets are reasonable estimates of their value.

2. Current assets (the pool of circulating cash assets available to be allocated to pay bills) *minus* current liabilities(the pool of obligations the business must pay in the near future) is an analytical amount called net working capital (NWC). NWC is a rough measure of the current assets left over if

the current liabilities were paid. The NWC to total assets ratio estimates the proportion of assets in net current assets, another name for NWC:

$$\text{NWC/total asset ratio} = \text{net working capital} \div \text{total assets}$$

3. The current ratio is the classic liquidity ratio, but is merely a variation of the idea above--what pool of circulating assets is available relative to the pool of current obligations:

$$\text{Current ratio} = \text{current assets} \div \text{current liabilities}$$

4. Continuing the theme of assets available to pay obligations, the quick or acid-test ratio eliminates inventories, the least liquid current asset, from current assets:

$$\text{Quick ratio} = (\text{cash} + \text{marketable securities} + \text{receivables}) \div \text{current liabilities}$$

5. The cash ratio eliminates inventories and receivables from current assets to review the cash assets relative to the current liabilities:

$$\text{Cash ratio} = (\text{cash} + \text{marketable securities}) \div \text{current liabilities}$$

6. The interval measure of liquidity measures the firm's pool of liquid, quick assets (above) to the daily expenditures from operations and gives an estimate of the number of days' obligations that are circulating in the quick assets. The more days, the greater the ability to meet obligations:

$$\text{Interval measure} = (\text{cash} + \text{marketable securities} + \text{receivables}) \div \text{average daily expenses from operations}$$

The denominator represents annual cash (not depreciation) expenses divided by 365.

D. Efficiency Ratios

1. Another area of financial analysis, efficiency ratios, measures how effectively the business is using its assets. "Using" relates to liquidity or profitability or performance. The numerators used in efficiency ratios are activity-based items, such as sales, cost of sales, etc., while the denominators are generally some average balance sheet amount. Turnover ratios are often converted to a time-line focus by dividing turnovers ratios into 365 days.

2.   The asset turnover ratio measures the sales activity derived from total assets, or the revenue generated per dollar of total assets. The asset turnover is also an important component of asset profitability studied later, measuring the revenue per dollar invested:

$$\text{Asset turnover ratio} = \text{sales} \div \text{average total assets}$$

Sales, a measure of activity, may be compared to a variety of balance sheet accounts (e.g. fixed assets, net working capital, stockholders equity, etc.) to measure the revenue generating efficiency of the account.

3.   The inventory turnover ratio, using the cost of goods sold representing the cumulative amount of inventory sold in a period as the numerator and average inventory (beginning plus ending divided by two) as the denominator, measures the number of times the value of inventory turns over in a period:

$$\text{Inventory turnover} = \text{cost of goods sold} \div \text{average inventory}$$

The inventory turnover may be converted to a time line concept, the number of day sales in inventories, by finding the reciprocal $(1/x)$ of the inventory turnover times 365 or:

$$\text{Days' sales in inventories} = \text{average inventory} \div (\text{cost of sales}/365)$$
$$\text{or } = 1 \div (\text{inventory turnover} \times 365)$$

4.   The average collection period applies the same concept above to accounts receivables. The average collection period is the estimated number of days it takes to collect receivables:

$$\text{Average collection period} = \text{average receivables} \div \text{average daily sales}$$

The more days' sales outstanding, the greater amount of capital is tied up in accounts receivables relative to sales.

E.   **Profitability Ratios**

1.   Profitability refers to some measure of profit relative to revenue or an amount invested. The net profit margin measures the proportion of sales revenue that is profit available for sources of funds (EBIT - tax). Net profits after taxes is commonly used in this ratio, but net profits is biased by the relative amount of leveraging or debt financing in the business:

$$\text{Net profit margin} = (\text{EBIT - tax}) \div \text{sales}$$

2.	A good performance ratio is the return on total assets (current and fixed), or the EBIT - tax earned per dollar of average assets. This ratio is featured later in the Du Pont analysis:

$$\text{Return on assets} = (\text{EBIT - tax}) \div \text{average total assets}$$

3.	The return on equity measures the profitability of the common stockholder's equity or return per dollar of invested equity capital:

$$\text{Return on equity} = \text{earnings available for common} \div \text{average equity}$$

The earnings available for common (EAC) is the net income less any preferred dividends, if applicable.

4.	The proportion of earnings that is paid out as dividends is called the payout ratio:

$$\text{Payout ratio} = \text{dividends} \div \text{earnings}$$

The complement of the payout ratio is the plowback ratio studied earlier, or the proportion of earnings retained in the period:

$$\text{Plowback ratio} = 1 - \text{payout ratio}$$

$$= (\text{earnings - dividends}) \div \text{earnings}$$

$$= \text{earnings retained in period} \div \text{earnings}$$

The plowback ratio times the return on equity (ROE) is an estimate of the growth rate in common equity from internally generated earnings, or the sustainable growth rate in assets that the business can support from internal earnings without changing the total debt/total asset ratio:

$$\text{Growth in equity from plowback} = \text{earnings retained in period} \div \text{equity}$$
$$= (\text{earnings retained} \div \text{earnings}) \times (\text{earnings} \div \text{equity})$$

$$= \text{plowback ratio} \times \text{ROE}$$

II. THE DU PONT SYSTEM

A. The **Du Pont System** is a process of analyzing component ratios (also called decomposition) of the ROA and ROE to explain their level or changes.

B. The ROA is comprised of the product of the profit margin, what the firm earns on every dollar of sales, times the asset turnover or the extent to which a business utilizes its assets:

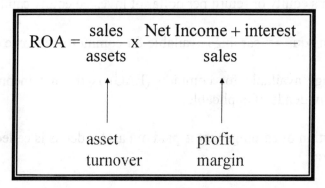

$$ROA = \frac{sales}{assets} \times \frac{Net\ Income + interest}{sales}$$

asset turnover   profit margin

Both the profit margin and asset turnover can be broken down in sub-components (decomposed) to assess the cause of the level or changes in the ROA. The ability to earn on assets is comprised of expense control per sales (profit margin) and the effective use of assets to generate revenue (asset turnover). A level of ROA can be generated or changed by affecting the margin or turnover.

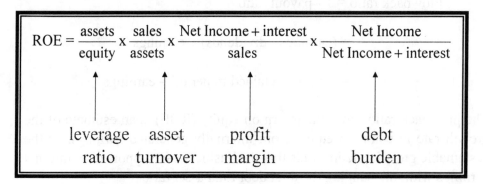

$$ROE = \frac{assets}{equity} \times \frac{sales}{assets} \times \frac{Net\ Income + interest}{sales} \times \frac{Net\ Income}{Net\ Income + interest}$$

leverage ratio   asset turnover   profit margin   debt burden

C. The ROE is comprised of the ROA *times* the leverage ratio *times* the debt-burden ratio, or the ROE is related to the effective, profitable use of assets, the extent of financial leverage, and the level of interest rates paid on debt:

Financial ratios for major industry groups, 2nd quarter, 1998				
	Petroleum and coal products	Machinery except electrical	Electrical and electronic equipment	Retail trade
Debt ratio	0.35	0.29	0.23	0.35
Net working capital to total assets	-0.03	0.17	0.12	0.16
Current ratio	0.85	1.57	1.45	1.55
Quick ratio	0.44	0.91	0.82	0.49
Sales to total assets	0.85	1.19	1.02	2.06
Net profit margin (%)	4.71	3.11	5.88	3.23
Return on total assets (%)	4.02	3.71	5.99	6.66
Return on equity (%)	14.39	15.47	12.23	12.57
Dividend payout ratio	0.67	0.31	0.34	0.44

III. USING FINANCIAL RATIOS

A. Cautions
1. Generally acceptable accounting principles have considerable leeway in accounting for asset/liability values and income, so that it is often difficult to make an absolute comparison of company ratio with other companies or the industry ratios.
2. Goodwill is difficult to assess. Some commitments to pay, such as pensions, lease obligations, and guarantees, are not always shown as a liability.

B. Choosing a Benchmark
1. Knowing reasonable ranges for the above ratios calculated requires practice, comparison of the trends over time, and compared to averages, a successful business or similar benchmark for comparison.
2. Industry ratios are available from a number of sources. Differences from averages or earlier trends is not wrong, but provides a beginning for understanding why the differences or changes occurred.

IV. MEASURING COMPANY PERFORMANCE

A. Efficient markets have come to realize that an accounting statement has limited use when determining the value of the firm. All the ratio analysis skills in the world can not tell you the market value of a firm. Nor can they tell you why market value of some firms continues to rise above expectations.

B. **Stern Stewart & Co.** employ two measurements to track just such information. **Market Value Added (MVA)** tells us The difference between the market value of common stock and its book value. Their other measurement, Economic Value

Added (traditionally referred to as residual income), tells us the net dollar return after deducting the cost of capital.

$$EVA = \text{Residual Income}$$
$$= \text{Income Earned - income required}$$
$$= \text{Income Earned -} \left[\text{Cost of Capital} \times \text{Investment}\right]$$

C. **THE ROLE OF FINANCIAL RATIOS**
    1.   Never forget that financial ratios can provide "invaluable" information about a firm, its health and its risks. At the same time, it does not necessarily lead us to "valuable" information either. Specifically, when it relates to market values and economic values.
    2.   The accountant tends to over emphasize ratios and the financial manager tends to under estimate them. Be mindful that the truth lies somewhere in the middle.

COMPLETION QUESTIONS

1.   The purpose of financial statement analysis (*is/is not*) to analyze a firm's overall performance and to assess its current financial standing.

2.   The five types of financial ratios are: _____, _____, _____, _____, and _____.

3.   (*Leverage/Liquidity*) ratios show how easily the firm can get cash.

4.   The (*balance sheet/income statement*) presents a snapshot of a firm at a given point in time.

5.   An example of asset not shown on the balance sheet is (*employees/trademarks*).

6.   Shareholders equity (*excludes/includes*) preferred stock.

7.   The common size balance sheet presents items as a percentage of (*assets/sales*).

8.   Financial leverage (*decreases/increases*) the riskiness of the rate of return on equity.

9.   The debt ratio (*excludes/includes*) the value of leases.

10.   The times interest ratio uses interest payments in the (*denominator/numerator*).

11. In the cash coverage ratio, _____ is added to the earnings before interest and taxes.

12. Liquidity refers to the ability to convert (*assets/liabilities*) to cash quickly and at low cost.

13. The difference between current assets and current liabilities is known as _____ _____ _____.

14. The quick or acid test ratio (*excludes/includes*) inventory.

15. The most liquid assets are cash and marketable _____.

16. The _____ measure indicates how many days a firm can pay its bills using only its cash and other liquid assets.

17. If a firm is operating at close to full capacity it likely will have a relatively (*high/low*) asset turnover ratio.

18. The inventory turnover ratio uses (*cost of goods sold/sales*) in the numerator.

19. The days' sales in inventory is the reciprocal of the inventory turnover ratio (*divided/ multiplied*) by 365.

20. The average accounts receivable divided by the average daily sales is called the average _____ _____.

21. The net profit margin equals earnings before (*interest/taxes*) divided by sales.

22. In order to measure returns on all assets, interest is (*added to/subtracted from*) net profits.

23. If earnings are highly variable, the firm will likely have a (*high/low*) target payout ratio.

24. The proportion of earnings that are reinvested in the firm is called the _____ ratio.

25. Shareholders' equity grows faster if (*less/more*) dividends are paid.

26. A high price/earnings ratio for a company indicates that investors expect (*high/low*) growth rate of dividends.

27. A high dividend yield indicates that investors expect (*high/low*) dividend growth or that they require a (*high/low*) return.

28. Book value equals the amount common stockholders have invested in the firm (*minus/ plus*) amounts that have been invested on their behalf.

29. A high Tobin's q, which is equal to the market value of a firm's assets (*divided/multiplied*) by the replacement cost of those assets, indicates investors are (*optimistic/pessimistic*) about the firm's future.

30. The Du Pont system of financial analysis links (*liquidity/profitability*) with (*efficiency/ market value*) ratios.

31. Competition usually results in trade-offs between (*profitability/turnover*) and (*plowback/ profitability*).

32. Incorporating a (*leverage/liquidity*) ratio in the Du Pont system allows one to analyze how financing choices affect returns to shareholders.

33. A company that has acquired another firm by paying more than book value will have goodwill on the (*balance sheet/income statement*).

34. In analyzing financial statements for a company, it is important to compare the ratios calculated with averages for the same (*industry/size*).

35. Studies have shown historical earnings are (*reliable/unreliable*) predictors of future earnings.

PROBLEMS

For problems 1-9 use the financial statements for Jennifer's Jai Alai and Jicama Corporation (JJAJC) as shown below:

BALANCE SHEET
(Millions of dollars)

Account	End of year	Start of year
Assets		
Cash	2	6
Accounts receivable	14	12
Inventory	21	17
Plant and equipment	63	48
Accumulated depreciation	(10)	(8)
Total	90	75
Liabilities and shareholders' equity		
Accounts payable	14	9
Notes payable	10	6
Other current liabilities	4	2
Long-term debt	5	2
Common stock (10 million shares)	24	18
Retained earnings	33	38
Total	90	75

INCOME STATEMENT
(Millions of dollars)

Sales	100
Cost of goods sold	44
Depreciation	2
Other expenses	<u>43</u>
Earnings before interest and taxes	11
Interest expense	<u>1</u>
Earnings before taxes	10
Taxes	<u>5</u>
Earnings after taxes	5
Common dividends	1

1. Calculate the following ratios for JJAJC:
   a. Times interest earned
   b. Long-term debt ratio
   c. Total debt ratio
   d. Cash coverage ratio
   e. Current ratio
   f. Quick ratio
   g. Net profit margin
   h. Inventory turnover
   I. Days in inventory
   j. Average collection period
   k. Return on equity
   l. Return on assets
   m. Payout ratio

2. If JJAJC shut down operations, how many days could it pay its bills?

3. What must have been the investment in new plant and equipment during the latest year?

4. If the market value of the stock was $84 million at the end of the latest year, what was the price-to-book ratio?

5. What were JJAJC's earnings per share?

6. What is the price-to-earnings ratio?

7. What must have been the price of JJAJC's common stock at year-end?

8. What were the dividends paid per share?

9. What was the dividend yield on the common stock?

10. A partial analysis of Paul Thomas Meats, Inc. reveals the following ratios:

Current	2.5
Quick	2.0
Inventory turnover	4.0
Net operating margin	.10

    If the current liabilities were $6 million and operating expenses were $15 million, what must have been the cost of goods sold if we ignore taxes?

11. What were PTM's sales for that year?

ANSWERS TO COMPLETION QUESTIONS

1. is
2. leverage, liquidity, efficiency, profitability, market value
3. Liquidity
4. balance sheet
5. employees
6. excludes
7. assets
8. increases
9. includes
10. denominator
11. depreciation
12. assets
13. net working capital
14. excludes
15. securities
16. interval
17. high
18. cost of goods sold

19. multiplied
20. collection period
21. interest
22. added to
23. low
24. plowback
25. less
26. high
27. low, high
28. plus
29. divided, optimistic
30. profitability, efficiency
31. turnover, profitability
32. leverage
33. balance sheet
34. industry
35. unreliable

SOLUTIONS TO PROBLEMS

1. a. Times interest earned = EBIT/interest = $11/$1

    = 11

    b. Long-term debt ratio = long-term debt/(long-term debt + equity)

    = $5/($5 + $57)

    = 0.081

    c. Total debt ratio = total liabilities/total assets

    = $33/$90

    = 0.367

    d. Cash coverage ratio = EBIT + depreciation/interest

    = ($11 + $2)/$1

    = 13

    e. Current ratio = current assets/current liabilities

    = $37/$28

    = 1.32

    f. Quick ratio = (current assets - inventories)/current liabilities

    = ($37 - $21)/$28

    = 0.571

    g. Net profit margin = (EBIT - taxes)/sales

    =($11 - $5)/$100

    = 0.06

h. Inventory turnover = cost of goods sold/average inventory
$$= \$44 \div \{(\$21 - \$17)/2\}$$
$$= 2.32$$

I. Days in inventory = average inventory/cost of goods sold per day
$$= \$19 \div (\$44/365)$$
$$= 158 \text{ days}$$

j. Average collection period = average accounts receivable/sales per day
$$= \frac{(\$14 + \$12)}{2} \div \$100/365$$
$$= 47.5 \text{ days}$$

k. Return on equity = net income/average equity
$$= \$5 \div \{(\$57 + \$56)/2\}$$
$$= 0.088$$

l. Return on assets = EBIT - taxes/average assets
$$= \$11 \div \{ (\$90 + \$75)/2\}$$
$$= 0.133$$

m. Payout ratio = dividends/net income
$$= \$1/\$5$$
$$= 0.20$$

2. The interval measure is the cash on hand plus accounts receivable divided by the total cash expenses per day. The cash expenses equal the cost of goods sold plus the other expenses. In this case the interval measure is
$$= (\$2 + \$14) \div \{(\$44 + \$45)/365\}$$
$$= 65.6 \text{ days}$$

3. The new investment in plant and equipment must have been the increase in plant and equipment during the year. If only net plant and equipment was shown on the balance sheet, depreciation would be added to the change in the net amount during the year. In this case new investment = $63 - $48 or $15 million.

4. The book value of the stock at year end was $57 million which, if divided into the market value of the stock outstanding of $84 million yields a price to book ratio of 1.47.

5. Earnings per share equals net income divided by the number of shares outstanding. For JJAJC it is $5 million/10 million shares or $0.50 per share.

6. The price-to-earnings ratio is the market value divided by the net income. This is:
$$= \$84/\$5$$
$$= 16.8$$

7. The stock price would be the market value divided by the number of shares outstanding. For JJAJC it would be $84/10 or $8.40 per share.

8. The total dividends paid were $1 million on the 10 million shares so the dividends per share would be $1/10 or $0.10.

9. The dividend yield would be $0.10/$8.40 = 0.012 or 1.2 percent.

10. The key to this problem is to write various ratios to solve for the missing amounts. For example, we know:

    current ratio = current assets/current liabilities
    2.5 = current assets /$6
    current assets = 2.5 × $6 = $15 million.

    Next we can find the inventory by remembering that the quick ratio equals current assets less inventories divided by current liabilities. This yields:

    2.0 = ($15 - inventory)/$6
    inventory = $15 - ($6 × 2) = $3 million

    In the last step we use the inventory turnover ratio as being the cost of goods sold divided by the inventory. For PTM it is:

    4 = cost of goods sold/$3
    cost of goods sold = 4 × $3 = $12 million

11. Sales can be found from the answer to problem 10 and by knowing that the net operating margin equals sales less total expenses divided by the sales. The total expenses are the sum of the cost of goods sold and the operating expenses or $12 + $15 = $27 million.
    The net operating margin = 0.10 = (sales - $27)/sales. Sales = $30 million.

FINANCIAL PLANNING

INTRODUCTION

This second of three working capital management chapters focuses on the concepts of financial planning. Beginning with an assumption of volume (sales, production), the financial planning process, top-down or down-up, focuses all estimates and iterations in financial terms to a certain point in the future (balance sheet) or during the period (income statement or statement of cash flows). Every business person becomes involved in the planning process, formally or informally, so the financial planning concepts covered here have considerable value to students of all majors. Just like other chapters, the concepts of this chapter are easily applied to your own personal financial planning.

After an introduction to the planning process, the authors use the percentage of sales financial planning model to demonstrate the general framework of a financial plan. The general assumption is that specific asset levels are directly related to the level of sales. Given sales, asset needs for the future can be estimated. Some current liabilities, such as accounts payables, are directly related to inventory levels and increase with increased inventories. The difference between assets needed at some future point and financing provided, including any new retained earnings, is the funds needed or plug amount of financing that the financial manager must provide.

Estimating the amount of funds needed and when funds are needed are valuable inputs for the financial manager. The key issue in financial planning is not the single right estimate of what will exactly take place (that seldom occurs), but reviewing and understanding a series of likely scenarios is the real value of planning for the financial manager. Being ready, financially, for whatever happens in the sales and production areas is the crucial function of the financial manager.

The last section of the chapter interrelates investment policy, debt policy, dividend policy, and growth policy into a financial planning format. The concepts of internal growth rate (maximum sales or asset growth rate without external financing) and the sustainable growth rate (maximum growth rate within specific debt and dividend policy) are valuable concepts that tie several important financial policy areas together.

LEARNING CHECKLIST

After studying this chapter you should be able to:

_____1. Describe the steps involved in preparing a financial plan.

_____2. Construct a simple financial planning model.

_____3. Estimate the effect of growth (sales and assets) on the need for external financing.

SOURCES OF BUSINESS INFORMATION

Almanac Of Business and Industrial Ratios. Another valuable source of industry financial ratios is Troy's <u>Almanac Of Business and Industrial Financial Ratios</u>. The <u>Almanac</u>, published annually, compiles operating factors and financial ratios for approximately 160 industries including manufacturing, wholesaling, retailing, banks, and financial services. Troy analyzes each industry group under a two-table format. Each industry is divided into twelve categories based on size of a company's assets. Several categories of ratios are presented and include the current ratio, quick ratio, sales to net working capital, coverage ratio, asset turnover, and debt to net worth ratio. The ROA and ROE are also provided for each category.

Business Job Finder. One of the better finance career sites on the web, the Business Job Finder, like the Financial Data Finder, is also published and maintained by the Finance Department of Ohio State University. From a description of various finance careers, there are links to many career web sites.

CHAPTER OUTLINE, KEY CONCEPTS AND TERMS

I.   **WHAT IS FINANCIAL PLANNING?**

     A.   **Financial Planning is a process consisting of:**
          1.   Analyzing the investment and financing choices available to the business.
          2.   Projecting the future consequences of current decisions under varying scenarios.
          3.   Deciding which alternative to undertake.
          4.   Later, measuring performance or results with the goals of the financial plan--the planning and control cycle.

     B.   **Planning Horizon** -- The time line of financial planning includes both short-term planning, perhaps the next twelve months with a focus on cash flow timing, and long-term financial planning where the **planning horizon** or time associated with the plan is around five years or longer.

     C.   **Financial Planning Focuses on the Big Picture**
          1.   Financial plans include the strategic plan of the business or a "big picture" perspective, rather than the implications of individual investments and other decisions.

2. Alternative business plans might consider three scenarios relating to *best case, normal growth,* or *worst case* or *retrenchment.*
3. Planning may consider a variety of alternative opportunities or future options.
4. Financial plans often interrelate a level of activity such as sales to the level of assets needed, which in turn determines the amount of funds needed to finance the added investment.
5. Added sales increases the need for current assets, increases some current liabilities (accounts payable) or *netting* the two determines an added level of net working capital needed to fund asset growth.
6. Dividend policy is a factor in a financial plan, for the dividend/retention decision affects the level of earnings paid out or retained in the business to finance new assets needed.
7. A firm has financial slack if the level of expected financing is greater than the funds needed for a period. Debt may be repaid, dividends increased, or stock repurchased when long-term financial slack exists.
8. Businesses estimating rapid sales and asset growth beyond the funding ability of earnings, must prepare to raise external capital from banks, bonds, or common stock issues.

D. **Financial Planning Is Not Just Forecasting**
1. Forecasting attempts to estimate the most likely future outcome, such as a level of sales.
2. Financial planning considers a variety of future outcomes and prepares for each should they occur.
3. "What if" analysis is a major part of financial planning from changing a single variable in a plan (sensitivity analysis) and noting the effect on funds needed, to scenario analysis, where a situation involving a number of variables (recession) is analyzed to estimate the ability to serve customers and earn expected returns to equity should the scenario develop.

E. **Three Requirements for Effective Planning**
1. The *three* requirements for effective planning include forecasting, the process of choosing the best or optimal plan and watching the plan unfold, and comparing actual to the plan and addressing variances.
2. Forecasting focuses on the most likely outcome and is not financial planning. However, a good forecast always is a good start for the financial plan. Anticipating competitive responses should be considered in the plan.
3. After considering several scenarios, the financial manager must choose a plan which will direct the efforts of the business. Financial plans are often in accounting terms, not shareholders, such as total return. Shareholder interests should be represented in decisions and strategy, not accounting performance indicators.

4. Financial plans are dated with the short passage of time, so a plan must be easily adapted as events and opportunities occur. Plans may serve a standard to compare experience.

II.   FINANCIAL PLANNING MODELS

A.   A financial planning model establishes relationships between economic activity (sales), business policies, such as a credit policy, and the resulting resources needed, including assets, employees, or financial capital.

B.   The equations or relationships in the financial model may be derived from past relationships (correlations) or expected relationships based on forecasts.

C.   Financial models using spreadsheet programs enable the planner to study a wide range of possible outcomes and prepare the firm to handle *what will occur*.

D.   **Components of a Financial Planning Model**
1.   Financial plans include *three* components: inputs, the planning model, and outputs.

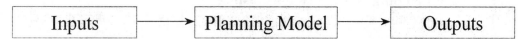

2.   The inputs include current financial statements and forecasts. In most financial plans, expected sales is the major independent variable which drives the plan. Other variables, such as assets (inventories) are related to expected sales.
3.   The planning model, with the established relationships between sales and assets, etc., calculates the estimated levels of resources needed, the expected amount of financing needed, and the expected profit and cash flow.
4.   The output of the financial plans includes estimated financial statements based on the assumptions and relationships of the plan, called **pro forma** financial statements. Financial ratios, based on the pro forma financial statements, are usually calculated.

Income Statement	
Sales	$1,200
Costs	1,000
Net Income	200

Balance	*Sheet (YTD)*		
Assets	$2,000	Debt	$ 800
		Equity	1,200
Total	$2,000	Total	$2,000

E. **An Example of a Planning Model**

1. The **percentage of sales model** is a financial planning model in which the future level of asset investment, and subsequent financing needs, is a function of forecasted sales. The assumption is that sales drives assets which drives the financing needed. See Tables 18.1-18.3.

2. A simple percentage of sales model assumes no spare capacity in the asset(production) structure, so increased sales will require added current assets, fixed assets, perhaps some spontaneous financing from current liabilities, and added equity financing via retained earnings (net income minus dividends).

3. The pro forma balance sheet associated with the percentage of sales financial planning model uses any one of a number of ledger accounts as a variable to "balance" the balance sheet. Dividends paid, a financing decision, may be the **balancing item** as might the debt/equity ratio, bank financing, or a generic "funds needed" liability account.

Income Statement	
Sales	$1,320
Costs	1,100
Net Income	220

Balance Sheet			
Assets	$2,200	Debt	$ 800
		Equity	1,320
Total	$2,200	Total	$2,200

Balance Sheet			
Assets	$2,200	Debt	$ 960
		Equity	1,240
Total	$2,200	Total	$2,200

F. **An Improved Model**

1. The Executive Fruit Company pro forma example, Tables 18.4-18.7 is a good example of the percentage of sales financial planning model.

2. A relationship between sales and specific balance sheet dependent variables are established before the planning begins.

3. Sales is estimated for the coming periods. Sales, the independent variable, drives the level of assets needed and the estimated required external financing needed.

4. The next stage of the plan focuses on the debt/equity mix and specific types of financing the firms may seek.

5. Alternative estimates of financing needed, given varied sales estimates, provide a range of possible outcomes that the financial manager should be prepared to handle.

III. PLANNERS BEWARE

    A.   **Pitfalls in Model Design**
        1.   Will a more sophisticated financial planning model give the financial manager an improved forecast of funds needed in the future? Is having "the" right forecast the real purpose of financial planning, or is financial planning really about estimating the range of possible outcomes?
        2.   The value of the financial plan is to prepare for a variety of outcomes, not build the ultimate, realistic financial planning model.

    B.   **Shortcomings of Percentage of Sales Models**
        1.   Though a good "rough" first estimate for financial planning, the percentage of sales model is limited in that many estimated variables, such as assets, are not or are not always proportional to sales.
        2.   Fixed assets are not easily added in small amounts, but are more economically added in large investments. Thus, the firm must plan based on expected production utilization rates. Asset investment is not usually proportional to sales in a shorter time span, and is better related over a longer planning horizon.

    C.   **There Is No Finance in Financial Planning Models**
        1.   Financial planning models estimate accounting statements, and do not focus on financial decision tools such as incremental cash flows, time value, market risk, etc.
        2.   Financial planning models are not focused on financial decisions which would increase market value, though the debt/equity standards of the firm and the dividend policy of the business are built into financial planning.

IV. EXTERNAL FINANCING AND GROWTH

> Required external financing = new investment - retained earnings
> = (growth rate x assets) - retained earnings

    A.   Financial planning produces consistency between growth, investment, and financing goals of the business, for all are included in the plan. This section studies the relationships between growth objectives and requirements for external financing.

    B.   The general idea is that the faster the firm grows, the more financing, and probably more external financing, will be needed. The extent of external financing will be related to the asset intensity of the firm, the profitability of the firm and the debt/equity and dividend policies of the firm.

C. Sales growth drives asset growth drives funds needed. The higher the sales growth, the more assets/sales needed, the lower the profitability of the firm, the higher the dividend payout, the *greater* the more likely external funds (debt or equity) will be needed.

D. The **internal growth rate** of the firm is the maximum rate of growth *without* external financing. Where the upward sloping (slope related to profitability and dividend policy) line intersects the horizontal line (growth rate scale) is the internal growth rate, or the maximum growth rate at which the firm can grow and finance all its needs from internal sources (equity). The internal growth rate is the ratio of retained earnings divided by assets. The higher the historic contribution of retained earnings to finance assets, the higher the growth rate the firm can maintain without external capital.

$$\text{Internal growth rate} = \frac{\text{retained earnings}}{\text{assets}}$$

$$= \frac{\text{retained earnings}}{\text{net income}} \times \frac{\text{net income}}{\text{equity}} \times \frac{\text{equity}}{\text{assets}}$$

E. The internal growth rate is the product of the plowback ratio times the ROE times the leverage ratio or: Internal growth rate

= (retained earnings ÷ net income) x (net income ÷ equity) × (equity ÷ assets)

The higher the plowback ratio (lower dividend payout), the higher the profitability (ROE) and the higher the proportion of assets financed by equity, the greater the internal growth rate.

F. The **sustainable growth rate** is the maximum growth rate (sales or assets) the firm can maintain without changing the debt/equity ratio and without any external equity financing (sale of stock). While the internal growth rate is the maximum growth rate without *any external financing* (debt or equity), the sustainable growth rate is the maximum growth rate sustainable without *any external equity financing*.

$$\text{Sustainable growth rate} = \text{plowback ratio x retrun on equity}$$

G. The sustainable growth rate will be greater than the internal growth rate for the former considers added debt financing along with added equity financing provided by earnings retained (not paid in dividends) in the period.

H.   The sustainable growth rate is the product of the plowback ratio (proportion of net income retained in the firm) times the return on equity (ROE).

COMPLETION QUESTIONS

1.   Financial planning is a process designed to (*minimize/take appropriate*) risks.

2.   The planning horizon is (*short- and long-/long-*) term.

3.   Often separate plans are submitted for the best case, normal growth, and (*exceptional growth/retrenchment*).

4.   Sensitivity analysis and scenario analysis are used for (*how-to/what-if*) questions.

5.   Forecasting is (*a part of/the same as*) planning.

6.   When forecasts come from different areas of the company it (*is/is not*) important to have consistent assumptions for influencing variables such as inflation and economic growth.

7.   The optimal financial plan typically (*is/is not*) developed by setting a goal of profit margin.

8.   Long-term plans (*should/should not*) be revised periodically.

9.   The three parts of all financial plans are inputs, outputs and (*cash flows/planning models*).

10. Projected or forecasted financial statements are called _____ _____ statements.

11. The planning model in which sales forecasts are the driving variables is called the _____ of sales model.

12. A variable that is adjusted to maintain consistency in a proforma statement is called a balancing item or _____.

13. A firm that forecasts the need for an additional $100 of assets to support an increase in sales which are expected to generate total profits of $60 will need to acquire new financing of _____.

14. In the early steps of financial planning the (*amount/mix*) of financing is determined.

15. In estimating future financing requirements, amounts for depreciation of fixed assets (*add to/subtract from*) the projected needs.

16. The percentage of sales models of forecasting are (*less/more*) accurate because many variables are not proportional to sales.

17. Financial planning models (*do/do not*) emphasize tools of financial analysis.

18. The internal growth rate is the (*maximum/minimum*) rate of growth without external financing.

19. The sustainable growth rate is the maximum growth rate that a firm can maintain without (*decreasing/increasing*) leverage.

20. Unless a company does not borrow money, its internal growth rate will be (*less/more*) than the sustainable growth rate.

PROBLEMS

1. Why do businesses make financial plans?

2. Why are individual investment projects usually not considered separately in a financial plan?

3. How is uncertainty about the future incorporated into financial planning?

4. Discuss how inconsistencies may affect financial planning?

5. Matthew Tyler Stamps, Ltd. (MTSL) expects sales next year to be $10 million. Past experience indicates that the cost of goods sold will be 70 percent of sales, that operating expenses will be 10 percent of sales, that interest expense will be $0.4 million, and that the income tax rate will be 40 percent. Develop the pro forma income statement for the coming year.

6. If the total assets for MTSL are projected to be $25 million next year and liabilities and equity are predicted to be $20 million, what is the estimated amount of funds required?

7. Suppose MTSL needs a minimum cash balance of $1 million. How would this affect the amount of financing required as determined in problem 6?

8. Suppose MTSL's assets, excluding cash, has been $3 million less than the total of predicted liabilities and equity. What would this mean?

9.   The retained earnings at the end of MTSL's latest year of operation were $2.5 million. Using the other information from problem 5 and a target payout ratio of 40 percent, what is the expected balance in the retained earnings account at the end of next year?

10.   How does the answer in problem 9 affect the amount of financing needed?

ANSWERS TO COMPLETION QUESTIONS

1.   take appropriate
2.   short- and long-
3.   retrenchment
4.   what-if
5.   a part of
6.   is
7.   is not
8.   should
9.   planning models
10.   pro forma
11.   percentage
12.   plug
13. $40
14.   amount
15.   subtract from
16.   less
17.   do not
18.   maximum
19.   increasing
20.   less

SOLUTIONS TO PROBLEMS

1.   A major reason for financial planning is as an aid in anticipating the financial future of a company. By developing a sense of financial requirements in advance of their occurrence, more alternatives will likely be available. Financial problem solving in a crisis is not a remedy for long-term viability. Banks do not like surprises from their lending customers. They react by either reducing the loan amounts, raising the interest rate, adding restriction on the firm, or not even making the loans at all. Bottlenecks can be recognized early while there is still time to make adjustments. Another reason for planning is to establish some bench marks to measure progress.

2.   The nature of financial planning is to not show too much detail. This is why projects are often grouped into categories. The emphasis is on aggregate accounts. Unless a specific project is exceptionally large, its cash flows are best incorporated with others of a similar nature. Also as the time horizon is extended the precision of individual and small projections becomes blurred.

3.   Typical ways of allowing for an uncertain future are to develop several forecasts and accompanying financial plans. For example, a conservative case, a most likely case, and a strong growth case may be prepared. This is basis for scenario analysis. It provides a range of possible outcomes and alerts management to difficulties that can arise if the best guess case does not happen.

4.   Financial planning is a complex exercise involving many different people. A major concern is problems that arise because each person providing input to the process may not be using the same set of assumptions about key variables that affect the projections being made. For example, one division was expecting a downturn in the economy it would most likely influence the size of their forecasts. Another part of the firm could be highly optimistic about the future and base their projections on strong growth of the market. Other differences in the important variables are found in the expected changes in the cost of living, labor costs, prices of raw materials etc. This is why most financial plans are developed using a set of common assumptions about critical variables that affect the major lines of business of a firm.

5.   Using the information in the problem will develop the following projection:

PRO FORMA INCOME STATEMENT FOR
MATTHEW TYLER STAMPS, Ltd.

(Millions of dollars)

Sales	10.0
Cost of goods sold (70% of sales)	7.0
Gross income	3.0
Operating expenses (10% of sales)	1.0
Interest expense	.40
Earnings before taxes	1.60
Income taxes (40%)	.64
Earnings after taxes	.96

6.	The plug or balancing account is determined by subtracting the liabilities and equity from assets:

$$\$25 \text{ million} - \$20 \text{ million} = \$5 \text{ million}$$

This means projected asset needs exceed the projected financing sources so the firm must raise the difference in order to support the projected level of sales.

7.	The amount of financing required must include a working cash balance. The information given does not specify what MTSL has initially so we must assume that the $1 million for the cash account must be added on to the fund needs making the total requirement as $6 million.

8.	In this case the predicted cash balance would be $3 million. If this is too much, the excess could be used to pay off liabilities, to pay more dividends, to buy more plant, to invest in marketable securities, etc. The point is that the financial manager will be able to provide top management with some pleasant alternatives.

9.	From problem 5 we learned that the net profits were $0.96 million. The payout will be 40 percent of this or $0.384 million. The addition to retained earnings will be $0.96 - $0.384 or $0.576 million. Since MTSL has $2.5 million to start the year, the retained earnings account will be $2.5 + $0.576 = $3.076 million at the end of the next year.

10.	The amount of retained earnings reduces the amount of financing needed. The total amount of retained earnings is a source of financing. It is referred to as internally generated funds.

CHAPTER 19

WORKING CAPITAL MANAGEMENT AND SHORT-TERM PLANNING

INTRODUCTION

The early part of the text is focused on the value creating aspects of business: investment, debt policy, and maybe, dividend policy. While value building is not generally associated with working capital management today, value may be negatively impacted by working capital inefficiencies, illiquidity, and policies adversely affecting customer relationships. This chapter opens with a general discussion of working capital, the net working capital concept, followed by the flow concept of the working capital and cash conversion cycles. The time line is used to discuss these concepts. Instead of a point-in-time, balance sheet perspective, the time line presentation of the cash conversion cycle, etc., puts working capital management into a "flow" perspective. Money flows through the firm and the financial manager must keep it flowing. When the time line lengthens, the balance sheet levels increase, reducing profitability and more financing. Think of a business as a "flow," or in a dynamic sense, rather than from a static, balance sheet perspective.

The second section of the chapter studies the short-term versus long-term financing tradeoffs. Presented with a seasonal variation in asset needs or a long-term trend, how should working capital (current assets) be financed? Short-term financing rates average well below long-term rates, but must be rolled over or refinanced frequently if one is financing permanent working capital needs. Long-term financing costs more but fewer trips to the market are necessary. Three alternative financing strategies are discussed.

The third section of the chapter is directed toward short-term planning using the sources and uses of cash and cash budget formats. Note that the cash budget includes only cash flows. Given a time period, such as a month, cash inflows and outflows are assumed to occur proportionally throughout the month. As we both know, cash inflows and outflows are not even throughout the month. One must shorten the time period considered, such as a week, to plan more specific cash flows.

The last section of the chapter centers on the financing of working capital. From negotiated loans from banks and finance companies to issuing commercial paper in direct financial markets, firms have several options and several "effective rates," for each financing option selected.

LEARNING CHECKLIST

After preparing this chapter you should be able to:

_____1. Understand why a business must invest in working capital and how net working capital finances current assets.

_____2. Show how long-term financing policy affects short-term financing requirements.

_____3. Trace a business's sources and uses of cash and evaluate its need for short-term borrowing.

_____4. Develop a short-term financing plan for future cash needs.

SOURCES OF BUSINESS INFORMATION

Robert Morris Annual Statement Studies. The Robert Morris Annual Statement Studies is an excellent source of medium and small business industry ratios. Covering many industries, classified by size of firm, financial and operating data and financial ratios are provided. A common-size or percentage composition format for balance sheet and income data is excellent.

Government Agencies and Information Search Engines. Two very good search engines will link you to almost all federal and state governmental agencies and information. The World Wide Web Virtual Library: US Government Information Sources (http://www.nttc.edu/gov_res.html) is maintained by the National Technology Transfer Center. It is linked to over 900 government sites, including agencies, Congress, White House, Treasury, Justice Department, and other executive branches, Supreme Court, U.S. Census Bureau, and many more. The FedWorld Information Network, maintained by the Department of Commerce is another massive listings, from federal job availability to the effective Government Information Locator Service. It is located at http://www.fedworld.gov/.

CHAPTER OUTLINE, KEY CONCEPTS AND TERMS

I.   **WORKING CAPITAL**

    A.   **The Components of Working Capital**
        1.   Short-term circulating current assets, invested to support long-term fixed assets, and current liabilities are called working capital.
        2.   Current assets, composed of cash accounts, marketable securities, accounts receivables, and inventories represent an important level of asset investment for business that must be financed. See Table 19.1.
        3.   There are advantages of having plenty of current assets, such as having plenty of ready cash, promoting sales with generous credit terms (accounts receivable), and large amounts of inventories.

4. There are disadvantages of having too much invested in working capital. The profitability of assets is lowered if too much cash assets are idle, too generous credit terms may bring losses, and inventory investments are unable to earn their opportunity rate of return.
5. Current liabilities are short-term obligations to pay suppliers (accounts payable), employees and borrowed funds (accrued expenses), and short-term lenders such as commercial banks.

B. **Working Capital and the Cash Conversion Cycle**
1. The difference between current assets and current liabilities is called **net working capital** (NWC). The term NWC is often used interchangeably with working capital discussed above. NWC is the extent that the circulating current asset pool exceeds the current liabilities and is often thought of as the net liquidity of the business.
2. NWC is also the extent to which current assets is financed by long-term, noncurrent liabilities, sources of financing.
3. Working capital needs fluctuate with changes in sales, changes in credit policies, changes in production techniques, types of products produced, desired finished goods stocks desired, the credit terms of suppliers, the pay periods of employees, and many other variables which are related to business policies, the type of the business, and the external operating environment.
4. Four key dates in the production cycle affect the level of investment in working capital. The longer the periods, the larger the investment. See Figure 19.1.

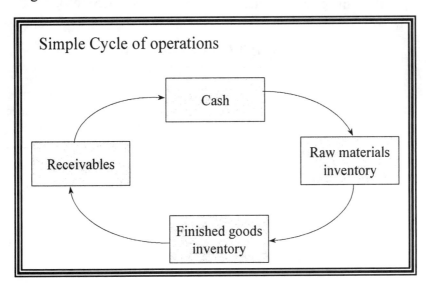

5.	The first time period is the accounts payable period, the length of time the firm has between purchasing materials and the payment date for the materials. The longer the period, the larger the accounts payable balance and the shorter the cash conversion cycle.

6.	The second key period is the inventory period, the time between the purchase of raw materials and the sale of the finished goods. The longer the time period, the greater the investment in inventory.

7.	The third key period is the accounts receivable period, the time period from the sale of the goods (on credit) to when the cash is collected from the customer. Again, the longer the period, the larger the investment in accounts receivable.

8.	The fourth key period is the **cash conversion cycle** or the time between the payment for raw materials and the collection of cash from the customer. Note that the accounts payable period, or the credit offered by suppliers, provides some financing for the working capital cycle, but the longer the cash conversion cycle, the larger the investment in working capital. Cash conversion cycle:

	= (inventory period + receivables period) - accounts payable period

9.	The length of the inventory period is the average inventory divided by the daily cost of sales (CGS/365). The accounts receivable period is the average accounts receivables divided by the daily sales rate (sales/365). The accounts payables period is the average accounts payables divided by the daily cost of goods sold or purchases (CGS/365).

Cash Conversion Cycle

242

C. **The Working Capital Trade-Off**
   1. The cash conversion cycle is influenced by management policies, such as credit policy, levels of inventory, and credit policies of suppliers.
   2. The higher the level of working capital, the *greater* the **carrying costs** or the costs of maintaining current assets, including the opportunity cost of capital to finance the current assets.
   3. The lower the level of working capital, the *greater* the **shortage costs** or the costs incurred from shortages in current assets, such as inventory stock outs and lost sales from a restrictive credit policy.
   4. The financial manager must attempt to minimize the total opposing carrying and shortage costs.

II. **LINKS BETWEEN LONG-TERM AND SHORT-TERM FINANCING**

   A. The cost of total assets in the firm is called the total capital requirement. The total capital requirements change over time, increasing steadily in a growing company, varying seasonally as in lawn and garden stores, and decreasing as a firm is slowly liquidated. See Figure 19.3.

   B. The financial manager has a choice of financing the total capital requirement with debt or equity (discussed earlier) or short-term or long-term financing. *Three* variations of short/long financing are studied here. There is a risk/return tradeoff between the extremes. See Figure 19.4.

   C. The "relaxed strategy" is a conservative, mostly long-term financing with few payoff requirements in the short run. This strategy has considerable cash assets at times and emphasizes liquidity. The current ratio and level of net working capital would be very high, but the return on assets will likely be lower, because this strategy favors liquidity over profitability.

   D. The "restrictive strategy" uses the matched maturity approach and finances long-term assets with long-term financing and short-term assets with short-term financing. At times there will be a high level of short-term financing providing funds for a seasonal increase in inventory and accounts receivable. The current ratio will fluctuate considerably with the seasonal fluctuation in current assets and current liabilities, as will profitability as interest financing rates move up and down. This strategy is more profitability focused, but also more risky. Short-term financing may not always be affordable or available.

   E. The "middle-of-the-road" policy recognizes that a certain minimum level of current asset investment is always present or is permanent. Using the matching policy, the firm would finance the permanent portion of current asset investment with long-term financing and the short-term current asset needs with short-term financing. There are times in the seasonal cycle when the firm will borrow short-term, and there are times when idle funds will be invested in marketable securities waiting for the next seasonal cycle. In this case the firm will use the liquidity from *both* marketable securities and short-term financing.

III. TRACING CHANGES IN CASH AND WORKING CAPITAL

A. Comparing two balance sheets (points in time) enables the financial manager to see the changes or flows that occurred in the period between the two balance sheets.

Example - Dynamic Mattress Company

Assets	1999	2000	Liabilities & Equity	1999	2000
Current Assets	4	5	Current Liabilities		
Cash	4	5	Bank Loans	5	0
Mark Securities	0	5	Accts Payable	20	27
Inventory	26	25	Total Curr Liab	25	27
Accts Recv	25	30	Long Term Debt	5	12
Total Curr Assets	55	65	Net Worth	65	76
Fixed Assets					
Gross investment	56	70			
less Depr	16	20			
Net Fixed Assets	40	50	Total Liab and		
Total Assets	95	115	owner's equity	95	115

B. The sources and uses of cash statement (Table 19.5) are constructed by first noting the change in each of the balance sheet accounts (Table 19.3) and several items from the income statement.

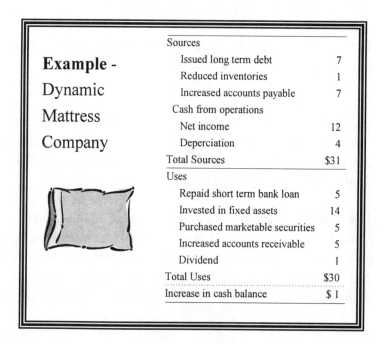

Example - Dynamic Mattress Company

Sources	
Issued long term debt	7
Reduced inventories	1
Increased accounts payable	7
Cash from operations	
Net income	12
Deperciation	4
Total Sources	$31
Uses	
Repaid short term bank loan	5
Invested in fixed assets	14
Purchased marketable securities	5
Increased accounts receivable	5
Dividend	1
Total Uses	$30
Increase in cash balance	$ 1

C. Sources of funds are indicated by the cash flows from operations, decreases in assets, and increases in liability and equity accounts.

D. Uses of funds are indicated by the increases in assets and decreases in liabilities and equity, including dividends paid.

IV. CASH BUDGETING

A. The cash budget estimates sources and uses of funds in future periods and provides information related to future cash needs and a plan for future cash flows.

B. **Cash Inflows**
   1. A sales forecast is the primary independent variable behind a cash budget.
   2. Cash inflows are derived primarily from the collections of accounts receivable which is related to the credit terms, the payment practices of customers, the collection efforts of the firms, and the level of credit sales. An estimate of the collections lag behind sales is an important estimate. See Table 19.6.
   3. Other cash inflows are added to each period considered which could be weekly, monthly, or here, quarterly.

C. **Cash Outflows**
   1. Cash outflow estimates in the coming periods include payments of accounts payables, labor and administrative costs and other expenses, capital expenditures, taxes, interest, principal payments on loans, and dividends.

Example - Dynamic Mattress Company

Dynamic collections on AR

	Qtr			
	1st	2nd	3rd	4th
1. Beginning receivables	30.0	32.5	30.7	38.2
2. Sales	87.5	78.5	116.0	131.0
3. Collections				
. Sales in current Qtr (80%)	70	62.8	92.8	104.8
. Sales in previous Qtr (20%)	15.0	17.5	15.7	23.2
Total collections	85.0	80.3	108.5	128.0
4. Receivables at end of period				
. (4 = 1 + 2 - 3)	$32.5	$30.7	$38.2	$41.2

2.   Delaying payment or stretching payables offers the benefit of saving cash but the cost of discounts missed and possible termination of the supplier relationship.

D.   **The Cash Balance**

1.   The cash budget is usually comprised of a starting cash position in each period, followed by the net cash flow in the period giving the cash at the end of the period.

2.   A minimum cash balance is assumed and a cumulative cash surplus or shortage (borrowing needed) balance is estimated. The changes in the cumulative account is caused by the net cash flow in each period adjusted for borrowing and lending. See Table 19.8.

Example - Dynamic Mattress Company

Dynamic short term financing requirements

Cash at start of period	5	- 40	- 55	- 29
+ Net cash flow	- 45	- 15	+ 26	+ 35
= Cash at end of period	- 40	- 55	- 29	+ 6
Min operating cash balance	5	5	5	5
Cumulative short term financing required (minimum cash balance minus caash at end of period)	$45	$60	$34	- $1

V.   **A SHORT-TERM FINANCING PLAN**

A.   The options for short-term financing include trade credit (accounts payable), accruals (delay in the receipt of services such as labor before payment), and negotiated, short-term borrowing.

B.   Stretching payables is costly if discounts are missed, but must be compared with taking the discounts and financing the early payments at the bank.

VI. SOURCES OF SHORT-TERM FINANCING

A. Bank Loans

1. A business interested in bank financing should establish a **line of credit** with the bank, an agreement by a bank that a company may borrow at any time up to an established limit.

Example - Dynamic Mattress Company- *Financing Plan*

	Qtr			
	1st	2nd	3rd	4th
Cash Requirements				
1. Cash for operations	45	15	- 26	- 35
2. Interest on bank loan	0	.8	.8	.6
3. Interest on stretechd payables	0	0	.8	0
4. Total cash required	45	15.8	- 24.4	- 34.4
Cash Raised				
5. Bank loan	40	0	0	0
6. Stretched payables	0	15.8	0	0
7. Securities sold	5	0	0	0
8. Total cash raised	45	15.8	0	0
Repayments				
9. Of stretched payables	0	0	15.8	0
10. Of line of credit	0	0	8.6	31.4
Increase in cash balances				
11. Addition to cash balances	0	0	0	3
Line of credit				
12. Beginning of quarter	0	40	40	31.4
13. End of quarter	40	40	31.4	0

2. A revolving credit arrangement is a line of credit that establishes, for a fee to the bank, a level of credit that the business may borrow at any time during the period.

3. Lines of credit may be associated with a minimum deposit balance requirement for the business called a compensating balance. Compensating balances, because they force the business to borrow more or use less of the loan, may increase the effective cost of the loan.

B. Commercial Paper

1. A larger business with a high quality credit rating may issue short-term, unsecured notes, called **commercial paper**, in financial markets.

2. The credit quality of commercial paper is enhanced by backup lines of credit from commercial banks, which would provide loans to the borrowing business to pay-off the commercial paper if credit problems arose and new commercial paper could not be sold to the market.

C. **Secured Loans**
    1.   Current assets such as inventory and accounts receivables are often used as security for business loans.
    2.   Accounts receivables may be pledged or assigned as security for a loan or sold or factored to shorten the cash conversion cycle.
    3.   Standardized, identifiable inventory, such as autos, make excellent collateral for loans, whereas perishable low value items are less likely to serve as security for a loan.
    4.   A lender must establish some control over inventory pledge for a loan. The lender may have a general lien on inventory, hold title as with autos, store in a warehouse away from the business, or set certain inventory items aside in a field warehouse to limit access by the borrower.

VII. THE COST OF BANK LOANS

A. **Bank Loan Terms**
    1.   The loan rate may be fixed or constant during the loan term, or...
    2.   The loan rate may vary (variable) based on changes in a specific market rate or rate index.

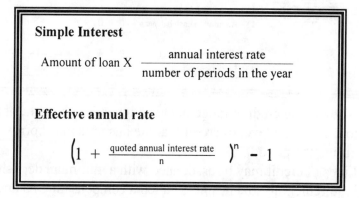

Simple Interest

$$\text{Amount of loan} \times \frac{\text{annual interest rate}}{\text{number of periods in the year}}$$

Effective annual rate

$$\left(1 + \frac{\text{quoted annual interest rate}}{n}\right)^n - 1$$

B. **Interest Rate Calculations**
    1.   Interest charged and paid at the end of each interest period is called simple interest and is calculated as principal x periodic rate(annual rate/number of interest periods in a year) x time.
    2.   Compound interest involves monthly interest not paid each month being added to the principal and charged interest the next month. The effective rate of interest is higher than the simple rate because of the compounding of interest on interest. The effective rate is $(1 + \text{periodic rate})^n - 1$. A stated simple rate of 12 per cent compounded monthly (paid at end of year) would have an effective rate of $(1 + .12/12)^{12} - 1$ or 12.68 per cent. The one in the equation is the compounder, representing any amount of loan.
    3.   Loans with discount interest terms means the lender subtracts the entire interest amount at the beginning, lessening the amount of borrowed

principal received or requiring the borrower to borrow more to net the amount needed. The effective rate on a discounted loan is higher than a non-discounted loan.

C. **Interest With Compensating Balances**
1. Compensating balances represent added deposits in the bank as requirements for the loan.
2. Compensating balances increase the amount borrowed (increase idle funds in a deposit account) and the effective rate of borrowing because it increases the amount of interest paid each period per the amount of usable funds, or:

Effective Rate (Comp.Balances) =

$$[(1 + \text{actual interest paid} \div \text{borrowed funds available})^n - 1]$$

COMPLETION QUESTIONS

1. Capital budgeting and capital structure are (*long-/short-*) term financial decisions which (*are/are not*) easily reversed.

2. Short-term assets and liabilities are called _____ _____.

3. Trade credit and/or consumer credit extended by a firm is reflected in its accounts (*payable/receivable*).

4. The cash conversion cycle is equal to the inventory period (*minus/plus*) the receivables period (*minus/plus*) the accounts payable period.

5. The inventory period is also called the (*days'/years'*) sales in inventory.

6. Costs of maintaining current assets, including opportunity costs, are called _____ costs.

7. Shortage costs are incurred when the levels of different current assets are too (*high/low*).

8. Assets like plant and equipment are usually financed with (*long-/short-*) term sources.

9. In an extension of the matching principle, most firms finance (*permanent/temporary*) working capital requirements with long-term sources.

10. An increase in accounts (*payable/receivable*) is a source of funds.

11. When a firm uses cash to buy inventory, net working capital will (*decrease/increase/stay the same*).

12. Cash inflows come from (*collections of accounts receivable/credit sales*).

13. Stretching payables or delaying payment is a (*source/use*) of financing.

14. If suppliers offer discounts for prompt payment it is likely that stretching payables due to these vendors will be a very (*cheap/expensive*) financing source.

15. The simplest and most common source of short-term financing is (*secured/unsecured*) bank loans.

16. An agreement by a bank to permit a company to borrow at any time up to an established limit is called (*a line of/trade*) credit.

17. A revolving line of credit is usually for a (*longer/shorter*) time period compared to a line of credit.

18. A compensating balance requirement will (*lower/raise*) the effective cost to the borrower.

19. Commercial paper is issued (*by large, safe, and well-known firms/in bath rooms*).

20. A firm may raise funds by selling its accounts receivable to a financial institution known as a _____.

21. A field warehouse is an arrangement used in (*inventory/unsecured*) financing.

PROBLEMS

1. Indicate how each of the following transactions will affect cash and net working capital by using + for an increase, - for a decrease, or 0 for no change:
   a. Federal income tax due for the previous year is paid.
   b. A fixed asset is sold for less than book value.
   c. Merchandise is sold on credit.
   d. Short-term notes receivable are sold to pay off short-term notes payable.

2. Musselman Kennels had sales for the months of January through April of $150, $100, $120, and $200, respectively. The firm receives cash payments of 10 percent in the month of sale, 60 percent one month later and the remaining 30 percent two months after the sale. What will be the cash inflows for April?

3. Tell how each of the following transactions will affect the current ratio (CR) and the net profits (NP) by using + for an increase, - for a decrease, and 0 for no change. Assume the current ratio is above one before each transaction.
    a. A fixed asset is sold for more than book value.
    b. Payment is made to trade creditors for previous purchases.
    c. Cash is obtained through bank short-term bank loans.
    d. Advances are made to employees.

4. Refer to the balance sheet and income statements used at the beginning of the problems for Chapter 18 of this Study Guide and prepare a Sources and Uses of Funds statement for JJAJC.

5. Rosenfeld, Inc. has a line of credit at 12 percent and a compensating balance requirement of 20 percent. How much will it need to borrow on the credit line if it needs $100,000?

6. Suppose another bank makes an offer to Rosenfeld for a line of credit without a compensating balance requirement. However, the interest rate would be 14 percent. Which bank is offering the best interest rate?

7. What is the cash conversion cycle? What is the purpose of this concept in working capital management?

8. Explain what the effect of each of the following actions would likely be on the cash conversion cycle:
    a. Implementation of just-in-time techniques in the production process.
    b. Addition of staff to the accounts receivable department who will focus their attention on managing the collection process.
    c. Obtain agreement from major suppliers that allows 45 days payment instead of 30 days as has been the practice.

9. David's Computer Graphic's, Inc. had sales of $100,000 last year. The cost of goods sold was $60,000. The firm's average inventory, receivables, and payables during the year were $5,000, $10,000. and $9,000, respectively. What was David's cash conversion cycle?

10. Austin's firm pays its suppliers on the 15th day after receiving the invoice. What share of purchases will be paid:
    a. In the current quarter?
    b. In the following quarter?

ANSWERS TO COMPLETION QUESTIONS

1. long, are not
2. working capital
3. receivable
4. plus, minus
5. days'
6. carrying
7. low
8. long
9. permanent
10. payable
11. stay the same
12. collections of accounts receivable
13. source
14. expensive
15. unsecured
16. line of
17. longer
18. raise
19. by large, safe and well-known firms
20. factor
21. inventory

SOLUTIONS TO PROBLEMS

1. This problem will test knowledge of accounting. The answers below show the sign for change in the cash balance and the net working capital (NWC), respectively.
    a. - cash and 0 NWC. Federal income tax due is a current liability. It will drop by the same amount as the cash paid out.
    b. + cash and + NWC. Cash will increase from the sale and liabilities are unchanged.
    c. 0 cash and + NWC. Assuming this is a profitable company, they will sell items for above cost. The latter amount is the inventory value so the accounts receivable will increase by more than the decline in inventory. Cash and liabilities are not affected.
    d. 0 cash and 0 NWC. The notes receivable will decline by the same amount as the notes payable.

2. In April, 10 percent of that month's sales or $20 will be collected. Also 60 percent of the March sales or $72 will be received in cash. The other cash inflow will be 30 percent of February sales which is $30. The total for April will be $20 + $72 + $30 or $122.

3. a. + CR and + NP. Cash is the only current account to be affected and by definition, the transaction was profitable.
    b. + CR and 0 NP. Cash and accounts payable will decrease by the same amount but the ratio of current assets to current liabilities will increase. This is difficult to see without assuming amounts for the cash account and the accounts payable before and after the transaction. As the problem states, the beginning current ratio was above 1 so the end ratio will increase.

    c. - CR and 0 NP. This transaction has the opposite effect on the current ratio by the same logic as described in part b. above. Again profits are not impacted by the transaction.
    d. 0 CR and 0 NP. Cash will decrease by the same amount that the other current asset account (advances to employees) increases. Nothing else is affected.

4. Decreases in assets and increases in liabilities and/or equity are sources of funds. Increases in assets and decreases in liabilities and/or equity are uses of funds. From these relationships the following statement can be prepared:

Sources and Uses of Funds for JJAJC
(Millions of dollars)

Sources of funds

Decrease in cash	4
Increase in accumulated depreciation	2
Increase in accounts payable	5
Increase in notes payable	4
Increase in other current liabilities	2
Increase in bonds	3
Increase in common stock	6
Total	26

Uses of funds

Increase in accounts receivable	2
Increase in inventory	4
Increase in plant and equipment	15
Decrease in retained earnings	4
Total	26

5. Since the firm can use only 80 percent of the amount borrowed it will need to arrange for a loan that is higher. Let X = the amount needed. Then:

$$0.8X = \$100,000$$
$$X = \$125,000$$

6. The effective interest rate offered by the bank with the compensating balance requirement is 12/.8 or 15 percent. Rosenfeld should choose the bank without the compensating balance requirement since the interest rate is only 14 percent.

7. The cash conversion cycle represents the time and amount of funds tied up in inventory and receivables less the time funds are provided by suppliers. It equals the days in inventory plus the days in accounts receivable minus the days in account payable. Focusing attention on the cash conversion cycle helps the financial manager to identify ways of shortening the time it takes for cash to make the cycle from purchases of materials to collections from sales of the finished goods..

8. a. Just-in-time is an important technique that involves having suppliers of raw materials deliver those items at the same time they are needed in the production process. The goal of passing the goods through the production process with minimal waiting time cuts the investment in inventory and thereby reduces the cash conversion cycle.
   b. The additional personnel will speed up collections which will reduce the investment in accounts receivable. This will also shorten the cash conversion cycle.
   c. Stretching out the time when accounts payable must be paid has the effect of securing additional financing from suppliers. This helps to reduce the cash conversion cycle.

9.   The cash conversion cycle is computed from the accounts receivable period, the inventory period, and the accounts payable period.

Accounts receivable period = ($10,000/$100,000) × 365
$$= 36.5 \text{ days}$$

Inventory period = ($5,000/$60,000) × 365
$$= 30.4 \text{ days}$$

Accounts payable period = ($9,000/$60,000) × 365
$$= 54.8 \text{ days}$$

The cash conversion cycle = (36.5 + 30.4) - 54.8
$$= 12.1 \text{ days}$$

10.   a.   The 15 day period is 1/6 of a quarter so 5/6 or 83.3 percent will be paid in the current quarter.

b.   The remaining 1/6 or 16.7 percent will be paid in the following quarter.

CASH AND INVENTORY MANAGEMENT

INTRODUCTION

This is the first chapter of a two-part section entitled "Short-Term Financial Decisions." Cash and inventory investment considerations are discussed here; accounts receivables are covered in the next chapter. The level of cash and inventories are investment decisions that are approached in similar ways. Financial managers are seeking returns on added investment that exceed the opportunity cost of capital. The optimal cash level provides liquidity and operational support. Too little cash and securities selling or borrowing costs are incurred. Too much cash in the bank or in the mail and profitability ratios (ROA) are adversely affected. Inventory levels, whether related to raw material, work in progress, or finished goods are approached in the same way. Too little and stock outs (opportunity cost of lost margins) and production down-time increases. Too much and efficiency is hindered.

The opposing cost decision models discussed here are similar for cash and inventory. The optimal point is that level that minimizes the sum of the two opposing costs.

Working capital balances have a tendency to increase quickly to control limits. Sales wants ready inventory and generous credit, production managers want to avoid down-time. As the cash cycle time increases, so does the level of investment and the eventual conflict between the financial manager or credit manager and production and sales.

The "flow" concepts developed in the last chapter related to working capital management are extended here. The business is a constant flow of values and managers must work to shorten and reduce the time line (reduce the level) needed to serve the capital assets.

LEARNING CHECKLIST

After studying this chapter you should be able to:

_____1. Define the various types of float, how it arises, and how it can be controlled.

_____2. Calculate the value of changes in float.

_____3. Understand the costs and benefits of holding inventories.

_____4. List the costs and benefits of holding cash balances.

_____5. Understand how cost minimizing models are applied to both inventory and cash investments.

SOURCES OF BUSINESS INFORMATION

CPI Detailed Report. What are the housing costs in Denver? How much has clothing costs changed in the last five years? All these rather practical questions and others may be answered from the CPI Detailed Report, a monthly periodical published by the Bureau of Labor Statistics, U.S. Department of Labor and available, if not in your library, from the Government Printing Office near you. The CPI Detailed Report provides a complete breakdown of the popular Consumer Price Index. By category, by geographical location, the prices of new goods and services are indexed each month. It is an important reference for keeping up with inflation levels and adjusting data for the effects of inflation. CPI information is also available online from the Department of Labor web site.

THOMAS--U.S. Congress on the Internet. Want to know the current status of a bill in Congress or look over the current version of a bill. Find it at THOMAS (http://thomas.loc.gov/). Perhaps you would like to view the work of previous Congresses from 1973 to current. Want to see what your congressperson said on a bill? Find it in the Congressional Record. Is their a bill in Committee that you would like to follow? Perhaps you would like to read the Declaration of Independence again?? Find it in the Historical Documents section of this great web site!

CHAPTER OUTLINE, KEY CONCEPTS AND TERMS

I. **CASH COLLECTION, DISBURSEMENT, AND FLOAT**

    A. Businesses keep their cash in the form of bank deposits and pay and receive funds via checks and other forms of value transfer.

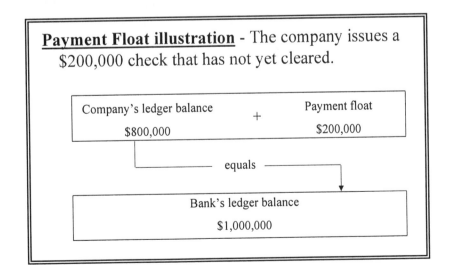

B.   Because checks must be physically presented to the bank for payment, there are lags or delays in the movement of checks through a business, through the mail, and through the bank clearing system.

C.   **Float**
1.   The lag or delay in the check delivery and clearing system is called float.
2.   When a company has written a check on its bank account and mailed the payment, it deducts the balance from its checking ledger. **Payment float** is the time lag between the time the check was sent to when it is presented against (debited) the checking account. The bank account balance (recorded by the bank) is the sum of the business' ledger balance plus the float, or the float is the difference between the bank's balance and the checkbook's balance.

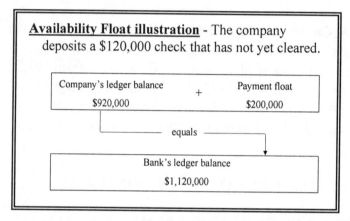

3.   When checks are deposited, the funds are often not immediately available. This lag or time delay is called **availability float**. The bank delays the availability because its funds availability is delayed when it sends the check to the Federal Reserve Bank or other bank for clearing. The company's bank balance is the sum of what is available plus what is deferred for a time (availability float).

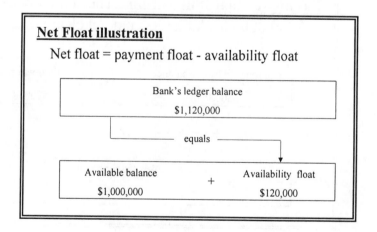

4.   The **net float** for a business is the payment float less the availability float or the funds the firm has paid but has not cleared less the funds due the business but deferred by the bank.

D.   **Valuing Float**
1.   Float has a value because of the opportunity cost of funds. Money due the firm cannot be invested until "available," and checks sent to suppliers but still "floating" may be used or invested until the check is presented at the bank.
2.   Payment float results from the delay between writing a check and the reduction in the checking account. The level of payment float is related to the *size* of the average check and the *length* (days) of the float. The payment float is the product of the average daily checks written times the number of days float. The benefit of the payment float to the business is the total float times the opportunity rate of return for the period. The availability float is a cost to the receiving firm and the cost is the total float (average deposits delayed times the number of days delayed) times the opportunity rate of return. A business may have a net payment or net availability float.
3.   Reducing the float provides (availability float) or reduces (payment float) the net float saving (costing) the business a *one time* amount of funds available or lost for investment. The present value of a permanent reduction in net availability float is the amount by which the float is reduced.

Managing Float

II.   **MANAGING FLOAT**

A.   Several kinds of delays or floats occur in the check payment system: mail, processing, and clearing as depicted in Figure 20.1.

B.	The sum of the three floats above are associated with receiving a payment: the mailing time, the company processing time to get the check to the bank, and the clearing (availability) delays of the banking system.

C.	Efforts to speed up collections are usually countered by efforts by payers to delay disbursements, but the Federal Reserve System is dedicated to reducing clearing float.

D.	**Speeding Up Collections**
	1.	**Concentration banking**, a system of regional collection centers which transfers balances to one bank, is one method of speeding up collections and reducing mail, processing, and clearing float.
	2.	Concentration banking reduces mail float and clearing float, because the depository bank is located close to the paying customer.
	3.	Consolidating many balances in a single bank for possible overnight investment is a good cash management technique.
	4.	Balances may be transferred via the bank wire system or through the use of depository transfer checks.
	5.	A **lock-box system** directs the customer to make payments to a post office box, the bank picks up the mail, quickly processes the check into the clearing system, and the customer posting is finished last.
	6.	A lock-box system reduces float, increases investable funds which may now earn a rate of return, but is profitable only if the annual added rate of return exceeds the annual cost of the lock-box.

E.	**Controlling Disbursements**
	1.	Controlling disbursements is a process for lengthening the payment float or time it takes a mailed check to a supplier to reach the payer's bank.
	2.	Remote disbursement, or mailing checks from a location distant from the supplier lengthens the mail float portion of the payment float. The clearing float may be lengthened by writing checks on banks in remote geographic areas far away from Federal Reserve Banks or larger clearing banks.
	3.	A **zero-balance account**, or account to which a paying business keeps only the daily amount of checks presented, may be a part of the remote disbursement system.

F. Electronic Funds Transfer
   1. Computerized automation has enhanced our ability to manager cash. Since funds can be transferred electronically from one account to another, many new issues arise. Each issue is good, or bad, depending on what side of the transaction you assume.
   2. An almost paperless transfer can occur. Unfortunately, paperless can also be difficult to trace.
   3. Electronic transfers occur instantly. Unfortunately, some firm's rely on the snails pace of normal cash transfers and check clearing.

   4. The cost of an electronic transfer is also much lower than traditional methods. Unfortunately, or should we say curiously, banks often charge more for these cheaper and more efficient transactions.

III. INVENTORIES AND CASH BALANCES

A. Cash and inventory are similar in that to have them costs money and to not have enough costs money. Excess working capital reduces the return on assets; too little working capital loses sales, slows production, and chances illiquidity. The same analytical techniques used to assess the "right" balance that minimizes the total cost may be used with both inventory and cash management.

B. Cash management is a tradeoff of having too little cash and possibly incurring cost of selling interest-bearing securities, paying commissions, and taking losses, to having too much cash in an idle, non-earning account.

C. Inventory management has similar tradeoffs. Too little inventory minimizes carrying costs but customer service and missed sales hurt the business. Too much investment in inventory maximizes sales, but requires added capital and incurs carrying costs.

D. **Managing Inventories**
   1. Carrying costs increase as inventory investment increases; ordering costs decrease as fewer orders are made during a period of time.
   2. The **economic order quantity** is a cost minimization model which computes the EOQ which minimizes total inventory costs, the sum of carrying and ordering costs. The EOQ is the square root of the product of two times the total inventory used in a period (sales) times the cost per order divided by the carrying cost.

$$\text{Economic Order Quantity} = \sqrt{\frac{2 \times \text{annual sales} \times \text{cost per order}}{\text{carrying cost}}}$$

E. **Managing Inventories of Cash: The Baumol Model**
1. The Baumol model applies the EOQ model to cash management and determines the amount of securities to be sold at one time to replenish cash accounts. The business is assumed to have its cash resources in either non-earning cash(checking account) or short-term securities. At an assumed rate of cash usage, an assumed interest rate on the securities, and a cost of selling the securities (note opposing costs of earning and selling), there is a level of securities one must sell each time to minimize the total costs of cash versus securities.
2. The Baumol model calculates the optimum amount of securities to be sold as the square root of two times the annual cash disbursements times the cost per sale of securities divided by the earning interest rate on securities. The total costs of trading securities versus the opportunity costs of having cash and not securities are minimized at the Q^*.

Determination of optimal order size

F. **Uncertain Cash Flows: The Miller-Orr Model**
1. The Baumol model assumes a certain, steady cash outflow without any random variations. The Miller-Orr model considers cash inflows and outflows with random, unpredictable changes.
2. The Miller-Orr model establishes a permissible range of cash balances and actions (sell/buy securities) that only occur if an upper/lower balance is reached. The range between the upper and lower limits is established by three factors: daily variance of cash flows, cost of buying or selling securities, and the rate of interest on the securities.
3. When the daily variation in cash flow is small, the cost of buying/selling low, or the interest rate high, the upper/lower limits should be narrow. With the variation low, it will seldom hit the limits. With the trading cost low, it will not cost much to buy (upper limit) or sell (lower limit).

Finally, with interest rates high the cost of high cash balances encourages a narrow range.

4. The return point (replenished cash level) in the Miller-Orr model is one-third of the range up from the lower limit (point where one would sell securities), making it more likely to hit the lower limit.

5. The Miller-Orr model return point minimizes the sum of transaction costs and opportunity interest costs (money not made by being in cash).

G. **Cash Management in the Largest Corporations**
1. For large balances normally associated with large businesses, the cost of selling securities to replenish cash is a very low proportional cost, so the average cash balance should normally be quite low.

2. Large firms do hold cash balances as compensating balances for banking services and, with many decentralized plants and divisions operating around the country, each with a bank account, the balances sum to a rather large amount.

3. Efficient cash management implies that centralization of balances for efficient investment or allocation is necessary.

H. **Investing Idle Cash: The Money Market**
1. When excess cash is present, securities are purchased. When funds are needed, securities are sold. The securities normally used for temporary investments are usually purchased in the **money market** where short-term, high quality, marketable securities are traded.

2. When cash needs are known, securities of specific short-term maturity may be selected. If cash is needed, money market securities may be sold quickly, and because there is little price variability if market interest rates change, the cost of selling the securities is kept at a minimum.

3. One choice of short-term, high quality investment is commercial paper, the short-term notes (maturities usually less than 270 days) issued by industrial and financial corporations.

4. Certificates of deposits (CDS) are short-term notes issued by commercial banks.

5. Repurchase agreements (repos), the purchase of securities under agreement to resell (at a higher price), are issued by commercial banks when the checking account of the business is higher than desired. The money stays in the bank and the business has a temporary earning investment.

COMPLETION QUESTIONS

1. In principle, companies want to hold cash balances up to the point where the value of additional liquidity is equal to the value of interest (*earned/foregone*).

2. The amount of funds represented by checks written that (*have/have not*) cleared is called payment float.

3. Checks deposited that have not cleared is called _____ float.

4. When payment float exceeds availability float a firm will have a (*negative/positive*) net float.

5. To minimize having too much cash on hand the financial manager should maximize (*availability/payment*) float.

6. A principle of cash management is to (*slow down/speed up*) collections and to (*slow down/speed up*) payments.

7. Retail stores can reduce delays from receiving payments by encouraging customers to use (*credit/debit*) cards.

8. Preauthorized payments with customers are arrangements used by companies to (*decrease/increase*) float.

9. A system that has customers make payments to a bank in the customers' geographic area and then has the bank transfer the funds to one of that firm's principal banks is called (*concentration/investment*) banking.

10. Preprinted depository transfer checks are (*faster/slower*) than wire transfers.

11. A system that has customers sending payments to a local post office box so that a local bank can process the checks is called a _____ - _____.

12. Remote disbursement is a method of (*decreasing/increasing*) payment float.

13. In a zero-balance account, funds flow (*from/to*) the firms's concentration account (*from/to*) its disbursement account.

14. Inventory management is similar to cash management in that there is a _____ between costs and benefits from holding a balance.

15. Total costs of inventory are equal to carrying costs (*minus/plus*) order costs.

16. The order size that minimizes total inventory costs is called the _____ _____ quantity.

17. The time that it takes to place an order and have it delivered should be incorporated into the (*economic order quantity/reorder point*).

18. Just-in-time inventory management systems involve (*almost no/substantial*) safety stocks.

19. According to the Baumol model for determining optimal cash balances, higher interest rates available on liquid investments will (*lower/raise*) the optimal level cash balances.

20. In the Miller and Orr model of cash management, the cash balance is allowed to vary within certain limits. When it reaches the maximum, securities are (*bought/sold*) to bring the cash level to its return point.

21. According to the Miller and Orr model, spread between upper and lower limits is (*directly/inversely*) proportional to transaction costs and uncertainty of the cash flow pattern and (directly/inversely) related to the level of interest rates on liquid securities.

22. If the cost of borrowing is high relative to the return on liquid investments, firms should borrow relatively (*less/more*).

23. Large firms should favor (*centralized/decentralized*) bank accounts.

24. The market for fixed income securities with maturities of less than one-year is called the (*capital/money*) market.

25. Appropriate investments for amounts of temporary, idle cash are(*long-/short-*) term securities because they have little interest rate risk and are issued by organizations having (*considerable/little*) financial strength.

26. _____ agreements are in effect loans that are collateralized with Treasury bills.

PROBLEMS

1. DRD Corp. has a ledger balance of $80,000 in its bank checking account at the end of the day; has written and mailed three checks today totaling $35,000; and yesterday deposited two checks totaling $15,000. The bank will credit DRD Corp.'s account for the deposits tomorrow.
   a. What is the current checking account ledger balance of DRD?
   b. What is DRD Corp.'s current bank balance according to the bank?
   c. What is the payment float of DRD Corp.?

d. What is the availability float of DRD Corp.?

e. What is the current net float of DRD Corp.?

2. ATM Corp. has just called the bank and was told that their current bank balance was $54,000. The current ledger balance of their account is $42,000 and $15,000 in checks were recently mailed. No other checks are outstanding. No other deposits have been made recently. What is the likely amount of yesterday's deposit which has not yet been made available at the bank? What is the net float of ATM Corp.?

3. Zoo Corp. has a checking account ledger balance of $41,000, and after calling the bank, found that the bank balance was $47,000. A deposit of $5,000 was made this morning and has not yet been credited by the bank. What explains the difference between the bank balance of Zoo Corp. and their ledger balance?

4. In an attempt to reduce mail, processing, and availability float, AU Corp. is considering a lock-box arrangement with First National Bank. With a current annual rate of investment return of 6% available on any funds made available from the lock-box system, a cost $25 per day on currently used depository transfer checks, AU Corp. estimates that it can reduce its float by two days with the lock-box system. The bank charges $10 per day for the lock-box system. What is the break-even amount of collections per day that would equate the new lock-box system with the current depository transfer check system? (**Hint**: The break-even amount made available for investment at a daily rate (365 day year) that would equal the $25 cost of the current depository transfer system.)

5. With reference to the question above, if AU Corp. has a daily receipts amount of $125,000, should they adopt the new lock-box system?

6. Heather is reviewing a lock-box proposal just presented to her by a local bank. The lock-box system is designed to reduce the mail, check processing, and availability float of the 95 checks received daily by Heather's firm, Dolls, Inc. The average invoice is $800, the current annual rate on invested funds is 10%, and it estimated that the lock-box system will save three days float for Dolls, Inc. The bank charges $.30 per check processing fee for the service. What is the estimated daily savings with the new lock-box system? What should Anna recommend? (**Hint**: One must compare the added return on the cash made available compared to the bank charges for the new system).

7. In the question above, what is the minimum reduction in float time to collect and process the checks of Anna's business that is needed to justify the adoption of the new lock-box system?

8. One year ago, Allstar, Inc. began disbursing checks to suppliers from a small bank in Montana. The annual amount of disbursements was $20 million dollars with 10,000 checks. Assuming an annual investment rate of 8% on investable funds made available, an extension of Allstar's float by six days, and a cost of the check disbursement system of $7,000 per year plus $.15 per check processed, has this been a profitable venture by Allstar? Assume a 205 business day year.

9. In the question above, what is the value of the increase in float if the benefits are expected to be permanent? Are there any other costs of this system that Allstar should consider?

10. Jason's Computer center uses 515 boxes of paper every year, but has limited space and some pilferage so the carrying costs per box is estimated at $2 per box. The average cost per order each time new paper is ordered is estimated to be $15.03.
   a. What is the economic order quantity (EOQ) that minimizes total ordering and carrying costs?
   b. How many orders should the computer center place per year?
   c. What is the average inventory of paper in the computer center?
   d. As order costs, carrying costs, and total usage increases, what is the effect on the EOQ?

11. Financial Corp. has an erratic cash flow pattern that offers an opportunity to invest in money market securities, and once in a while, a need to sell the money market securities to meet obligations. The current investment rate in money market securities is 6 percent and the cost of selling securities is currently $34.70 per sale. The firm pays out cash at the rate of $2,000,000 per month. Using the Baumol Model, what is the optimal amount of securities that should be sold each time to minimize the cost of investing cash?

12. With reference to the question above, as interest rates and security transaction charges increase, what is the impact on the optimal level of securities to sell each time cash is needed? What are the assumptions of the Baumol Model?

13. With reference to the Financial Corp. above, and now including an assumed variability of cash inflows and outflows (Miller/Orr Model), if the standard deviation of cash flows is $8000 and the minimum cash balance is $150,000,
   a. Calculate the spread between the upper and lower cash balance limits?
   b. Calculate the upper limit where securities would be purchased (upper) and the lower limits where securities would be sold. **Hint**: Assume a 365 day year.

14. With reference to the question above, what is the impact of lower interest rates, increased variability of cash flows, and a decrease in securities transaction costs on Financial Corp.'s cash balance.

15. The cost of keeping cash balances is the interest opportunity cost of securities, now 6 percent. If the bank borrowing cost, should cash be needed, is 10 percent, the cash balances should be adjusted to a level so that the probability of borrowing from the bank is what?

ANSWERS TO COMPLETION QUESTIONS

1.   foregone
2.   have not
3.   availability
4.   positive
5.   payment
6.   speed up, slow down
7.   debit
8.   decrease
9.   concentration
10. slower
11. lock-box
12. increasing
13. from
14. tradeoff
15. plus
16. economic order
17. reorder point
18. almost no
19. lower
20. bought
21. directly, inversely
22. less
23. centralized
24. money
25. short-
26. Repurchase

SOLUTIONS TO PROBLEMS

1.   The checkbook ledger balance (an asset account) of DRD Corp. differs from its bank balance by the net float (amount of outstanding checks and deposits not yet credited to the bank balance). DRD has debited (added) the amount of its deposits and has credited (subtracted) the amount of checks written to determine its ledger balance.

a. DRD Corp.'s ledger balance is its current checkbook balance of $80,000.
b. The bank balance equals DRD ledger balance minus deposits not yet credited by the bank plus checks written, not yet cleared.

Bank Balance = $80,000 - $15,000 + $35,000 = $100,000

c. The payment float represents checks written by DRD Corp. that have not cleared or $35,000.
d. The availability float or checks already deposited that have not yet been posted to the account is $15,000.
e. The net float is the payment float (outstanding checks) less the availability floats (unavailable deposits) or $35,000 less $15,000 or $20,000. When positive net float is a net payment float (ledger < bank); if negative, a net availability float (ledger > bank).

2. The amount of yesterday's deposit was $3,000. The difference between ATM's ledger (checkbook) balance and bank balance is the net float, which is the difference between the payment float and the availability float (the deposit).

Bank - Ledger = Net Float = Payment Float - Availability Float

$54,000 - $42,000 = $12,000 = $15,000 - Availability Float (Deposit)

Availability Float (Deposit) = $3,000

Another way?   Use the standard checkbook reconciliation method:

$54,000 Bank balance
+$3,000 Deposit made, not credited by bank
$57,000 Bank balance before outstanding checks
-$15,000 Checks written, not cleared
$42,000 ATM ledger (checkbook) balance

3. The difference between Zoo Corp.'s ledger (checkbook) balance and the balance recorded by the bank is the net float, the net amount of checks written by Zoo (deducted from their ledger account), but not yet back to the bank, and the deposit made by Zoo (and added to their checkbook amount), but not yet credited to their account by the bank. The difference between the bank balance and ledger balance, $6,000, is not explained by the $5,000 deposit. Zoo has checks outstanding or payment float of $11,000 which has been deducted from their ledger account and a $5,000 deposit which they have added to their account. The net difference, $6,000, is the difference between the bank and ledger balances.

Bank - Ledger = Net Float = Payment Float - Availability Float

$47,000 - $41,000 = $6,000 = Payment Float - $5,000

Payment Float = $11,000

4. The daily interest savings (rate x time x amount?) on some amount of funds made available by the new lock-box system must cover the daily cost of the lock-box system and equal the $25 current charge of the depository transfer check system.

Break-even = net cost of lock-box = cost of depository checks
If "x" equals the size of daily cash transfers;

$(.06/365)\ (2\ days)\ (x) - \$10.00 = \$25.00$

$.0001644\ (2)\ (x) = \$35.00$

$x = \$106,458$

The break-even daily cash flow made available and invested for two days plus $10 necessary to match the cost of the current payment process is $106,458.

5. With any average cash disbursement above $106,458 the new lock-box system should be adopted. The added investment return ($125,000 x 2 days x .06/365)

$125,000\ x\ 2\ x\ .06/365 - \$10.00 = \$31.09$ net daily return

The $31.10 added daily profit exceeds the $25 daily cost of the prior depository transfer check by $56.10. The new lock-box system is advantageous. The bank could charge up to $16.09 per day for the lock-box system before AU Corp. would go back to its current system.

$\$125,000(2)(.06/365) - x = \$25.00$

$x = \$16.09$

6. Average number of daily payments to lock-box = 95

Average size of payment = $800

Rate of interest/day = .10/365 = .0002739

Float savings with new system = 3 days

The daily savings is the added interest return on the funds available less the cost of the lock-box system.

95 items/day x $800/item x 3 days = $228,000 funds available for investment.

$228,000 x .0002739 = $62.45 investment return/day

The daily cost of the lock-box system proposed is 95 items/day x $.30/check charge = $28.50. The daily earnings from the cash made available, $62.47, exceeds the daily cost of the proposed lock-box system. The new system should be adopted.

7. The break-even point float time saved is the number of days float saved that just equals the daily cost of the system or $28.50.

Solve for the unknown, Days

95 items/day x $800/item x Days x .0002739 = $28.50

20.8219 Days = $28.50

Days = 1.37

A float reduction of 1.4 days or 33 hours will cover the charges for the lock-box system.

8. The analysis compares the investment return on the invested cash emanating from delayed disbursement to the cost of the delayed-disbursement system.

Daily Disbursement = $20 mil. per year/205 = $97,561

$97,561 daily disbursements x 6 days x .08 = $46,829 added investment return

$10,000 checks/year x $.25 + $7,000 = $9,500 cost of system

The delayed disbursement program has saved Allstar $46,829 - $9,500 = $37,329 per year.

9. The value of the float increase is, assuming a perpetuity:

$97,561 daily disbursement x 6 days = $585,366 cash saved and available or:

PV = $46,829 added invested return/.08 = $585,366

While speeding cash returns to a firm is the "white-knight," positive aspect of cash management systems, remote disbursements is a "black-knight," negative side, that many firms play without discussion. Suppliers are most likely to feel the impact of delayed

271

payments. Supplier credit terms may be changed or other sanctions applied unless, of course, Allstar is a valuable customer!

10.   a. The EOQ for the computer center is:

$$Q^* = \sqrt{\frac{2 \text{ x unit sales x cost per order}}{\text{unit carrying cost}}}$$

$$= (2 \text{ x } 515 \text{ x } 15.03/2)^{.5} = 88$$

    b. The number of orders per year is 440/88 = 5

    c. The average inventory is the EOQ/2 = 88/2 = 44 boxes

    d. As order costs increase, the EOQ increases and the computer center will place fewer orders and hold a larger inventory of paper. As carrying costs increase, more orders will be placed or less inventory will be on hand at any time. As total usage increases, the EOQ increases.

11.   The value of short-term securities sold, Q^*, each time the cash balance is replenished is:

$$Q^* = \sqrt{\frac{2 \text{ x annual cash disbursements x cost per sale}}{\text{interest rate}}}$$

$$= \{2 \text{ x (\$2 million x 12 months) x } \$34.70/.06\}^{.5}$$

$$= \$166{,}613$$

The amount of T-bills sold each time, ($2 million/$166,613) = 12 or once per month with an average cash balance (inventory) of $166,613/2 = $83,307.

12.   The level of T-bills to sell each time cash is needed is directly related to the annual cash disbursement level and the cost of selling securities and inversely related to the T-bill interest rate. Selling $167,000 in securities minimizes the transaction cost of selling securities and the opportunity cost of selling securities (interest given up by selling securities). The Baumol model assumes steady use of cash with little variability of cash flows. Thus we study the Miller-Orr model for more practical problems of cash flow variability.

a. The spread between the upper and lower cash balance limits is:

$$\text{spread} = 3^{.33} \sqrt{\frac{.75 \times \text{transactioncosts} \times \text{variance}}{\text{interest rate}}}$$

$$= 3\{.75(\$34.70 \times 8000^2)/.06\}^{.33}$$

$$= \$8,384$$

Upper limit = lower limit ($150,000) + $9,084 = $159,084

Return point = lower limit + spread/3

   = $150,000 + $9,084/3

   = $153,028

Lower limit = $150,000 minimum cash balance

b. If the cash balance reaches $159,084, then $6,056 in securities ($159,084 - $153,028) will be purchased, bringing the cash balance to the return point of $153,028. If the cash balance drops to the minimum level, $3,028 in securities ($153,028 - $150,000) will be sold to bring the balance to the return level of $153,028.

The lower the interest rates, the higher is the allowable spread between the upper and lower limits. This is so because the opportunity cost of cash is lower. Cash flow variability and transaction costs are directly related to the spread. As transaction costs and variability increases, so does the cash/securities adjustment.

Cost of cash balances/Cost of borrowing
= 6/10 = 0.6

The best cash balance depends upon the cost of borrowing and the extent of uncertainty about future cash flow. If the cost of borrowing (denominator) is high relative to the opportunity cost of cash balances (numerator), the probability of borrowing the high cost funds should be low.

CREDIT MANAGEMENT AND BANKRUPTCY

INTRODUCTION

In this third working capital management chapter, credit management is the focal point. Accounts receivable represents a significant investment for many businesses. Why give credit? Credit is a competitive necessity, and combined with the product or service, is a major factor influencing sales. Like investment in capital assets, working capital investments should, at the margin, provide returns in excess of the firm's minimum required rate of return. This investment level is affected by who receives credit, the level of sales, the terms of sales, and the paying practices and/or collection efforts of the firm.

This chapter provides many of you with your first and only look at credit management concepts. While most of you will not work in the credit-granting area of a business, almost all of you working in business must work with the credit operation and that of other businesses during your career.

LEARNING CHECKLIST

After studying this chapter you should be able to:

_____1. Measure the implicit interest rate charged for credit.

_____2. Understand the range of credit and IOU arrangements that a business and customer might have.

_____3. Understand the process by which a credit applicant's credit record is assessed.

_____4. Summarize the bankruptcy procedures available to debtors and creditors.

SOURCES OF BUSINESS INFORMATION

Most business periodicals have special, quarterly or annual issues which analyze and summarize the previous period. These are valuable for they concentrate a lot of information into one source. Fortune, Business Week, Forbes, Barron's, The Wall Street Journal, and others have special editions that summarize and/or highlight special topics, such as technological developments, the economy, and the investment outlook, or, as in the case of Fortune and Business Week, create lists of corporations by size, sales, market value, etc. Look for editions just after the end of each quarter or, of course, at the end of the year. Most have indexes that list where specific companies are discussed in the edition. This is helpful if you are studying a specific company.

Board of Governors of the Federal Reserve System. The financial markets wait in anticipation for the comments of the Chairman of the Board of Governors of the Federal Reserve System, currently Alan Greenspan. The Federal Reserve System is charged with maintaining price stability, maintaining the country's payments system, regulates bank holding companies and "member commercial banks, enforces many federal laws related to consumer credit protection, etc. All this information and links to all twelve Federal Reserve District Banks are available at http://www.bog.frb.fed.us/. At the "Fed In Print" link, all the publications of the Federal Reserve Board and District Banks. All twelve District Banks have excellent web sites.

CHAPTER OUTLINE, KEY CONCEPTS AND TERMS

I.   TERMS OF SALE

A.   Credit **terms of sale** vary between industries and are directly related to the credit rating of the customer, the size of the account, the durability of the product, and the length of time it takes the customer to sell the product.

Example - On a $100 sale, with terms 5/10 net 60, what is the implied interest rate on the credit given?

Effective annual rate

$$= \left(1 + \frac{\text{discount}}{\text{discounted price}}\right)^{365/\text{extra days credit}} - 1$$

$$= \left(1 + \frac{5}{95}\right)^{365/50} - 1 = .454, \text{ or } 45.4\%$$

B.   Credit terms range from cash before delivery (CBD), cash on delivery (COD), net terms without trade discounts and with trade discounts for early, or timely payments. End of the month (EOM) billing and terms is common with continuous purchase/shipment activity.

C.   Trade credit terms of 2/10, net 30 allow a 2 percent discount if paid within ten days of the invoice, with the net due in thirty days.

D.   The effective annual cost of passing the discount on the tenth day and paying twenty days later is 1 +(discount rate/1 - discount rate) raised to the power of

365/n minus 1, where "n" is the number of days "borrowed" by not paying on the tenth. In the above example, if the discount is passed on the tenth for the added twenty days, the effective rate is:

$$44.6\% = 1 + [.02/(1 - .02)]^{365/20}$$

E. The cost of discounts missed is usually much higher than commercial bank lending rates. Business should, if needed, borrow on the tenth, pay the discount, and lower their costs of discounts missed.

F. High effective rates for discounts missed penalizes firms that stretch their payables.

II. CREDIT AGREEMENTS

A. Credit agreements between supplier and customer vary from very informal to formal IOUs.

B. An **open account** is a trade credit agreement without any formal debt contract. A promissory note formalizes the obligation, as does an accepted commercial draft called a trade acceptance, which is an acknowledgment of payments due on receipt of goods (sight draft) or later (time draft). If the customer's bank accepts the customer's obligation as their own, the trade acceptance becomes a banker's acceptance.

C. A conditional sales agreement maintains title to goods until payment is made.

III. CREDIT ANALYSIS

A. The procedure to determine if the customer is likely to pay for goods shipped or services rendered is called **credit analysis**.

B. Prior payment practices, high ratings from credit analysis firms such as Dun and Bradstreet, rating agencies such as Moody's, and credit bureaus help discriminate payers from non-payers.

C. **Financial Ratio Analysis**
1. A supplier providing trade credit may assess the ability and willingness to pay by performing their own financial analyses with their customers' financial data.
2. With reference to Chapter 17, the liquidity, debt capacity, and long-term profitability of a customer is assessed.

D. **Numerical Credit Scoring**
  1.   The scope of a financial analysis includes an assessment of the customer with regard to the "five Cs of credit": character, capacity to pay, capital, collateral, and conditions.
  2.   Numerical credit scoring models are developed and used to discriminate between characteristics of those who pay as agreed and those customers who do not. See Example 21.2.
  3.   The credit scoring model is an effective screening device for low-risk and high-risk customers, with the latter undergoing substantial credit analysis.
  4.   Considerable research effort, including classic research by E. I. Altman and the *Z score* has been devoted to this area.

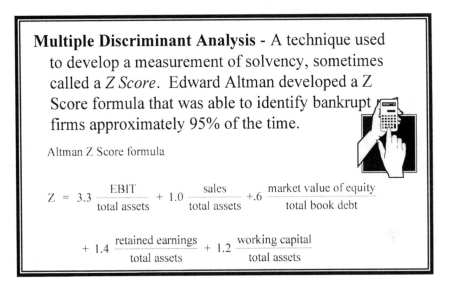

Multiple Discriminant Analysis - A technique used to develop a measurement of solvency, sometimes called a *Z Score*. Edward Altman developed a Z Score formula that was able to identify bankrupt firms approximately 95% of the time.

Altman Z Score formula

$$Z = 3.3 \frac{EBIT}{total\ assets} + 1.0 \frac{sales}{total\ assets} + .6 \frac{market\ value\ of\ equity}{total\ book\ debt}$$

$$+ 1.4 \frac{retained\ earnings}{total\ assets} + 1.2 \frac{working\ capital}{total\ assets}$$

E. **When to Stop Looking for Clues**
  1.   Credit analysis costs money and there are two general rules as to when to stop.
  2.   The two rules are 1) do not undertake a full credit analysis unless the order is large enough to justify it, and 2) undertake a full credit analysis for the doubtful or higher risk customers only.

IV.   THE CREDIT DECISION

A.   **Credit policy** establishes standards determining the amount and type of credit terms to extend to customers. The review of the credit decision process is shown in Figure 21.1.

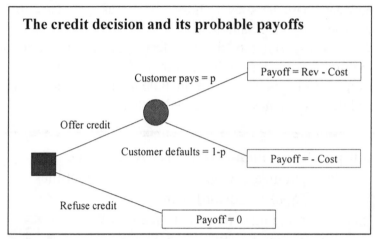

The credit decision and its probable payoffs

- Customer pays = p → Payoff = Rev - Cost
- Offer credit
- Customer defaults = 1-p → Payoff = - Cost
- Refuse credit → Payoff = 0

B.   Credit should be extended if the expected profit from the credit sale is greater than the expected profit from refusing credit. If paid as agreed, the profit margin will be realized on the sale; if payment is not received, the firm loses the cost of sales. Refusing credit makes no profit.

C.   **Credit Decisions with Repeat Orders** -- The chance of repeat orders and future profits from a credit customer increases the expected value of granting credit and encourages credit extension.

D.   **Some General Principles**
   1.   The job of the credit manager is to maximize profits, not minimize losses. Tight credit terms turn away good repeat customers, so some losses are expected.
   2.   Concentrate efforts on large order, high-risk accounts.
   3.   Consider a new account as a possible long-term customer. Offer small amounts of credit to high-risk customers until a good payment record is established.

V.   COLLECTIONS POLICY

A.   Slow payers impose two costs on a business: collection expenses and a greater investment in working capital, specifically accounts receivable.

B.   The investment in accounts receivables is the product of the daily sales rate times the average collection period. As the collection period is extended by slow payers or no payers, the investment increases and required opportunity cost of capital is incurred.

C.   **Collections policy** includes the procedures to collect and monitor receivables.

D.   An **aging schedule** classifies accounts receivable by the length of time they are outstanding. See Table 21.1.

Sample aging schedule for accounts receivable

Customer's Name	Less than 1 month	1 - 2 months	2 - 3 months	More than 3 months	Total Owed
A	10,000	0	0	0	10,000
B	8,000	3,000	0	0	11,000
*	*	*	*	*	*
*	*	*	*	*	*
*	*	*	*	*	*
Z	5,000	4,000	6,000	15,000	30,000
Total	$200,000	$40,000	$15,000	$43,000	$298,000

E.   Collections efforts range from friendly reminders to collection agency and court actions.

F.   There is always a conflict of interest between sales, who desire generous credit terms, and the collections department who "remind" good-customer deadbeats of their payment practices or the financial manager who must control the level of accounts receivable investment in order to maximize value.

VI.   BANKRUPTCY

A.   **Bankruptcy** is the court-directed procedure whereby a failing business is reorganized or liquidated.

B.   **Bankruptcy Procedures**
       1.   A problem business and their creditors have a range of options before bankruptcy, including extension of time for payment, or a possible composition of obligations which reduces the amount to be paid by some proportion.

2. These informal arrangements above, taken before bankruptcy, are referred to as a **workout**.
3. Bankruptcy results in either a **liquidation** or sale of a business' assets to generate money for claimants, or a **reorganization**, which restructures the financial claims on a business in an attempt to keep it operating.
4. In a bankruptcy liquidation, there is an official order of claimants.
5. During bankruptcy, the creditor claims and individual efforts to collect are suspended and the operation of the business, through management or a court appointed trustee, are monitored by the bankruptcy court.
6. A reorganization plan evaluates and selects the higher of the value of the business as liquidated or as a reorganized business.
7. A reorganization plan must be approved by creditors and confirmed by the bankruptcy court.

C. **The Choice between Liquidation and Reorganization**
1. In theory, the liquidation/reorganization decision should be based on which produces the higher value.
2. Other factors, including tax considerations, cash flow considerations of reorganization, and time delays, are variables in the court decisions.

COMPLETION QUESTIONS

1. The credit, discount, and payment terms are called the _____ _____ _____ .

2. Manufacturers sometimes delay dating invoices for products sold unevenly during the year in a practice known as _____ _____ .

3. The longer the period after the discount period lapses, the (*higher/lower*) is the cost of using trade credit.

4. Open account sales are an agreement whereby sales are made with (*a/no*) formal debt contract.

5. A _____ draft requires payment immediately.

6. A trade acceptance is signed by the (*bank/purchaser*).

7. _____ acceptances are often used in international trade.

8. The procedure to determine the likelihood that a customer will pay its bills is known as a (*cash flow/credit*) analysis.

9. The 5 Cs of credit are _____, _____, _____, _____, and _____.

10. In numerical credit scoring systems, the applicant's sex and race (*may/may not*) be used.

11. Credit scoring systems favor large (*families/incomes*).

12. An important indicator of potential bankruptcy for a firm is a (*high/low*) EBIT to total asset ratio.

13. More intensive analysis is recommended for (*large/small*) orders and (*strong/weak*) customers.

14. Credit decisions are based on expected (*collections/profits*).

15. When considering long-run sales to a customer, the higher discount rates will favor (*higher/lower*) break-even probabilities.

16. An aging schedule is helpful when establishing a (*collection/payment*) policy.

17. The situation in which a firm that cannot pay its debts is reorganized or liquidated is called _____ .

18. In a workout, the troubled firm (*avoids/declares*) bankruptcy.

19. An extension or a composition are arrangements negotiated (*prior to/during*) bankruptcy.

20. The restructuring of financial claims to keep a firm operating occurs in a _____.

21. Shareholders and junior creditors usually have strong reasons for preferring (*liquidation/reorganization*).

PROBLEMS

1. Company A sells on terms of 2/10, net 45 basis. Debi buys goods with an invoice of $10,000.
   a. How much will Debi pay if she pays by the 10th day of the month?
   b. How many extra days can Debi receive if she gives up the discount and pays according to terms?
   c. If Debi passes the discount, what is the effective annual rate of interest paid her if she pays on the net date?

2. With reference to Question 1 above, if Customer B is able to finance the purchase at an effective annual rate of 14 percent, how much will they pay ($) for the financing?

3. Which of the following credit terms has the highest effective annual rate (cost) of discounts missed?
   a. 2/10, net 30
   b. 1/5, net 60
   c. 3/20, net 45

4. With reference to Question 2 above, if customers had opportunities to finance at a bank at an effective rate of 12 percent, under what credit terms above are businesses likely to borrow and pay the invoice on the discount date?

5. Jordan Inc. purchases $60,000 worth of goods from Wall's Inc. every month. Wall's has recently changed its credit terms from 2.5/10, net 30, to 2/10, net 45. Jordan Inc. has always paid on the 10th, but now is asking you for your opinion?

6. Kellen Corp. has recently changed its credit terms from 1/10, net 60 to 2/10, net 40. What has this action done to the effective cost of discounts missed for its customers and the likely impact upon its level of accounts receivables?

7. Greg's Golfing Store that has always sold its merchandise for cash is considering adopting a net 30, EOM policy, in line with larger competitors. The business feels that, while its merchandise is superior to that of competitors, it is losing sales because of its "cash basis" policy. It is estimated that sales/month would increase 10 percent from the current level of $2000/month. The price per unit is $130 and the cost (in present value terms) is $65. The current interest rate is 9 percent per year. Should the new credit policy be adopted?

8. With reference to Question 7 above, if it is estimated that 1 percent of all customers will not pay, should the new credit policy be adopted?

9.	Econopools sells portable swimming pools to retailers for $1000. Each pool costs $500 to make. With credit terms of net 30 and estimates of bad debts of 4 percent, should Econopools accept a one-time order on credit? The current interest rate is 1 percent per month.

10.	In the above Question 9, what is the break-even probability of collection?

11.	With reference to Econopools in Question 9 above:
	a.	If after paying for its first pool order, the customer places an identical order each month forever. With little chance of default, should credit be extended for these additional orders?
	b.	What is the break-even probability of collection with this repeat-sale customer?

12.	Microven, Inc. manufactures a miniature microwave oven for reheating coffee. It costs $50 to produce and sells for $80. The bad debt proportion is estimated to be 5 percent and the firm offers terms of net 30. An order from Wallpark for 2000 units has just arrived. Assuming interest rates of 9 percent annually, should Microven, Inc. take this one-time order? Assume the customer will pay the invoice or nothing at all.

13.	With reference to the Microven, Inc. problem above, what is the break-even probability of collections?

14.	Youth Bouncebeds, Inc. has been selling trampoline beds for "active" children for many years. It is currently studying a proposal to tighten credit policy in an attempt to reduce its bad debt expense ratio, now 5 percent to 3 percent. Sales are estimated to decline by 10 percent. The cost of sales is 80 percent of the selling price. Should the company adopt this new credit policy?

15.	Reemay sells $50,000 of product to Gardner's Fair each month. Gardner's Fair has always borrowed and paid on the tenth day of the month in response to Reemay's 1.5/10, net 30, and Gardner's Fair is now considering payment on the net date. What do you advise? Gardner's Fair has an investment in money market securities earning 5 percent.

ANSWERS TO COMPLETION QUESTIONS

1.	terms of sale
2.	seasonal dating
3.	lower
4.	no
5.	sight
6.	purchaser
7.	Banker's

8. credit
9. character capacity capital collateral, conditions
10. may not
11. incomes
12. low
13. small, weak
14. profits
15. high
16. collection
17. bankruptcy
18. avoids
19. prior to
20. reorganization
21. reorganization

SOLUTIONS TO PROBLEMS

1. a. If the invoice is postmarked by the 10th, Debi will receive a 2 percent discount or .02 x $10,000 = $200, and will pay $9,800.
    b. For $200, Debi can delay payment for 35 days (45 - 10).

    c. If the discount is passed, the effective annual rate of discounts missed is:

    $$(1 + \$200/\$9,800)^{365/35} - 1 = (1.0204)^{365/35} - 1 = 23.5\%$$

2. If Debi passes the discount, it will cost them $200 for 35 days at an effective cost of 23.5 percent. (See Question 1 above) An effective borrowing rate of 14 percent is $(1.14)^{35/365}$ - 1 or 1.264 percent times ($9,800 cost of invoice on 10th) = $123.91 interest cost for 35 days. The $123.91 interest cost is less than the $200 offered by Company A for 35 days. Debi should borrow and pay the invoice by the 10th.

3. The effective annual rate of discounts missed are:
    a. 2/10, net 30

        One gives up 2 percent for 30 - 10 = 20 days added time to finance 100 - 2 = 98 percent of any invoice amount on an annualized basis.

        $$(1 + 2/98)^{365/20} - 1 = (1.020408)^{18.25} - 1 = 44.6 \text{ percent}$$

    b. 1/5, net 60
        $$(1 + 1/99)^{365/55} - 1 = (1.0101)^{6.636} - 1 = 6.9 \text{ percent}$$

c. 3/20, net 45

$$(1 + 3/97)^{365/25} - 1 = (1.03092)^{2.6} - 1 = 8.24 \text{ percent}$$

The 2/10, net 30 is the most punitive if the discount is passed.

4. With a 12 percent borrowing rate available, borrowing on the 10th and paying the invoice for the 2/10, net 30 terms would save considerable amounts of money. It is cheaper to pay on the net date for "b" and "c."

5. The effective annual rate of discounts missed has changed from:
   a. 2.5/10, net 30

$$(1 + 2.5/97.5)^{365/20} - 1 = (1.02564)^{18.25} - 1 = 58.7\%$$

   b. 2/5, net 60

$$(1 + 2/98)^{365/55} - 1 = (1.0204)^{6.64} - 1 = 14.3\%$$

The prior terms with an effective cost of missing the discount of 58.7 percent, meant that Jordan's Inc. was likely to pay on the 10th each month. The new terms warrant an analysis. If the bank charges an effective rate of 14.3 percent or more, borrow and take the discount. If the bank rate is greater than 14.3 percent, pass the discount and pay on the net date. Under the new terms the discount of ($60,000 x .02) = $1200 buys 55 days. If the bank had a 14.3 percent rate, Jordan's Inc. would pay $1184 for the 55 days of borrowing $(1.143475)^{55/365} - 1 = .020408($58,000) = 1184 in interest, approximating the $1200 discount ($60,000 x .02).

6. When Kellen changed its credit terms from 1/10, net 60 to 2/10, net 40, the cost of discounts missed changed.

Cost of discounts missed:

1/10, net 60

$$(1 + 1/99)^{365/50} - 1 = 7.6 \text{ percent}$$

2/10, net 40

$$(1 + 2/98)^{365/30} - 1 = 27.9 \text{ percent}$$

This policy change was intended to encourage customers to take the discount and pay by the 10th of every month. The policy change should reduce accounts receivables by about 50 days and free up capital to be invested elsewhere, at a cost of one percent of their margin. Customers, on the other hand, now face a shift from net terms (60) to borrowing and taking the discount on the 10th. Their accounts payable should decline by 50 days and borrowing costs increase somewhat (difference between 7.6 percent effective cost of merchandise before to whatever the bank rate might be, most likely under 27.9 percent).

7.   The current value of a cash sale is the units sold times the profit/unit or:

2000 units x ($130 - 65) = $130,000 current value of sales

If one month (30 days) credit is given, the present value of revenue falls from its current value of $130 (cash received now) to 130/1.0075 = $129.03 per unit ($130 discounted one month--.09/12 = .0075).

If both existing and new customers now take the net credit terms, the value of the sales, now 10 percent higher, is:

2000 (1.10) ($129.03 - $65) = $140,866

Adopting the new credit terms would increase the value of sales. The new credit policy should be adopted.

8.   If in the question above, we now add a 1 percent bad debt expense to the issue, the expected value (probability times dollars) of the sales is now:

2200 [.99 ($129.03 - $65) - .01($65)] =

2200 ($63.3897 - .$65) = $138,027

The one percent bad debt expense associated with the new credit policy still adds to the value of sales, compared to the $130,000 value before the credit policy change. What bad debt expense ratio, "x," would hold the value of sales at $130,000. Hint: Let "x" equal bad debt loss rate and (1 - x) be the probability of a paid sale.

2200[(1 - x)($129.03 - $65) - x ($65)] = $130,000

9.   The present value of cost is $500.

The present value of revenue (PV of revenue collected in one month) is $1000/1.01 = $990.10.

The value of a sale of one unit is $450.50.

.96($990.10 - $500) - .04($500) = $470.50 - $20 = $450.50

The new credit terms have a positive value and should be adopted.

10. The break-even probability of a collection is the point where the expected value equals zero.

Let x = probability of collections
1 - x = probability of default

x($990.10 - $500) - (1-x)500 = 0
$490.10x - $500 + 500x = 0
$990.10x = $500
x = 50.5 percent
1 - x = 49.5 percent

Econopools, with a good profit margin, could lose up to 1 - .505 = .495 or 49.5 percent of its sales before the value of sales would fall below zero.

11. a. A paying customer is a cash flow profit stream forever per month of ($990.10 - $500) = $490.10). The PV of this $490.10 perpetuity is $490.10/.01 = $49,010. The PV of a sale, given a 4 percent loss rate is:

.96($49,010) - .04($500) = $47,050 - $20 = $47,030

It clearly makes sense to make the repeat sale on credit. The PV, $47,030, is greater than zero.

b. The break-even probability of collection, p, is found by solving for:

p($49,010) - (1 - p)$500 = 0
$49,010p - 500 + 500p = 0
$49,510p = $500
p = .01

The probability of collections need only be 1 percent for the credit policy to break even.

12. The present value per unit of revenue is $80/1.0075 = $79.40, where the one month discount rate is .09/12 = .0075. The cost is $50.

The value of the sale is:

$$.95(\$79.40 - \$50) - .05(\$50) = (\$28.025 - \$2.50) =$$

$25.525 per unit or $51,050 value of the 2000 unit order.

13.   The break-even probability of collection for Microven, Inc. is:

$$p(\$79.40 - \$50.00) - (1 - p)\$50.00 = 0$$
$$\$29.40p - \$50.00 + 50p = 0$$
$$\$79.40p = \$50.00$$
$$p = .63$$

The probability of collection must be approximately 63 percent for the sale to break even.

14.   The expected profit margin under the existing and the new, tighter credit policy is outlined below:

	Present	New	
Sales	100.00	90.00	
- Bad debt exp.	5.00	- 2.70	(.03 x 90)
- cost of sales	80.00	-72.00	(.8 x 90)
Profit	15.00	15.30	

The new policy increases expected profits and should be adopted.

15.   Under the current terms the annualized cost of discounts missed is:

$$(1 + 1.5/97.5)^{365/20} - 1 = 32 \text{ percent}$$

It is obvious that Gardner's Fair would always borrow and take the discount on the 10th of every month. Now with .5/10, net 30, the effective annualized cost of discounts missed is:

$$(1 + .5/99.5)^{365/20} - 1 = 9.6 \text{ percent}$$

Paying on the net date increases the cost of the merchandise by $250 from a discount-assuming base of $49,750 for 20 days, a cost of $(1 + 250/49,750)^{365/20} - 1 = 9.6$ percent.

As long as the bank's annualized effective rate is **above** 9.6 percent, Gardner's Fair should pay on the net date. If bank rates are less than 9.6 percent, they should borrow on the 10th of every month and take the discount. With liquid securities available for sale, the cost of taking the discount on the 10th is only 5 percent, the opportunity cost of securities.

MERGERS, ACQUISITIONS, AND CORPORATE CONTROL

INTRODUCTION

Just as there are markets for securities and commodities, so is there a market for corporate control, the buying and selling of controlling influence over business. The transactions are mergers, acquisitions, leveraged buy-outs, and other similar terms. The deals are carried out in smoke-filled rooms, annual meetings, in the mail for proxies, and in large expensive ads in The Wall Street Journal. This chapter provides the terminology and concepts related to the market for corporate control. It is an extensive, intuitive chapter centering on one of the two exciting activities of financial management. The other is going public, covered in an earlier chapter. There is always a good proxy fight occurring in the newspapers during each semester to provide a good current event discussion and assignment.

LEARNING CHECKLIST

After studying this chapter you should be able to:

____1. Describe ways that companies change their ownership or management.

____2. Explain the motivations for merger. What are the gains from merger?

____3. Describe how the gains from merger are divided among the sellers and buyers.

____4. Describe several takeover defenses.

____5. Summarize the evidence related to whether mergers enhance efficiency.

SOURCES OF BUSINESS INFORMATION

Have you thought about the type of business or industry in which you would like to spend your life? Just as families and relationships vary in tempo, stress, etc., so do businesses. There are a number of references and periodicals that frequently list the "Best Companies to Work For." A popular reference is Robert Levering and Milton Moskowitz, The 100 Best Companies to Work for in America, (1994: ISBN: 0452271231). Business Week often has a cover feature related to the same topic. Look at the criteria by which they select their companies. It can help you in your career planning.

Beige Book--Current State Of The Economy. At the same Federal Reserve Board site, discussed in the last chapter and from many web sites, the link to the current Beige Book. Every six weeks the Federal Open Market Committee of the Federal Reserve System meets in Washington D.C. to discuss the current state of the U.S. economy. In preparation for this meeting, all twelve district banks file a report on the economy of their district. If you are considering moving to Ohio and are wondering how the economy in the eastern Midwest is doing, check out the most recent Beige Book. Incidently the name of the report is derived from the color of the cover that used to be attached to it!

CHAPTER OUTLINE, KEY CONCEPTS AND TERMS

I. **THE MARKET FOR CORPORATE CONTROL**

    A.   In a small corporation the stockholders, directors, and managers are likely to be the same people, unlike in the major corporations that dominate business.

    B.   Shareholders elect the board of directors who in turn appoint management. Control of the business is vested in management, with the board left to an oversight role.

    C.   Ownership and control of businesses change. The market place where this exchange takes place is called the market for corporate control.

    D.   There are four ways that the management of a corporation can change: a proxy contest, merger, leveraged buy-out, and divestiture.

    E.   In any business transaction, including mergers, one must distinguish between what is purchased, what is used for payment and how much is paid for it, and how or who will manage the assets/business in the future.

    F.   **Proxy Contests**
        1.   Existing management may be changed or replaced by the board of directors, or failing that, by changing the board of directors who are elected by the shareholders.
        2.   A **proxy contest** is an attempt to replace the board, and later management, by an outsider group or owners or other interested parties. Shareholders may delegate or "proxy" their vote on issues to others. A group may wage a proxy fight to elect directors. Control is decided by shareholders by how they vote or to whom they proxy their vote.
        3.   Most proxy fights by outsiders fail for existing managers have the advantages of company funding and inertia.

G. Mergers and Acquisitions

1. Corporate control is more likely to be changed through acquisition via three ways. Something is purchased and something is given in consideration.

2. **Merger**, the combination of two firms into one, is the first method of acquisition with the purchases assuming the assets and liabilities of the target firm. The acquired firm ceases to exist and the former shareholders are given cash or securities, perhaps in the acquiring firm.

Year	Buying Company	Selling Company	Payment ($bil)
1999	MCI WorldCom	Sprint	115
1999	Viacom	CBS	35
1999	AT&T	MediaOne Group	54
1999	Travelers	Citicorp	83
1999	Exxon	Mobil	80
1999	TotalFina (France)	Elf Aquitaine (France)	55
1999	Olivetti (Italy)	Telecom Italia (Italy)	58
1999	Vodafone (UK)	Air Touc Comm.	61
1998	British Petroleum (UK)	Amoco Corp.	48
1998	Daimler-Benz (Germany)	Chrysler	38
1998	Zeneca (UK)	Astra (Sweden)	35
1998	Nationsbank Corp.	BankAmerica Corp.	62
1998	WorldCom Inc.	MCI Communications	42
1998	Norwest Corp.	Wells Fargo & Co.	34

3. Another means by which a firm is acquired is by the purchase of the target company's stock. Cash or securities is paid, stockholders change places, and change is affected via board and management changes. A **tender offer** is where an unwanted acquirer invites shareholders to offer or tender their shares at a specified price to the acquirer.

4. The third way to acquire control over a company's assets is to purchase the assets directly from the selling company. Again cash and/or securities are the likely consideration.

H. Leveraged Buy-Outs

1. When a firm's assets or stock is purchased by a private group using borrowed funds, the change in corporate control is called a **leveraged buy-out (LBO)**.

2. When the buyers are current or former managers, the term **management buy-out (MBO)** is used.

I.

Divestitures and Spin-Offs -- Divisions, subsidiary corporations, and assets may be sold to other businesses (divestiture) or sold or spun-off to the general public or new owner group.

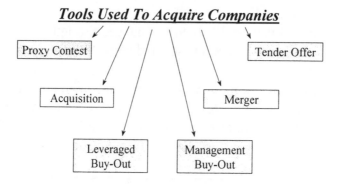

Tools Used To Acquire Companies

Proxy Contest

Tender Offer

Acquisition

Merger

Leveraged Buy-Out

Management Buy-Out

II.   SENSIBLE MOTIVES FOR MERGERS

A.   Mergers are categorized as horizontal, vertical, or conglomerate, depending upon the nature of the business acquired.

B.   If a firm in a similar line of business is acquired, the merger is called a horizontal merger. If a supplier or a customer is acquired (vertical in the supply chain), it is a vertical merger. A conglomerate merger is the acquisition of an unrelated line of business.

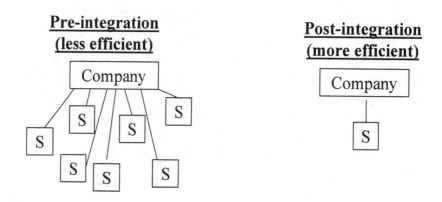

Pre-integration (less efficient)

Post-integration (more efficient)

C.   The motives for acquiring another business or its assets include the desire to replace existing management, and to improve efficiency or to produce synergies. The synergies or the value added by combining businesses may be explained by the following four areas.

D.   **Economies of Scale**
1.   The ability to derive reduced cost efficiencies through larger operations is an often quoted benefit of mergers.
2.   Horizontal mergers, in the same line of business, and from centralizing such functions as finance and accounting is likely to produce economies of scale.

E.   **Economies of Vertical Integration**
1.   Efficiencies related to controlling raw material supplies and final customer contact may benefit some industries.
2.   Benefits in this area are often questionable.

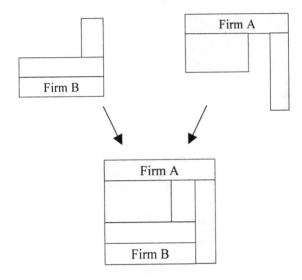

F.   **Combining Complementary Resources**
1.   Some mergers involve firms where each has valuable assets which complement the other so the total becomes more efficient or better serves the customer.

G.   **Mergers as a Use of Surplus Funds**
1.   The presence of free cash flow in a mature firm often motivates managers to purchase other firms.
2.   Unless the merger contributes positive NPVs, increased dividends or stock repurchase via downsizing is the better option for shareholders.

III.   **DUBIOUS REASONS FOR MERGERS**

A.   **Diversification**
1.   It is easier for shareholders to diversify than businesses via asset investment.
2.   Diversification by itself is a poor reason for mergers, unless the merger is likely to produce value added (positive NPV's).

B.   The Bootstrap Game
    1.   The bootstrap effect is the arithmetical result of a higher post-merger earnings per share created when the acquiring firm has a higher price/earnings ratio.
    2.   Bootstrapping merger-oriented firms are able to produce high earnings growth rates, attract added demand for shares and increased stock prices, and maintain higher P/Es which continues until the market assesses the actual added value of the mergers. The market usually is able to see through the "smoke and mirrors."

IV.   EVALUATING MERGERS

A.   All merger analysis centers around two fundamental questions.
    1.   Does the merger create economic gain?
    2.   Do the terms of the merger make my company's shareholders better off?

B.   If given a simple answer to each, there would be no magic in the analysis of a merger. Unfortunately, the answers are usually less than obvious.

$$\text{Economic Gain} = \text{PV(increased earnings)}$$

$$= \frac{\text{New cash flows from synergies}}{\text{discount rate}}$$

C.   **Estimating the Gain**
    1.   Economic gain from merger occurs only if the two firms are worth more together than apart. Estimating and evaluating the economic gain is the central focus of merger analysis.
    2.   The economic gain is shared between the selling shareholders and the purchasing shareholders with the share to each determined by the price paid or negotiated.
    3.   The focus of a merger evaluation is the estimated amount of economic gain produced by the merger and the sharing of the gain between seller and buyer.
    4.   The cost of a merger is the share of economic gain given to the selling shareholders. The sellers' gain is the buyers' cost.

D. **Mergers Financed By Cash**
  1. The merger should be effected by the acquirer if the economic gain (the added value of the combination) exceeds the cost (the share of the gain given to the selling shareholders). The cost of the merger is often difficult to assess.
  2. When the compensation for selling shareholders is cash, the distribution of the gain is thought to be easily determined versus the difficult problem of assessing the value of securities used as payment.
  3. When cash is used as compensation to the selling shareholders, the cost is not affected by the actual economic gain from the merger. It is fixed, for the good or bad of it.

E. **Mergers Financed By Stock**
  1. The cost(gain given up by the buyer) is difficult to determine because the price of the selling stock may include some of the estimated premium (cost) paid by the buyer.
  2. When securities are used as compensation to the selling shareholders, the value of securities given are related to the economic gain to be derived. Thus, the cost is related to the future economic gain derived, because the economic gains that occur will be included in the share prices.

F. **WARNINGS**
  1. The key to successful mergers is the estimation of the gain and the negotiation of the share of the gain.
  2. When evaluating the economic gain, instead of estimating the target firm's future cash flows, the analyst should estimate the current value of the target firm and adjust this value by the estimated changes in future cash flows after the merger.
  3. Incremental economic gain from the merger will be derived from the value added (positive NPVs from added cash flows) produced after the merger.
  4. The market evaluates all mergers, the estimated gain and the sharing of the gain.

V. MERGER TACTICS

A. **Takeover Defenses**
  1. Takeover defenses are commonly approved by shareholders or legislated by states to "protect" their businesses (managers) from unwanted takeovers.

  2. Two takeover defenses commonly used are generally named **shark repellent** where shareholders approve amendments to the charter and bylaws that require a large majority of shareholders to approve a merger,

or make changes in the number of directors number and/or how directors are elected.

3. The second takeover defense is commonly called the **poison pill** and involves contingency plans to distribute large numbers of common stock to friendly shareholders if an unwanted takeover offer occurs.

4. A **White Knight** is often used to fend off an undesired takeover. The White Knight is defined as a takeover, but with a friendly face. While it is still a takeover, the terms are usually much more generous to existing management.

B. **Who Gets the Gains?**

1. Who benefits from mergers or who receives the economic gain, if any, from a merger?

2. Research indicates that target or selling shareholders have taken the larger share of the "gain."

3. Acquiring shareholders have received the smaller share of the gains or seem to break even.

4. Sellers receive the larger share because of competitor bidding. A firm receiving an unwanted takeover bid often invites other firms to bid, or uses legal and other defenses to force the bid higher. "Professionals," such as accountants, lawyers, etc., seem to get their share of the gain, as do speculators and insiders who buy/sell on anticipation of merger activity.

VI. **LEVERAGED BUY-OUTS**

A. An acquisition in which the majority of the compensation to selling shareholder is borrowed by the takeover group is called a leveraged buy-out.

B. Publicly owned (large number of shareholders) corporations are taken "private" when managers (management buy-out or MBO) borrow and buy the outstanding shares of the company. They become owner/managers with large obligations over their heads. They work harder, cut costs, and compete more effectively.

C. The RJR Nabisco LBO by KKR was a more notorious LBO case where entrenched management was outbid in their LBO attempt by an outside investor group.

D. **RJR Nabisco**
1. KKR expected to repay the enormous debt incurred to buy the RJR Nabisco stock and realize economic gains with the expected interest tax shields, favorable financing rates, availability in the junk bond market, reduced capital expenditure (free cash flow theory) and operating expenses, and the sale of some parts of RJR Nabisco.
2. The decline in the available high-risk bond market and in the increased cost of borrowing at the time forced KKR to add equity to the deal.

E. **Barbarians at the Gate?**
1. The LBO activity of the late 1980s had considerable negative press but has some redeeming features.
2. Sellers seem to have received most of the economic gain, not the buyers or raiders.
3. LBO activities were driven by the relatively cheap and available junk bond markets.
4. While an LBO generates more borrowing or debt, the benefits of LBOs seem to come from benefits other than tax benefits and leverage benefits.
5. Bondholders seemed to lose at the expense of selling stockholders in the LBO period. High rated bonds became junk as massive debt levels were added to finance the repurchase of stock.
6. LBOs provide considerable incentives to the owner/manager to improve economic efficiency.
7. The presence of free cash flows in mature industries was a major, but not the only, incentive for LBO activity.

VII. MERGERS AND THE ECONOMY

A. **Merger Waves**
1. Merger activity has occurred in cycles in this century, coinciding with periods of increased stock prices.
2. Are mergers driven by economic opportunity or cheap financing? Probably both.

B. Do Mergers Generate Net Benefits?
1. Mergers tend to benefit selling shareholders.
2. Mergers tend to improve real productivity.
3. While mergers may reward selling stockholders, the LBO movement of the 1980s tended to reward these selling stockholders and "professionals" at the expense of bondholders, IRS tax revenues, and perhaps employees at takeover firms.
4. The possibility of takeovers provides incentives for firm managers to manage efficiently, but are there other incentives for business productivity?

COMPLETION QUESTIONS

1. In a _____ contest, outsiders compete with management for shareholders' votes.

2. Institutional investors have (decreased/increased) managerial accountability.

3. A combination of two firms into one with the acquiring company assuming all of the assets and liabilities of the other is known as a _____.

4. In a leveraged buy-out a group takes the firm (private/public).

5. When a firm sells a part of its business it is a _____; when it distributes stock in a part of its business it is a _____.

6. The acquisition of one computer firm by another computer firm is called a _____.

7. The acquisition of a wood door manufacture by a company with sawmills is an example of a _____ merger.

8. A _____ merger occurs when a movie firm buys an oil company.

9. Economies from larger operations, vertical integration, and combinations of complementary resources are sources of _____.

10. Diversification is easier and cheaper for (companies/shareholders).

11. The incentive for firms selling at high price earnings ratios to acquire firms with low price earnings ratios is called the _____ game.

12. When the present value of a combined firm is worth more than the present value of each separate firm, the result is (capital/economic) gain.

13. The NPV of a merger is equal to the gain from the merger (minus/plus) the portion of the gain paid to the acquired firm's owners.

14. When stock is offered to purchase another firm, the (pre/post) -merger share price of the acquiring company should be used in figuring the cost of the acquired firm.

15. A friendly potential acquirer sought by a target company threatened by an unwelcome suitor is called a _____ _____.

16. Amendments made to a firm's charter to forestall takeover attempts are termed
_____ _____.

17. A provision offering selected shareholders a discount on the purchase of new shares when a bidder acquires a significant holding in the company is an example of a _____
_____.

18. Gains from mergers normally go mainly to the (buying/selling) firm.

19. Often times unwanted divisions of large firms are sold through a _____ but-out.

20. The junk bond market (enhances/inhibits) leveraged buy-outs.

21. High merger activity is related to (highs/lows) in the stock market.

22. Merger activity tends to result in (decreased/increased) operating efficiency.

PROBLEMS

1. Daytime, Inc., wants to acquire Nitetime, Ltd., because it feels the "whole can be worth more than the sum of the parts." Savings from the merger are estimated to be a one-time after-tax benefit of $100 million. Nitetime has 5 million shares outstanding at a current market price of $60 per share. What is the maximum cash price per share that could be paid for Nitetime stock?

2. Hot Foods, which has 1 million shares outstanding, wishes to merge with Cold Drinks with 2 million shares outstanding. The market prices for HF and CD are $40 and $15 per share, respectively. The merger could create an estimated savings of $600,000 annually for the indefinite future. If HF were willing to pay $20 per share for CD, and the appropriate cost of capital is 12 percent, what would be the:
   a. Present value of the merger benefit?
   b. Net cost of the cash offer?
   c. The net present value of the offer?

3. What is the major argument against seeking mergers as a strategy for diversifying to reduce risk?

4. Briefly identify the most valid reasons for mergers.

5. Tell why and how a proxy contest occurs.

6. What are LBOs?

7. Define the following terms:
   a. Poison pill.
   b. Shark repellent.
   c. White knight

8. East, Inc., is considering acquiring all of West's 1 million shares because it believes its methods of operation could increase West's compound annual growth rate of earnings and dividends from 10 percent to 12 percent. The market capitalization (share price × the number of shares outstanding) for East and West is currently $50 million and $20 million, respectively. If West is expected to pay $1 per share dividends in the coming year, what would be the estimated gain from the merger using the dividend growth model to value West?

ANSWERS TO COMPLETION QUESTIONS

1. proxy
2. increased
3. merger
4. private
5. divestiture, spin-off
6. horizontal
7. vertical
8. conglomerate
9. synergy
10. shareholders
11. bootstrap
12. economic
13. minus
14. post
15. white knight
16. shark repellent
17. poison pill
18. selling
19. management
20. enhances
21. highs
22. increased

SOLUTIONS TO PROBLEMS

1. The market value of Nitetime is $60 per share × 5 million shares or $300 million. The $100 million one-time benefit would be added to this making the value of Nitetime $400 million ÷ 5 million or $80 per share. If any more were paid the value of the combined entity would decline.

2. a. The gain from the merger would be the present value of the $600,000 annual savings. Because these are estimated to occur each year for the indefinite future they would be valued like a perpetuity as $600,000 ÷ 0.12 or $5,000,000.
    b. The offer for Cold Drinks would cost $20 per share × 2 million shares or $40 million. This is above the market value of $15 per share × 2 million shares or $30 million. The net cost would be $40 - $30 or $10 million.
    c. The net present value of the acquisition would be the outlay of $10 million less the $5 million NPV of the savings. The *negative* NPV of $5 million indicates too much is being paid for CD.

3. There is no doubt that volatility can be reduced by operating in businesses that act differently as the economy moves through expansion and contraction phases. However, it is easier and usually cheaper for individual investors to buy stocks in firms representing a wide range of business activities. This type of diversification results in a less risky portfolio because the returns will vary less than those received when the investment is concentrated in a few business sectors. It also allows investors to pick well-managed companies rather that to expect one firm to be able to excel in very different industries.

4. The basic idea behind mergers is the benefits of synergy. This is the notion that two firms can be worth more together than they are separately. The reasons for this include economies gained from: having larger scale operations; being vertically or horizontally integrated; capitalizing on unique strengths of each firm through the use of complementary resources; and the opportunity to better deploy cash being generated by a successful but mature firm.

5. When a group of investors becomes dissatisfied with the way a company is being run they can either sell their stock or they can try to effect a change in management. In the latter case they can seek to gain control of the firm by electing new directors. This is accomplished by convincing a sufficient number of shareholders to vote for the proposed slate of directors. Since shareholders vote using a proxy, a contest is created between the dissatisfied investors and the current board of directors. If the dissidents are successful in soliciting enough proxy votes in favor of their candidates, a new board will be elected, new policies established, and new management will be chosen to implement the board wishes.

6. An LBO, or leveraged buy-out, is the process of converting a public company into a private one. Before this happens, the shares are freely traded; after, they are held by a small number of investors. The financing for this to occur comes from debt. The relatively small group of investors borrow sufficient funds to buy all the stock held by the general public. Because this uses so much leverage, the debt is usually low grade (junk bonds). If the investors seeking the take-over are officers of the firm it is called a management buy-out.

7.
    a. A poison pill is measure that is designed to prevent an unwanted take-over from occurring. For example, the shareholders may pass a resolution that allows them the right to purchase additional shares at a substantial discount **if** an outside party acquires a substantial amount of the stock. The unfriendly bidder is not entitled to this privilege. When the new shares are issued, the bidder is further away from gaining control.
    b. Shark repellent is another advance step that discourages unwanted take-overs. For example, a provision could be passed by shareholders that requires a super-majority of votes to approve a merger.
    c. A white knight is a friendly acquirer that is sought when a firm is being threatened for take-over by an unfriendly suitor. When an unwanted bid is received, the target company seeks someone else (white knight) to buy it.

8. The current market price of West is $20 million ÷ 1 million shares or $20 per share. Using this figure and the dividend growth model, we can solve for the return (r) West investors are expecting on the shares that are growing at 10 percent and will pay $1.00 per share in dividends. This relationship is:

    $1.00 ÷ (r - 0.10) = $20
    r = 0.15 or 15 percent.

    With the new growth rate of 12 percent the shares would be valued at:
    $1.00 ÷ (0.15 - 0.12) or $33.33
    The gain from the merger would be:
    ($33.33 - $20.00) × 1 million shares $13.33 million.

INTERNATIONAL FINANCIAL MANAGEMENT

INTRODUCTION

When considering international cash and investment flows, foreign exchange rates and political risks are an added dimension for the financial manager. These risks are covered thoroughly in this chapter. Starting with a discussion of foreign exchange rates using the exchange rate table from The Wall Street Journal, a discussion of why spot and forward rates differ is presented. This section, featuring Figure 23.1, is a very effective method for explaining the interrelationship of spot and forward exchange rates, interest rates, and inflation rates. You will not find a better presentation on this topic and will use this reference for years to come.

LEARNING CHECKLIST

After studying this chapter you should be able to:

____1. Understand why spot and forward exchange rates differ.

____2. Understand the basic relationships between spot exchange rates, forward exchange rates, interest rates, and inflation rates.

____3. Describe simple strategies or procedures by which a business can protect itself against exchange rate risk.

____4. Perform an NPV analysis for projects with cash flows in foreign currencies.

SOURCES OF BUSINESS INFORMATION

The American Banker. The American Banker is a daily newspaper for executives of financial institutions and students who are interested in the banking industry. Covering the news and developments of banking, credit unions, savings and loans, finance companies, and payments systems, the American Banker focuses on companies and their managers. It is an excellent daily newspaper specifically related to commercial banking. Federal and state regulatory action including analysis of Federal Reserve System actions related to monetary policy and its impact upon banks are featured. The American Banker Index, available via the ABI Inform Index (newspapers index) is a useful addition for finding articles related to a bank, issue, or event you are researching. The American Bankers Association Banking Literature Index references all noteworthy journals and periodicals associated with the banking industry.

U.S. Census Bureau Web Site. The web site of the U.S. Census Bureau (http://www.census.gov), the agency that collects all that information about us all, including businesses, is an interesting site.

All of the data generated by the agency is available here, and the site links to instructionals about how to access, download, and import into your PC. Business people use the data from the Census Bureau to generate marketing reports and business strategy. As a future employee, you will likely be asked to generate economic and marketing information. Here is a good start.

CHAPTER OUTLINE, KEY CONCEPTS AND TERMS

I. **FOREIGN EXCHANGE MARKETS**

    A.   The electronic trading of foreign currencies between commercial banks, dealers, and businesses is called the foreign exchange market.

    B.   Unlike the New York Stock Exchange, the foreign exchange markets have no central marketplace, and participants trade via sophisticated communications systems.

    C.   The amount of one currency needed to purchase one unit of another currency is called the exchange rate.

    D.   Foreign exchange rates are quoted two ways. The "U.S. $ Equivalent" rate quotes the U.S. currency cost of one unit of foreign currency. This method is called the direct exchange rate.

    E.   An alternative (and reciprocal) exchange rate quote is the indirect or European quote(method used in the book discussions) and lists the amount of foreign currency that it takes to purchase one U.S. dollar (Currency per U.S. $).

    F.   The spot exchange rate is a quote for an immediate transaction, whereas a forward exchange rate is the price, determined today, of foreign currency delivered at some future date. The forward exchange rates may trade at a premium or discount relative to the spot rate. Using indirect exchange rate quotes, a spot/forward differential is equal to the spot minus the forward divided by the forward and annualized. When the forward rates buy less U.S., as in the text case of the yen, the differential is quoted at a yen forward premium (expected to appreciate against the $) and the dollar is at a forward discount (expected to depreciate against the yen). The sign (+ or -) of the foreign currency forward differential indicates a premium (+) or discount (-) or the expected direction of the value of the foreign currency.

$$\frac{\text{Forward Price} - \text{Spot Price}}{\text{Spot Price}} = \text{Premium or (-Discount)}$$

    G.   Foreign exchange futures contracts are traded on futures exchanges and are available for hedging foreign exchange risk.

II.   SOME BASIC RELATIONSHIPS

A.   There are several basic relationships between spot rates, forward rates, expected relative country inflation rates, and country interest rates that are fundamental to international financial management.

B.   The spot/forward differential reflects market expectations of relative country inflation rates. Interest rates differential reflects the spot/forward differential which reflects the expected relative country inflation rate. Investors are seeking a real, inflation adjusted, exchange rate adjusted, after-tax return, and price spot/forward differential to provide that return.

$$\boxed{\frac{1 + r_{foreign}}{1 + r_{\$}}} \quad equals \quad \boxed{\frac{1 + i_{foreign}}{1 + i_{\$}}}$$

$$equals \qquad\qquad\qquad equals$$

$$\boxed{\frac{f_{foreign/\$}}{S_{foreign/\$}}} \quad equals \quad \boxed{\frac{E(s_{foreign/\$})}{S_{foreign/\$}}}$$

C.   **Exchange Rates and Inflation**
  1.   The economic **law of one price** theory states that the prices of goods in all countries should be equal when translated to a common currency.
  2.   Inflation is the decline in purchasing power of a currency (or an increase in the price level in a currency).
  3.   For the law of one price to hold, exchange rates must vary with inflation to provide similar values for currencies or **purchasing power parity (PPP)** across countries. See Figure 23.2.
  4.   Estimated future spot exchange rates (forward rates) closely reflect estimated relative inflation rates between countries.

D.   **Inflation and Interest Rates**
  1.   Investors' real, nominal adjusted for inflation, return is the one that counts.
  2.   The **international Fisher effect** is a theory that says that real interest rates in all countries should be equal, with the differences in nominal rates reflecting differences in expected inflation.
  3.   Countries with high inflation rates tend to have high subsequent interest rates. See Figure 23.3.

E.   **Interest Rates and Exchange Rates**
  1.   International lending (investing) and borrowing entail transferring balances between currencies when lending and borrowing occurs. This concern of future exchange rate levels when the investment is complete or

when returns/payments are made forces most to buy forward exchange contracts for adverse exchange rate movements. Capital tends to flow to its highest real, risk adjusted rate of return.

2. Market forces and capital flows tend to provide **interest rate parity** among countries in that spot/forward foreign exchange rate differentials tend to offset interest rate differences between countries and tend toward offering investors nearly the same exchange rate adjusted, rate of return in all countries.

F. **The Forward Rate and the Expected Spot Rate**
1. Forward rates are expected future spot rates.
2. The percentage spot/forward differential (premium or discount) reflects the exchange markets' estimate of the percentage change in the exchange rate between two countries, and is called the expectations theory of exchange rates.
3. While forward rates are not good predictors of actual future spot rates, *on average* the forward rate is equal to the future spot rate.

G. **Some Implications**
1. The above four relationships are long run,"tending toward" relationships that tend to hold over the years.
2. International financial decision makers should implant those relationships and be wary when betting against them.

III. HEDGING EXCHANGE RATE RISK

A. Foreign exchange risk is the variability in returns and cash flows (gains and losses) which occurs when one must transfer values from one currency to another.

B. There are two types of foreign exchange risk. Contractual risk is the variability of outcomes occurring when a specified currency exchange must be made on a given date. Noncontractual risk includes the general business impact of changing exchange rates on importers and exporters, investors, etc.

C. One may assume foreign exchange risk and take the loss/gain consequences of changing foreign exchange rates or remove the impact of varying exchange rates by hedging.

D. One may hedge foreign exchange risk by trading in forward foreign exchange contracts, foreign exchange futures contracts, or financial futures option contracts. See the Enterprise Oil example in Table 23.4.

E.   The cost of the hedge is the difference between the forward rate and the expected spot rate when payments are made.

F.   Hedging foreign exchange risk makes sense for it focuses the business manager on "business" and not exchange rate forecasting and does not cost much.

IV.   INTERNATIONAL CAPITAL BUDGETING

A.   **Net Present Value Analysis**
   1.   The decision-making rules in international investments and currencies are essentially the same process as with domestic projects. If NPVs are positive, make the investment.
   2.   The exchange rate risk consideration may be handled two ways. First, the estimated foreign cash flows are converted to dollars at the projected exchange rates and discounted at the dollar cost of capital. Second, in order to avoid making estimates of future exchange rates, calculate the future foreign denominated cash flows and discount at the foreign cost of capital. The foreign currency NPVs are then converted to domestic currency at the current spot rate.
   3.   Under the assumptions developed above both evaluation methods should give the same investment decisions.
   4.   The key point is not to make investments dependent upon specific, estimated future exchange rate movements. Select the investment based on the NPV and hedge the foreign exchange rate.

B.   **The Cost of Capital for Foreign Investment**
   1.   An international investment is an additional investment to the total portfolio, so the relevant risk of the added investment is its effect on the total portfolio risk.
   2.   The discount rate on international investments should reflect this incremental risk effect on the total investment portfolio.

C.   **Avoiding Fudge Factors**
   1.   The usual international risk adjustment practice is adding an increment to the discount rate to cover the risks of expropriation, foreign exchange restrictions, and tax changes.
   2.   A better method is to specify the international risks and their likely impact on cash flows and reduce the expected future cash flows.

COMPLETION QUESTIONS

1. The amount of currency needed to purchase one unit of another currency is called the
_____ _____.

2. The _____ exchange rate is the price of currency for immediate delivery.

3. The _____ exchange rate is the price of currency delivery at some time in the future.

4. The theory that prices of goods in all countries should be equal when translated into a
common currency is the law of _____ _____.

5. The theory that the cost of living in different countries is equal and exchange rates adjust to
offset different exchange rates across countries is _____ _____
_____.

6. Countries with high inflation rates will tend to have their currencies (*appreciate/depreciate*).

7. The international Fisher effect is a theory that says real interest rates in all countries should
be equal with any differences in nominal rates reflecting differences in _____. (602)

8. The theory that says the interest rate differential must equal the differential between forward
and spot exchange rates is called _____ _____ parity.

9. When you receive fewer forward yen for a dollar compared to the amount when buying spot
yen, the yen is selling at a forward (*discount/premium*).

10. It is easier to hedge (*contractual/non-contractual*) exchange rate risk.

11. The hedge of a future dollar obligation can be accomplished by either borrowing in the
foreign currency and lending dollars or by buying (*forward/spot*) dollars.

12. When calculating net present values for capital budgeting a multinational firm (*should/should
not*) make currency forecasts.

13. The general principle of NPV calculations for international firms is to match the
(*discount/inflation*) rate with the specific cash flows in the corresponding currency.

14. The authors of the text recommend incorporating uncertainty by adjusting the (*discount
rate/expected cash flows*) for multinational capital budgeting.

15. One way of minimizing harmful changes in foreign government policies is for the domestic
parent company to invest in the (*debt/equity*) of its foreign subsidiary.

PROBLEMS

1. Refer to Table 23.1 of the textbook to determine:
    a. The number of Hong Kong dollars per U.S. dollar.
    b. The cost in US$ of a plastic replica of the statue of liberty selling in Hong Kong HK$60.
    c. If the 12-month forward exchange rate for the HK$ is $7.896. Is there a premium or discount relative to the U.S. dollar?
    d. The annual percentage of the premium or discount specified in part c. above.
    e. The implied 1-year interest rate in Hong Kong if the comparable rate in the U.S. is 4 percent.
    f. What is the expected spot rate for the HK$ in 12 months time according to the expectations theory of exchange rates?
    g. What is the expected difference in the rate of inflation in Hong Kong and the U.S. according to purchasing power parity.

2. Marlene returned from a trip abroad and with 30 Australian dollars, 45 Swiss francs, 350 Greek drachmas, 2500 Japanese yen, and 20 Swedish kronas. How much does this total in US$?

3. From Table 23.2 of the textbook you can see the cost of a Big Mac in US$ varies from $3.97 in Switzerland to $1.32 in Hong Kong. Does this variation refute the law of one price?

4. Ivan's Imports sells Mexican pottery. His next order will be for a one-year supply and he wants to lock-in the price now. His source in Mexico has agreed to a price in pesos today but does not require payment until the goods are shipped in three months' time. What should Ivan do if he wants to avoid the risk of the peso appreciating against the dollar?

5. Megan's Exports, Inc., sells gold jewelry in Germany. Her prices are quoted in Euros. How can Megan reduce her exposure to currency risk?

6. Suppose a U.S. firm expects to receive payment in Canadian dollars for a project it will complete there in four years. If its bankers do not want to offer an attractive forward contract that far into the future, how could the company hedge against a depreciation in the value of the Canadian dollar?

7. Consider the capital budgeting process for a multinational firm based in the U.S. If the potential investments are reviewed in U.S. dollars, which inflation and interest rates are relevant in the decision-making process?

8. Suppose you purchased 100 shares of an British company last year for 12.50 pounds per share when the exchange rate was 0.865 pounds per U.S. dollar. What is your percentage return using the British currency if the current stock price is 14.80 pounds per share?

9. What is the percentage return for the investment made in problem 8 if you calculate it in U.S. dollars and if the current exchange rate is 0.7022 pounds per dollar?

10. Refer to Table 23.1 of the textbook and calculate:
   a. The number of Swiss francs you could buy with 100 British pounds.
   b. The spot rate of Swiss francs in terms of Singapore dollars.

ANSWERS TO COMPLETION QUESTIONS

1. exchange rate
2. spot
3. forward
4. one price
5. purchasing power parity
6. depreciate
7. inflation
8. interest rate
9. premium
10. contractual
11. forward
12. should not
13. match
14. expected cash flows
15. debt

SOLUTIONS TO PROBLEMS

1. a. You will receive HK$7.7681 in exchange for each US$.
   b. HK$60 ÷ 7.7681 = US$7.72.
   c. The 12-month forward exchange rate is HK$7.896 per US$. Because you can receive more Hong Kong dollars they are said to be selling at a discount relative to the US$.
   d. ($7.896 - $7.7681) ÷ $7.7681 = 0.0165 or 1.65 percent.

e. The ratio of the forward to the spot exchange rates is equal to the ratio of the interest rates in the two countries. In this case, $(7.896/7.7681) = (X/1.04)$ where $X = 1 +$ the one-year interest rate in Hong Kong. $X = 1.057$ so the interest rate is 5.7 percent in Hong Kong.

f. The expected spot rate in 12 months time is HK$7.896 per US$.

g. According to purchasing power parity, the ratio of the growth in prices in the different countries is equal to the ratio of the forward to the spot exchange rate. Since $7.896/7.7681 = 1.0165$ the expected rate of inflation in Hong Kong over the next 12 months is 1.65 percent higher than the inflation rate in the U.S.

2.

		Foreign currency per US$	US$
30	Australian $	.6602	19.80
45	Swiss francs	.6727	30.27
350	Greek drachmas	.003261	1.14
2500	Japanese yen	.0093	23.25
20	Swedish kronas	.12285	2.45
	TOTAL	In US dollars	76.91

3. The law of one price states that, in theory, the same item should cost the same in all countries when the prices are translated into a common currency. The fact that the dollar cost of a Big Mac is different in every country shown in Table 23.2 would seem to refute this theory. This is because it is theoretically possible to buy Big Mac's where the price is cheap as in China and sell them in Switzerland where they would sell for more than 3 times as much. Of course this doesn't happen because the transport costs more than offset the potential gain. The law of one price works much better for commodities such as gold where the transportation costs are small relative to the value of the item. Services such as taxi rides and medical operations are not transportable at all and indeed their prices expressed in dollars do vary considerably. In summary, the law of one price explains the tendency for prices to be similar even though they will not be equal around the world. Each item is unique and price variations will exist due to specific circumstances in each country and in the nature of the particular good or service.

4. Ivan should buy forward pesos for delivery in three months. In so doing he will fix, today, the number of dollars he pays for the imports. No matter which way the peso moves, relative to the dollar, Ivan's outlay is a set and known figure.

5. If the dollar falls relative to the EURO, Ellen will lose money because the EURO she receives from sales in Germany will buy fewer dollars when she converts the EURO into dollars. In

theory she could simply raise prices in Germany to offset this loss but that would have a negative impact on her business. One way to minimize the currency problem would be to sell EURO forward so she could be assured of receiving a known amount of dollars for her jewelry.

6. The U.S. firm could arrange a four-year loan in Canada for the present value of its future payment in Canadian dollars. Then it would sell, on the spot market, the proceeds for U.S. dollars. These dollars would be invested in the U.S. debt market for four years. The Canadian dollar loan would be repaid in four years when the U.S. firm's Canadian customer paid its obligation. At the same time, the U.S. firm would have the proceeds from the sale of its debt investment in the U.S. Throughout this entire process the U.S. firm has been insulated against foreign exchange movements which was the purpose of the transactions.

7. To prepare cash flows from foreign projects, the estimates of future inflation rates in the foreign country and future exchange rates with that country are needed. In addition, current interest rates in the U.S. are required to help determine the domestic cost of capital.

8. In British pounds (L) the return is (L1480 - L1250) ÷ L1250 = .184 or 18.4 percent.

9. The cost of the 100 shares was 1250 pounds ÷ 0.865 pounds per US$ = $1445. The value today is 1480 pounds ÷ 0.7022 pounds per US$ = $2108. This makes the return:
$$= (\$2108 - \$1445) \div \$1445$$
$$= 0.459 \text{ or } 45.9 \text{ percent.}$$

10. a. The table does not show the Swiss franc to British pound conversion factor but the translation can be accomplished by converting the pounds into dollars and then the dollars into francs as follows:
$$100 \text{ pounds} \times \$1.6566 \text{ per pound} = \$165.66$$
$$\$165.66 \times 1.4865 \text{ Swiss francs per \$} = 246.25 \text{ Swiss francs.}$$
    b. 1.4865 Swiss francs per $US × $US 0.5956 per Singapore dollar
$$= 0.885 \text{ Swiss francs per Singapore dollar.}$$

CHAPTER 24

OPTIONS

INTRODUCTION

The growth of financial derivative securities for hedging and speculating has been dramatic. With lenient margin requirements, the speculator is provided an exciting place to play. For the risk manager, hedging with derivatives, the subject of the next chapter, has provided the opportunity to decide what risks to accept in the business and which to hedge.

In this first of two chapters associated with risk management, options, from traded exchanged-based to contract options in securities to imbedded options in real assets, are discussed. The "Financial Alchemy with Options" is an excellent section, along with Figure 23.4, for discussing investor payoff positioning. The discussion of option value factors provides insight as to what makes an option valuable.

Traditionally, financial management texts espoused financial flexibility. What were they talking about? Options, at some cost, provide the financial manager choices for the future. This chapter comes at the end of the textbook, but today represents the most dramatic and sophisticated aspect of finance. The recent losses in derivative positions by municipal governments (they were speculating) has now let the public know what we now know, that risk shows its ugly side about as often as the high returns associated with the risk.

LEARNING CHECKLIST

After studying this chapter you should be able to:

____1. Calculate the payoff to buyers and sellers of call and put options.

____2. Understand the determinants of option values.

____3. Recognize options in capital investment projects (real assets).

____4. Identify options that are provided in financial securities.

SOURCES OF BUSINESS INFORMATION

Compact Disclosure and Compustat PC+. The compact disk, read-only memory (CD-ROM) technology has emerged as a valuable source of business information. Everything that once was on paper will soon be offered on CD-ROM. The CD-ROM is capable of storing over 600 megabytes (600 million bytes) of data on a single disk. Currently Compact Disclosure and Moody's is using this technology to provide databases for students and researches. These databases contain extensive information on thousands of companies. For a single company, Compact Disclosure provides a complete description of the type of business and products, and provides a company history including debt issues, properties owned, histories of top management and directors, and letters to shareholders. In addition, the CD contains financial data from several previous years. This information includes income statements, balance sheets with financial notes, and statements of cash flow. Other features include the ability to download information and to export financial data directly to a spreadsheet.

Standard & Poor's Compustat has a more extensive CD-ROM package called Compustat PC Plus. PC Plus provides information and software sorting capability for over 7000 publicly traded companies, composites on 270 industries, information on 500 Canadian companies, twenty years of annual and monthly market data, twelve years of quarterly data, and five years of stock prices. Economic information is available. One is able to screen companies such as all firms with no debt and ROE greater than 20 percent. The PC Plus may be networked in student computer labs for class assignments.

CHAPTER OUTLINE, KEY CONCEPTS AND TERMS

I. **CALLS AND PUTS**

    A.   Options, the right to act within a specified period of time, are widespread in business, financing, and investment operations.

    B.   Options have value because they specify the ability to take action whether buying, selling, expanding, or doing nothing.

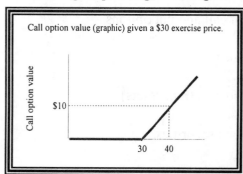
Call option value (graphic) given a $30 exercise price.

Call option payoff (to seller) given a $30 exercise price.

    C.   Standardized option contracts on a variety of financial assets began trading on the Chicago Board Options Exchange (CBOE) in 1973. Investors and businesses trade options to speculate and, more importantly for businesses and investors, to hedge price risk, the risk of unfavorable price movements in their business or portfolio.

D.   A **call option** gives the owner the right to buy an asset at a specified price on or before a specified date called the exercise date. A buyer of a call option may exercise the option in the option period or let it expire. In the case of the Compaq options, the owner of the call would exercise the call (right to buy Compaq at $30) if the price of Compaq exceeded $30. If the price remains below $30, the call will not likely be exercised.

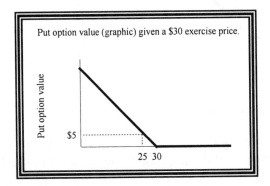

Put option value (graphic) given a $30 exercise price.

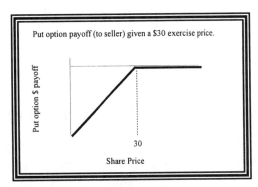

Put option payoff (to seller) given a $30 exercise price.

E.   A **put option** is a right to sell an asset at a specified exercise price on or before the exercise date. A buyer of a put would exercise if Compaq fell below $30 by buying Compaq below $30 and selling it for $30. If the price remains above $30, the put will not be exercised.

F.   Call and put options are often imbedded in contracts and are associated with ownership. The CBOE options, which have been extremely popular, are standard contracts for speculators and hedgers.

G.   **Selling Calls and Puts**
     1.   Traded options on the CBOE and other exchanges are issued by the call and put writers, usually investors. The positive/negative payoff of a call/put buyer is offset by call/put writers or option sellers.
     2.   The buyer of calls and puts has a limit on the negative payoff equal to the cost of the option paid to the writer. The writer's negative payoff potential may be very high, especially if the writer does not own the underlying asset (Compaq stock).

H.   **Financial Alchemy with Options**
     1.   Three possible conditions and payoffs are discussed to provide an indication of why investors may trade options.

2.	In Example 24.4, Portfolio Insurance, an investor owns stock and seeks to protect its current gains (protect against falling stock prices) by buying a put option on Compaq. For the cost of the option (insurance premium) the investor has upside price opportunity and downside protection. If the price falls, the gain in the option will offset the decline in the stock value.

3.	In Example 24.3, Profiting from Volatility, the owner of Compaq stock would buy two put options, thus establishing a position to gain via stock ownership if the price goes up and to gain if the stock declines via the high put position. In other words if the stock has volatility, enough to cover the cost of the options, the investor wins with volatility. If an investor did not own Compaq but wanted to gain from Compaq's increased volatility, it would establish a straddle position, buying both a put and a call.

## II.	WHAT DETERMINES OPTION VALUES?

### A.	Upper and Lower Limits on Option Values
1.	While an option is worthless when expired, why does an option have a positive value before expiration?
2.	The upper boundary on the value of a call option is the share price value, while the lower boundary on the value of a call is the payoff if exercised immediately.
3.	The value is related to the stock price. The call is always worth more than its value if exercised now (lower bound) and never worth more than the stock price itself (upper bound). See Figure 24.7 below.
4.	The value of the option lays between the upper and lower bounds. The value will lay on the curved upward sloping line in Figure 24.7.

B. **The Determinants of Option Value**
   1.   Given the exercise price, the value of a call option increases as the stock price increases.
   2.   Three key points on the option value curve, Figure 24.7, are important reference points.
   3.   At Point A, when the stock is worthless, the option is worthless. At Point B, when the stock price becomes very high, the option price approaches the stock price less the PV of the exercise price. The value of a call increases directly with increases in the rate of interest and the time to expiration. And at Point C, the option price always exceeds its minimum value, except when the stock price is zero. There is always a chance that the stock price will advance to the exercise price.
   4.   The value of an option is directly related to the stock price volatility. The greater the volatility, the greater the chance that the stock will move above the exercise price.

C. **Option-Valuation Models**
   1.   The best method for estimating the value of an option is to find a best combination of borrowing and making an investment in the stock.
   2.   Work by Black and Scholes developed this options value theory.

$$\text{Black-Scholes Option Pricing Model}$$
$$O_C = P_s[N(d_1)] - S[N(d_2)]e^{-rt}$$

III. SPOTTING THE OPTION

A.   Options, either explicit or implicit, are present everywhere in business and investments.

B.   The challenge is to identify the option present and to consider the value of the option.

C.   **Options on Real Assets**
   1.   **Real options** or the implicit (implied with ownership) options on real assets such as plant, land, etc., are present in any business setting.
   2.   The first real option is the option to expand an investment, such as a production facility, at a future date. This call option, option to buy more production facilities, is often called flexibility.

3. The business also has the option to abandon an investment. This option to sell (put) or quit is valuable, especially when the value of the underlying asset is volatile.
4. All aspects of project management from expansion, contraction, delay, or abandonment contain real options.

D. **Options on Financial Assets**
1. Options to participate in the common stock are often attached to debt securities. A **warrant** is a right to buy (call) shares from a company at a stipulated price before a set date.
2. The right to participate in the equity is valuable to the bondholder and the market. Warrants may be detachable and trade separate from the bonds.
3. A **convertible bond** is a bond that may be exchanged for a specified number of common shares. The convertible bond has a call option on a number of common shares. A conversion ratio of 26.7 shares on a $1000 bond has a conversion price of $37.45 (1000/26.7).
4. The value of a convertible bond is driven by the bond value when the stock price is low and becomes related to the stock value when the stock price approaches and passes the conversion price. The bond value establishes a floor or minimum price for the convertible bond; the upper bound is unlimited, dependent upon the value of the common stock. The value of the call option is equal to the difference between the convertible selling price and its bond value.
5. **Callable bonds** include a call option held by the borrower or issuer to repurchase or refund the bond before maturity at a specified call price.
6. Lenders are likely to lose their high rate callable bonds if interest rates decline, so they demand a higher rate of return. The value of the call option is the yield on the callable bond less the yield on a noncallable, similar bond.

COMPLETION QUESTIONS

1. A call option gives the owner the right to (buy/sell) stock at a fixed exercise price on or before a specified exercise date.

2. The value of a call option will be _____ if the stock price is less than the exercise price when the option expires.

3. An investor in put options is expecting share prices to (fall/rise).

4. Traded options (are/are not) sold by the companies themselves.

5. If you own a stock you can achieve portfolio insurance by buying a (call/put) for that some stock.

6. By (buying/selling) two puts in a stock you own you can create a situation of making a gross profit no matter which way the stock moves.

7. In the case of the situation described in question 6, you must (add/deduct) the cost of the call option premiums to compute the net profit.

8. If you sell two calls in a stock you own you will (gain/lose) form any stock price volatility.

9. The value of a call option (decreases/increases) as the stock price rises.

10. When the stock price is well (above/below) the call exercise price, buying that call is equivalent to buying the stock now with deferred payment and delivery.

11. The value of a call option will (decrease/increase) as interest rates increase and be (higher/lower) for longer as opposed to shorter times to expiration.

12. The greater the expected volatility in the stock price the (greater/less) will be the value of a call option.

13. As the exercise price increases, the value of a call option (decreases/increases).

14. It is possible to replicate the purchase of a call option by a bank (deposit/loan) and the purchase of the stock.

15. In capital budgeting, the projects being considered for investment are similar in concept to buying a (call/put) option.

16. The possibility of abandoning an existing project may be thought of as a (call/put) option.

17.   A warrant is a long-term (call/put) option.

18.   A _____ bond is a straight bond with a call option.

19.   If the stock price in the case of a convertible bond is (above/below) the conversion price, that convertible bond will always sell for more than its bond value.

20.   A callable bond is like a combination of a non-callable bond and a call option held by the (investor/issuer).

21.   (Risky/Safe) bonds are those where the asset value of the firm is less than the amount of debt outstanding.

PROBLEMS

1.   Suppose you own 100 shares of Neverfail, Inc. The firm is working on a project, which if successful, would result in a huge profit. However, if the project does not work out, the company could go bankrupt. Explain:
   a.   How you could use an option to protect against loss.
   b.   How the cost of insuring against the loss is related to the option price.

2.   What is the incentive for someone to write a put or a call option?

3.   If you bought a call option for $4 that had an exercise price of $70 per share, what would be the value of that option at its expiration if the stock was trading at:
   a. $70
   b. $75
   c. $65

4.   If you owned 100 shares of Slone Stoneworks, Inc., and then bought a put on that stock with an exercise price of $24, what would be the value of your holding if you closed out your position at the expiration date of the put and if the stock was trading at:
   a. $20
   b. $28

5. How much would be the payoff at the expiration date if you owned 100 shares of a stock and 2 puts for that stock with exercise prices of $46 when the market price for the shares are:
    a. $40
    b. $46
    c. $52

6. Discuss the major factors that influence the value of a call option.

7. What is the maximum potential loss if you buy a:
    a. put option?
    b. call option?

8. What is the maximum potential loss if you write a
    a. put option?
    b. call option?

9. Is the conversion feature on a convertible bond like a put or a call option?

10. What type of option is related to the case of a computer firm that forms a strategic alliance with a software developer by agreeing to advance $10 million for the rights to freely use a software program that is currently being written?

ANSWERS TO COMPLETION QUESTIONS

1. buy
2. zero
3. fall
4. are not
5. put
6. buying
7. deduct
8. lose
9. increases
10. above
11. increase, higher
12. greater
13. decreases
14. loan
15. call
16. put
17. call
18. convertible

19. above
20. issuer
21. Risky

SOLUTIONS TO PROBLEMS

1. a. To protect against the loss that would result if the stock price fell below the current market price, a put option could be purchased. This would allow the owner of the option to sell the stock at the exercise price on or before the exercise date. If the stock declined the investor would exercise the option and sell the 100 shares owned. This establishes a minimum value for the stock. On the other hand, if the stock price increased the owner would sell the stock at the higher price and realize a gain. The put option would be allowed to expire without being used since with a stock price rise, the investor would receive more by selling the stock in the open market as compared to selling it through the put option.
    b. The cost of insuring that a decline in the stock price will not hurt the owner of the 100 shares is the cost of buying the put option. This is similar to insuring a home or a car against a loss. You pay an insurance premium for that protection. In the case of the stockholder, the insurance premium is the price paid for the put option.

2. The incentive to be an option writer is much like the incentive to write insurance. You expect that the premiums received will cover the costs of claims, etc., and provide a profit. In other words, the insurance companies expect to be compensated for bearing the risk of loss. Option writers receive the premiums and hope those amounts will more than offset the losses they incur as a result of price moves in the wrong direction resulting in the writer having to pay more than the going market price when a put is exercised or to sell at the below the market price when the call they wrote is exercised.

3. a. The value of the call is equal to the exercise price minus the market price for the stock. With the stock selling at $70 the call option value is:
    $$= \$70 - \$70$$
    $$= \text{zero}$$
    b. With the stock selling at $75 the call option value is:
    $$= \$70 - \$75$$
    $$= -\$5.$$
    However, the option value will never be negative so the value in this case is zero.

    c. With the stock selling at $65 the call option value is:
    $$= \$70 - \$65$$
    $$= \$5$$

4.   a.   You would exercise the put and receive $100 \times \$24$ or $2,400$.
        b.   You would let the put go unused and sell the stock for $100 \times \$28$ or $2,800$. Notice that if your stock falls below the exercise price you receive the exercise price as the minimum or floor price. If the stock rises you participate in the appreciation.

5.   a.   The puts would have a positive value whenever the stock is below the exercise price. In this case you could sell your shares with one of the puts and receive $100 \times \$46$ or $4,600$. The other put could be sold in the market for its value of $(\$46 - \$40) \times 100$ or 600. Your total value would be $4,600 + 600$ or $5,200$.
        b.   At a market price of $46 for the stock, the puts would have zero value so the shares would be worth $100 \times \$46$ or $4,600$.
        c.   At $52, the puts would have zero value but the stock would be worth $100 \times \$52$ or $5,200$. So the value of the portfolio with 2 puts is at the minimum when the stock is trading at the exercise price. Whenever the stock goes up or down from that price the portfolio value will increase.

6.   The major factors that influence a call option's price are:
        a.   Exercise price--the lower this is, the higher the value of the call.
        b.   Stock price--the lower this is, the higher the value of the call.
        c.   Expiration date--the longer this is, the higher the value of the call.
        d.   Volatility of the stock--the more volatile the stock, the higher the value of the call.

7.   a.   The maximum loss you could incur if you purchased a put option would be the price paid for that option.
        b.   The maximum potential loss to the owner of a call option is the price paid for that option.

8.   a.   The maximum loss that could occur to the writer of a put option would be the exercise price for that option if the stock went to zero before the expiration date. Since options are written for 100 shares the maximum loss would be 100 times the exercise price.
        b.   The maximum potential loss to the writer of a call option would be unlimited in theory because the writer would have to deliver the stock if the call were exercised. This unlimited exposure is true only if the writer does not own the shares. That would be an uncovered position and would be very risky. Most writers of call options do so on shares they have in their portfolio. The loss they incur if the stock rises substantially is an opportunity loss since they could have sold their shares at the higher market price.

9.   In the case of a convertible bond, the owner has a call option because the bond can be exchanged for common stock at a predetermined price. In other words the convertible bond can exercise the right to "buy" common stock using the par value of the bond as the purchasing medium.

10.   By investing the $10 million now the computer company is fixing the price it will pay for the software program. This is similar to what an investor does when buying a call option.

RISK MANAGEMENT

INTRODUCTION

The business and financial risks faced by financial managers today are considerable, especially with the globalization of businesses and as competition increases. Today a manager must recognize what risks are faced, the range of outcomes, and the type and extent to which, and at what cost, the risks might be shifted to others, reduced, or accepted. The management of risk has always been a key financial manager function, but the orientation until recently was focused only on the pure risk faced by the business. Pure risk is the risk of loss on real assets from fire, theft, loss of use of assets, etc. A risk management approach to all business pure and financial risks is developing. This chapter is one of the first on the subject to appear in a financial management text. Soon the topic will be integrated throughout the chapters.

The financial manager that wishes to control the level of specific risks so identified may eliminate them by avoiding the risk, remove by contract, such as with contractual options, or hedge where cost justified and available, by using "off-balance sheet" or "off business" hedging tools such as futures, forwards, or SWAPS. Such hedging contracts are either exchange-based or are, as with forwards, negotiated with other parties with a mirror image risk to hedge or via a hedge dealer who will contract between parties as with SWAPS.

LEARNING CHECKLIST

After preparing this chapter you should be able to:

_____ 1. Understand why companies hedge to reduce risk.

_____ 2. Use options, futures, and forward contracts to devise simple hedging strategies.

_____ 3. Explain how companies can use SWAPs to change the risk of securities that they have issued.

SOURCES OF BUSINESS INFORMATION

Business Periodicals Index. Most of you are familiar with the classic <u>Business Periodicals Index</u>. If your library has computerized its card catalog, it likely has this information on CD-ROM. One other on-line source is the <u>ABI/INFORM</u>, which contains article abstracts from various periodicals such as <u>Fortune, Business Week</u>, etc., and the Newspaper Index, which provides synopsi newspaper articles from the <u>American Banker</u>, <u>The Wall Street Journal</u>, etc.

Business Search Engines. The Business Researcher's Interests....,Management & Techno Resource (http://www.brint.com) is an extensive search engines for business topics, espec technology-related information and sources. Inference FIND (http://www.inference.com) is a se engine that takes you search engines related to specific topics. Growing and expanding daily, will be very useful in locating "sites of sites" on a particular topic.

CHAPTER OUTLINE, KEY CONCEPTS AND TERMS

I.   **WHY HEDGE?**

      A.   Hedging involves incurring a cost to reduce the risk of adverse price movemen

      B.   Hedging makes financial planning easier and allows the manager to focus on internal, controllable production efficiency rather than external, noncontrollabl price speculation.

      C.   One tool for hedging involves contracting in financial derivatives, contracts wh value is derived from the value of other financial or real assets.

      D.   Hedging involves contracting to gain in a derivative contract if a loss or an opportunity loss should occur in the business, real assets, or securities. If the hedge is properly in place, any adverse business price changes will be offset by gain in the hedging contract, whether it is a futures contract, option on futures contract, swap, etc.

II.   **REDUCING RISK WITH OPTIONS**

      A.   Hedging with options provides adverse side price protection for a large number real and financial assets from wheat and oil to Treasury bonds.

      B.   The hedger selects the option exchange contract that is best associated with the price risk (risk of adverse price movements) at hand. There is also a large volur of option contracts written off of the exchanges between hedgers, who have pric risk in a commodity or financial asset and a speculator, who has no cash, curren or spot position in the asset.

      C.   Hedging is performed by taking a position in the option contract, or other hedgi contract, so that adverse price movements in the business (raw material costs increasing) is offset by gains in the hedging contract. It is assumed that the business or investor will continue their business by buying/selling in the spot or cash market.

D.   If a business will be adversely affected by rising prices, such as a processor of agricultural goods, a call option will offer one side price protection for a price, the price of the call. If raw prices rise for the business, they will rise to and above the strike price, providing option contract gains to offset business losses (opportunity costs of buying at a higher price). If prices fall, the call option holder will let the option expire.

E.   If a business, such as a farmer or manufacturer, has the risk of falling prices for its production, it may purchase put options or options to sell. If corn prices fall between planting and harvest, the economic loss in the business is offset by the gains in the put contract. The farmer is selling corn at a specified price when the puts are purchased. If prices fall, the option contract is in the money, offsetting the reduced margins in the business. If prices rise, the put option is never exercised. The cost of the option is the insurance premium spent to avoid adverse price movements.

F.   Option contracts may protect holders of financial assets. A Treasury bond investor may be worried about the Fed raising interest rates. If rates rise, bond prices will fall. How can an investor hedge the risk of interest rate increases or falling bond prices? Yes! Buying T-bond puts provides the downside protection. Focus on the direction of the adverse price movement and protect with a counter position in the option contract.

G.   Unlike futures contracts and forward contracts, hedging with options provides one-way insurance protection against adverse price movements.

III.   **FUTURES CONTRACTS**

A.   **Futures contracts**, exchange-traded contracts to buy or sell a standardized amount of an asset at a specified price at a specified date, are frequently used to hedge price risk.

Future	Exchange
U.S. Treasury notes	CBT
U.S. Treasury bonds	CBT
Eurodollar deposits	IMM
Standard and Poor' s Index	IMM
Euro	IMM
Yen	IMM
German Govt Bonds	Eurex

B.   For a small cost and a margin deposit, a farmer can protect against price declines by selling corn futures with total contracts approximating production. The maturity selected will be slightly longer than the period of price risk. If corn prices fall, the daily mark-to-market procedure of futures exchanges will add deposits to the farmer's account. Unlike option contracts, if prices for corn increase, the gain in the business is offset by losses on the sale (short position) of corn futures.

C. **The Mechanics of Futures Trading**
1. The futures contract with the exchange is highly liquid and can be reversed quickly should price risk in the business cease.
2. A financial manager, worried about higher interest rates during a heavy borrowing period, can hedge higher rates and lock in today's rates by selling T-bill or Eurodollar futures contracts. If rates rise, the business will pay more interest, but rising rates are associated with falling financial futures contract prices. As rates rise, the exchange will credit the financial manager's account. The manager is gaining for he or she has sold a contract that can be reversed later at a lower price, or hear she has locked in the cost of funds when the futures contract was sold and current rates are now higher.

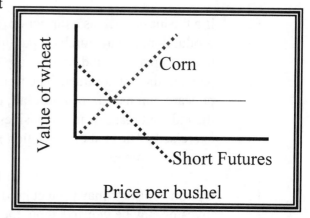

D. **Commodity and Financial Futures**
1. Commodity and financial futures exist in areas where there is extreme price variability. Futures began first in commodity markets, and became very popular later in the 1970s as interest rates became extremely volatile. Futures lock in prices today, avoiding *both* adverse and favorable future price movements.

IV. FORWARD CONTRACTS

A. **Forward contracts** are agreements to buy or sell an asset in the future at an agreed price. Forward contracts are designed specifically for the risk, amount, and period, whereas futures contracts are standardized contracts as to amount, time, and specific commodity or financial asset.

B. Forward contracts entail delivery; futures seldom entail delivery. Forwards are not marked to market daily like futures, but are settled at maturity which greatly increases the risk of default.

V. SWAPS

A. A **SWAP** is an arrangement between two traders to exchange a series of future payments on different terms.

B. A SWAP hedge entails trading a possible adverse price movement for known cash flows with a party that has the opposite need. In the chapter example Possum was able to improve the terms of its loan for its foreign subsidiary and reduce foreign exchange risk by borrowing in the U.S. at favorable rates and swapping the dollar loan commitment for a series of annual Deutsche marks.

C. SWAPS are often used to trade variable and fixed interest cash flows in the future. Like options and futures and other derivatives, they can be used to hedge business risk or to speculate on future price or interest rate movements.

D. Is "Derivative" A Four-Letter Word?
   1. Derivatives have become infamous to the general public due to the headlines created when investors lost money speculating.
   2. The vast majority of investors and businesses use derivatives to hedge the variety of risks they face. Alas, this information does not make splashy headlines.

COMPLETION QUESTIONS

1. _____ is the practice of taking off-setting risks.

2. A producer may wish to purchase a (call/put) option to hedge against a price decline.

3. A futures contract involves (a binding promise/an optional choice).

4. Use of futures contracts enables a producer to eliminate (price/quantity) risk.

5. When trading futures contracts the margin is the (borrowed/down payment) amount.

6. The requirement for futures contracts to pay for any loss or receive credit for any profit on a daily basis is called _____ to _____.

7. The ability to manage risks of changing interest rates, exchange rates, and security prices involves the use of _____ futures.

8. A (hedger/speculator) in futures markets takes on risk to provide others with insurance.

9. An agreement to buy or sell an asset in the future at an agreed price but without the marked to market requirement is called a _____ contract.

10. An agreement between two traders to exchange a series of future payments on different terms is called a _____ .

11. The majority of firms borrowing in the (domestic/international) bond market use currency and interest rate SWAPs.

PROBLEMS

1. What is the general principle of insurance?

2. What are the most frequent types of insurance used by businesses?

3. The chief financial officer of a firm wishes to refinance a long-term bond issue that his company has outstanding because interest rates have declined since the bonds were sold. However, since rates are still falling he thinks it is best to wait and thereby save more money. If he is wrong and interest rates increase he will have to pay more than he would have by refinancing now. How could he use Treasury bond futures contracts to hedge against a possible rise in interest rates?

4. Suppose Megan had a supply of silver that you planned to sell in 6 months. Today's price is $5 per ounce but she wants to be protected against a price decline. The price of silver for 6-months-ahead delivery is $5.25 per ounce. What be her strategy?

5. Could you have used a put or a call option instead of entering into a futures contract as described in problem 4?

6. What is the difference between a currency swap and an interest rate swap?

7. What is the difference between a futures contract for foreign exchange and an option to buy or sell foreign exchange?

8. Discuss how a maker of bread and a wheat farmer could use commodity markets to lessen risk?

9. What are the disadvantages of holding a commodity instead of selling it through the futures market?

ANSWERS TO COMPLETION QUESTIONS

1. Hedging
2. put
3. a binding promise
4. price
5. down payment
6. marked, market
7. financial
8. speculator
9. forward
10. swap
11. international

SOLUTIONS TO PROBLEMS

1. The general principle of insurance is to protect against a loss by paying a relatively small amount of money. This cost will reduce profitability but it will prevent a much larger disappointment if certain events happen. The key is to think not only in terms of traditional forms of protection offered by insurance companies but to consider a wide variety of business activities that can be protected by the use of certain financial instruments.

2. Businesses use insurance for protection of property damage due to fire, flood, wind, earthquake, theft, vandalism, war, etc. They insure against various liabilities and court judgements. This chapter considers the use of various financial instruments to help hedge against movements of commodity prices and financial related variables such as interest rates, foreign currencies' and stock prices.

3. The CFO could sell long-term bond futures with a delivery date of some months into the future. If interest rates increased the value of the bond futures would decline and create a profit, as measured by the difference between the original price received from selling the bond futures and the lower market price paid when covering the earlier sale. This profit would offset the opportunity loss by not refinancing the bonds at the current interest rate which turns out to be lower than the higher rate later. If interest rates had fallen, there would be a loss on the futures contract but this would be offset by the increased savings the company would realize by refinancing at the lower rate.

4. Megan should sell a 6-month futures contract at the $5.25 per ounce price. If she sold her inventory today she would receive the spot price of $5 per ounce. With the futures contract she will receive $5.25 but she will have incurred costs of storage and experienced the opportunity loss of not being able to invest the money if she had sold today.

5. If you purchased a put option, you would pay some amount based on the exercise price, the volatility of silver prices, expected direction for those price movements etc. This would be a cost of insurance. If silver increased above the exercise price your put would be worthless. If silver declined, you would make a profit from the option. The option gain or loss would offset most of the change in silver prices in comparison to the spot price.

CHAPTER 26

WHAT WE DO AND DO NOT KNOW ABOUT FINANCE

INTRODUCTION

No matter how far you get in the term, make sure that you read this last chapter. This is especially important if your instructor is giving a comprehensive final exam. The authors bring together the major issues developed in the course and focus on what work still remains related to our understanding of Finance. Several recent journal articles (Journal of Financial Practice and Education) also provide support for this last chapter.

SOURCES OF BUSINESS INFORMATION

Financial Management Association. The Financial Management Association is a professional association of business and academic professionals. The FMA also sponsors the local FMA Student Chapters and the FMA National Honor Society. In many business schools the FMA chapter is the student organization associated with Finance majors. The FMA web site (http://www.fma.org) has a great listing of "Finance-Related Links" that students of business finance ought to see. If you are interested in perusing careers in finance and, perhaps details of the FMA organization, take a look at this site. Finally, check out your local FMA Student Chapter and its activities.

CHAPTER OUTLINE, KEY CONCEPTS AND TERMS

I. WHAT WE DO KNOW: THE SIX MOST IMPORTANT IDEAS IN FINANCE

    A.   Net Present Value
        1.   The Net Present Value decision analysis method is a shareholder, value-creating process for selecting alternatives.
        2.   The NPV method considers cash flows, the timing of the cash flows, and the opportunity rate of return on capital, including the RRR of equity investors.
        3.   NPV is used in capital budgeting, merger analysis, bond refunding, and lease/buy analyses where cash flows over time are considered relative to an outlay today.
        4.   Maximize present value is a shareholder-focused, long-run decision criterion for managers.

B. Risk and Return
    1. Investors require added returns for added non-diversifiable risk assumed.
    2. An asset is seldom held by itself, but in portfolios. The risk of an asset is the change in risk to a portfolio when it is added. The CAPM approaches measuring relative risk by establishing a risk measure relative to the market portfolio called beta. The higher the beta of an asset, the higher the investor required rate of return.
    3. The relevant risk of an asset is non-diversifiable risk, the risk that cannot be diversified away.

C. Efficient Capital Markets
    1. Security prices accurately reflect available information and respond rapidly to new information. Three variations of available information, from weak-form (random walk), semi-strong, and strong form, are used to describe specific market situations.
    2. Competition is extremely keen in financial markets and information flows freely and efficiently. Security prices are fairly valued containing information about expected future cash flow, timing, and relative riskiness.

D. MM's Irrelevance Propositions
    1. Modigliani and Miller's (MM) theory of capital structure has been a significant contribution. What affects value is the cash flows from an asset, not how it is financed.
    2. Dividend policy does not affect value unless it affects the cash flow to shareholder.

E. Option Theory
    1. Option, contrived via derivatives, or embodied in assets and contracts, are valuable. This value ranges from the ability to "cash in at a strike price" to simple flexibility.
    2. Managers should recognize the presence of options and assess their value.

F. Agency Theory
    1. Managers are assumed to attempt to maximize present value for shareholders at all times. Conflicts in managers' focus to other stakeholders, including themselves, are difficult to resolve with simple compensation systems.
    2. These agency problems or conflicts of interest and remedies are of considerable interest to finance and financial managers.

II. WHAT WE DO NOT KNOW: SEVEN UNSOLVED PROBLEMS IN FINANCE

A.   How Are Major Financial Decisions Made? -- With such a variety of strategic financial decision-making processes, a common, general theory as to how managers make strategic financial decisions (debt or equity) is lacking in finance.

B.   What Determines Project Risk and Present Value?
       1.   Positive NPVs are associated with special value added or profitable ventures in the marketplace. How are these special opportunities created and how long do they last before competition removes them are questions that finance still asks.
       2.   How are relative project risks assessed? Differential fixed costs (operating leverage) and project beta determining methods are helpful, but the knowledge in the area is still at a beginning point.

C.   Risk and Return--Have We Missed Something?
       1.   While the CAPM has provided a good beginning for explaining the risk/return tradeoff, many statistical and theoretical questions are yet resolved.
       2.   Not all research supports the CAPM related to the relationship between risk and return and the impact of diversification.
       3.   The CAPM is built upon simplifying assumptions. When relaxed, the CAPM is less able to explain reality.
       4.   There are still unknown variables that explain the precise risk/return tradeoff.

D.   Are There Important Exceptions to the Efficient-Market Theory?
       1.   As mentioned in Chapter 11, there are several areas of financial markets that work counter to efficient-market theory and the reason why is not yet explained.
       2.   Stocks of small companies appear to yield returns higher than large company stocks with similar betas.
       3.   The January effect has provided extra returns per level of risk on small company stocks in the month of January.
       4.   If stocks were fairly priced, there would be no easy ways to make superior profits consistently over time. The "fairly priced" measure is difficult to assess.

E. How Can We Explain Capital Structure?
   1. While asset returns dominate in determining value, other "financing" factors affect the value of the business.
   2. The governmental tax shield shifts value from government to the business owners.
   3. The possible bankruptcy costs to business owners serve to affect value, limiting the continuous advantage of added borrowing for the tax shield.

F. How Can We Resolve the Dividend Controversy?
   1. Does dividend policy affect shareholder value? This is one area not resolved in financial theory.
   2. In MM's simplistic model dividends are irrelevant, but adding reality indicates that varied policy may have an effect on shareholder value.

G. How Can We Explain Merger Waves? -- Mergers have tended to occur in large numbers at various times and the reason for this is yet unresolved.

COMPLETION QUESTIONS

1. The idea behind net present value (NPV) is a means of analyzing if a project is worth (*less/more*) than it costs.

2. In computing NPV cash flows should be discounted at the (*opportunity/risk-free*) cost of capital.

3. The capital asset pricing model (CAPM) is a way of incorporating (*financing costs/risk*) into financial decisions.

4. Market risk is another name for (*diversifiable/non-diversifiable*) risk.

5. According to CAPM, beta is the measure of (*return/risk*) for a firm or a project.

6. According to CAPM, the only risk that matters is (*diversifiable/non-diversifiable*) risk.

7. The weak-form of _____ _____ theory is also called random-walk theory.

8. According to the strong-form of efficient market theory, prices reflect all (*acquirable/available*) information.

9. The propositions of Modigliani and Miller (MM) imply you (*can/cannot*) increase value of the firm by financing decisions unless cash flow is increased.

10. MM argue that dividend policy (*will/will not*) affect value of the firm.

11. The authors of the textbook argue that mergers solely for diversification purposes (*will/will not*) create benefits.

12. Company use of debt (*does/does not*) provide an option to default.

13. The analysis of potential conflicts among shareholders, management, employees, and creditors can be conducted within the framework of _____ theory.

14. The discipline of finance (*does/does not*) provide a general procedure for estimating project betas.

15. CAPM (*is/is not*) useful in explaining why people with different tastes can logically hold different portfolios.

16. Empirical data show small companies offer (*higher/lower*) returns for comparable risks.

17. The month of _____ has historically offered relatively higher returns.

PROBLEMS (There are no problems for this chapter. The authors hope the Study Guide helped readers to better understand the world of finance. We wish you both success and happiness.)

ANSWERS TO COMPLETION QUESTIONS

1. more
2. opportunity
3. risk
4. non-diversifiable
5. risk
6. non-diversifiable
7. efficient market
8. acquirable
9. cannot
10. will not
11. will not
12. does

13. agency
14. does not
15. is not
16. higher
17. January